The Long Journeys Home

NICK BELLANTONI

The Long Journeys Home

The Repatriations of Henry ʻŌpūkahaʻia and Albert Afraid of Hawk

WESLEYAN UNIVERSITY PRESS Middletown, Connecticut

Wesleyan University Press
Middletown CT 06459
www.wesleyan.edu/wespress

The Driftless Connecticut Series is funded by the
Beatrice Fox Auerbach Foundation Fund
at the Hartford Foundation for Public Giving.

Library of Congress Cataloging-in-Publication Data

Names: Bellantoni, Nicholas F., author.
Title: The Long Journeys Home : The Repatriations of Henry Opukahaia and
    Albert Afraid of Hawk / by Nick Bellantoni.
Description: Middletown, CT : Wesleyan University Press, 2018. | Series:
    Garnet books | Includes bibliographical references and index. |
    Description based on print version record and CIP data provided by
    publisher; resource not viewed.
Identifiers: LCCN 2017048410 (print) | LCCN 2018010232 (ebook) | ISBN
    9780819576859 (ebook) | ISBN 9780819576842 (cloth : alk. paper)
Subjects: LCSH: Obookiah, Henry, 1792-1818—Death and burial. |
    Afraid-of-Hawk, Albert, 1879-1900—Death and burial. | Human remains
    (Archaeology)—Repatriation—United States—Case studies. | Cultural
    property—Repatriation—United States—Case studies.
Classification: LCC CC79.5.H85 (ebook) | LCC CC79.5.H85 B45 2018 (print) |
    DDC 930.1—dc23
LC record available at https://lccn.loc.gov/2017048410

5 4 3 2 1

To four extraordinary women
who have inspired me and this book

Deborah Liʻikapeka Lee,
7th generation cousin descendant of Henry ʻŌpūkahaʻia

Marlis Afraid of Hawk,
grandniece of Albert Afraid of Hawk

my mother, Carmella

and

my wife, Angela

Contents

Illustrations

Maps

Acknowledgments

Upon completing this book, the reader will be aware that these narratives were a truly collaborative effort. Though written from a personal perspective, neither of the repatriations happens without multiple individuals contributing their expertise in the field, laboratory, and archives. Likewise, editorial processes require the dedication and commitment of so many people who give of their time and talents to improve the final product. Hence, readers, reviewers, editors, and researchers are critical to the process and deserve recognition. And, of course, without the Lee and Afraid of Hawk families, there are no stories to tell. Though I get my name on the title page as author, any book, and especially one like this, is rarely the effort of a single individual. As a result, we are grateful to acknowledge our numerous colleagues who believed in this project.

Likewise, field archaeology is a multi-disciplinary effort. With us in the field at Cornwall Cemetery for the ʻŌpūkahaʻia exhumation were David G. Cooke, Richard LaRose, Gary Hottin, Michael Alan Park, Bill and Kristen Keegan, David A. Poirier, Ruth Shapleigh-Brown, Shelley Smith, Jeffrey Bendremer, Nancy and John J. O'Donnell, Angela Bellantoni, Henry Fuqua, Rev. Carmen Wooster, Will Trowbridge, and William A. Dineen, Jr. In addition, we are indebted to the friendship and graciousness of Ben Gray and Amy Johnson, who have maintained the Foreign Mission School's Steward's House in Cornwall to its National Historic Landmark status. At Wooster Cemetery, Danbury, we were expertly assisted by the following individuals: Robert Young, Mary-Jo Young, Tania Porta, David Smith, Dan DeLuca, Kenneth Beatrice, Jeremy Pilver, Bruce Greene, William Morlock, Richard Red Elk, Wendell and Nancy Deer With Horns, Ed Sarabia, Deborah Surabian, Daniel Cruson, David Smith, the Danbury Civil Air Patrol, Gary Aronson, Dawn Petrocelli, Norma E. Vinchkoski, Tom Keane, and Christine Rose. In the forensic laboratories we were fortunate to have Michael Alan Park, Gary Aronson, David G. Cooke, Richard LaRose, William "Bill" Keegan, and Bruce Greene.

Archival research was conducted at a number of libraries and research centers throughout the country. We would like to acknowledge the assistance and cooperation of Stephen Rice and Kendall Wiggin, Connecticut State Library; Richard Malley, Connecticut Historical Society; Roger Thompson, Friends of the Office of State Archaeology; Gail Kruppa and Mark MacEachern, Torrington Historical Society; Rachel Guest and Jamie Cantoni, Cornwall Historical Society; Diane Hassan, Danbury Historical Society and Museum; Tawa Ducheneaux and Stella Iron Cloud, Oglala Lakota College Library; Elizabeth Thrond, Center for Western Studies, Augustana College; Deborah Adams, Buffalo Bill Center of the West; the Office of State Archaeology, Connecticut State Museum of Natural History; and staffs at the Federal Indian Archives in New York, the New York Public Library, and the Omaha Public Library.

We were lucky enough to take advantage of the exhaustive genealogical research into the Afraid of Hawk family conducted by Robert "Bob" Young. His friendship and permission to use his data in this book improved the accuracy of its content. Bob's passion for Albert Afraid of Hawk continues to motivate.

This book would never have been possible without the contributions of many reviewers and readers who took the time to inspect the text for editorial purposes and historical accuracy. I am totally indebted for the encouragement, criticisms, and comments of Marven Moss, Collin Harty, Bill and Kristen Keegan, Lucianne Lavin, Noenoe Silva, J. Kēhaulani Kauanui, Bob and Mary-Jo Young, and six anonymous readers who improved several drafts of this manuscript. We are grateful to Christopher L. Cook for sharing his extensive research into the life of Henry 'Ōpūkaha'ia. Technical support was provided by Bill Keegan (maps) and Brian Meyer (photos/index) whose cartographic and organizational abilities enhanced the final product. All these colleagues have improved this book in so many ways. I remain grateful for all their friendships and expertise.

Along with the technical contributions of reviewers and editors, I would also like to acknowledge the meaningful conversations I have had over the years in helping me formulate my thoughts on repatriation and understanding Native American and Hawaiian concerns about archaeology and its effect on Indigenous Peoples. In this regard, I am indebted to Ed Sarabia (Tlingit), Noenoe Silva and J. Kēhaulani Kauanui (Hawaiian), Rochelle Ripley, Stella Iron Cloud and Tawa Ducheneaux (Lakota), Rev. Kris Kua and Rev. Dionne Arakawa (Hawaiian). They have all taught me much and are not responsible for any misinterpretations on my part.

Any author needs to have the support, encouragement, and trust of their editors, especially a first time author, and I have benefited greatly from the professionalism of Parker Smathers, Suzanna Tamminen, Marla Zubel, and the staff at Wesleyan University Press. I can't thank them enough for their patience, criticisms, and conceptual ideas that have made this book a reality.

And, of course, there is no book without two extraordinary women: Deborah Liʻikapeka Lee and Marlis Afraid of Hawk, whose commitment and loyalty to family have been inspirational. It has been an honor to acknowledge them as friends and extended family. The power of their inner feelings and the responsibility of taking on the repatriations are examples to all of us of the importance of spirituality and heritage in our lives. I know that these selfless women would agree that the repatriations would never have been achieved were it not for the support of their loving families. The commitment of Debbie's parents, Elizabeth Kapeka Hoʻomanawanui and Kwai Wah Lee, to bringing Henry home and the strength of Marlis's father, Daniel Jay Afraid of Hawk, and her brother, John, are examples of the power and devotion of family for protecting and defining heritage, especially against overwhelming odds. And, of course, we must acknowledge Henry ʻŌpūkahaʻia and Albert Afraid of Hawk, whose courage to travel into the world of the cultural other we venerate.

My retirement as Connecticut State Archaeologist was, in part, to provide the time necessary to write this book. These stories resided inside me and simply had to come out. However, the hours and years devoted to this undertaking could never have been accomplished if it were not for my wife, Angela, whose advice, patience, and support have been my main inspiration. Her faith and unconditional love have made every page possible. I will love her forever.

Prologue

Deborah Li'ikapeka Lee, a young adult Native Hawaiian (*Kanaka Maoli*) woman, woke in the wee small hours of an October night in 1992 far from her homeland in Seattle, Washington, to an inner sensation, impossible to define and equally impossible to ignore. Alone and unsure of what was happening to her, she feared illness and anxiously rose from her bed searching for the comfort of her Bible. She felt as if she were being called to do something, but what? The sensation continued to well up inside her, forcing its way up and out, yielding a voice that spoke as clearly as if its source were standing in front of her. She heard five words: *"He wants to come home."*

Marlis Afraid of Hawk, an Oglala Lakota grandmother (*unci*), heard her call in the form of a midnight reverie on a warm spring night in 2012. She dreamt of a young Lakota man with flowing hair on horseback riding toward her, clothed traditionally, blowing melodiously on a flute. She was a child in her dream, standing immobilized, transfixed as the anonymous rider motioned toward her to follow, turning his horse and riding away, leaving the earth behind, galloping into the sky. To her amazement, she recognized ancestors and tribal members, dressed in regalia, emerging from the surrounding clouds falling in line behind the mysterious rider, dragging their dog-pulled *travois* into the heavens. Who was this Lakota who could command followers? Why had he come to her? Marlis spent days searching for the meaning of her dream from the spirit world. Ultimately, consulting with tribal elders, cloaked in ceremony, the message was revealed: the young man was her father's uncle, or in Lakota kinship, her grandfather (*lala*), who had left the reservation a long time ago, never to return. She was told: *"He wants to come home."*

Two Native women heard spiritual appeals that eventually led them to Connecticut and my office. As the Connecticut State Archaeologist, a position I held for almost thirty years, I had the responsibility of supervising, in hopefully a professional and respectful manner, the archaeological removal and the forensic identification of the surviving skeletal remains of Henry ʻŌpūkahaʻia and Albert Afraid of Hawk, young men who died and were buried in our state in the 19th century. We worked with the Lee and Afraid of Hawk families and a team of funeral directors, forensic scientists, archaeologists, and historians to conduct the exhumations and prepare the remains for the final leg of their journeys home. Our involvement is the bridge between these Hawaiian and Lakota narratives.

Henry ʻŌpūkahaʻia considered leaving the Big Island in the first decade of the 19th century "rather than live without a mother and father"[1] who had been brutally slain before his childhood eyes by Kamehameha's warriors. As a teenager, he secured passage onboard an American merchant ship, sailing halfway around the world hoping to replace pain and memory, attempting to outrun his survivor's guilt, seeking peace from the violence he experienced in his youth with its resultant despondency. His journey would take him to Connecticut, where he was introduced to Christianity, experienced a St. Paul-type revelation accepting Jesus as his personal savior leading to his study of the Bible in hopes of returning home as a missionary to convert Native Hawaiians to the Gospel, but tragically dying of typhus fever in Cornwall, Connecticut, on Feb. 17, 1818, and buried under frozen New England earth. Considered the first Christianized Native Hawaiian, Henry's journey stalled far from his birthplace until Debbie Lee, Henry's cousin seven generations removed, heard in the still of the night his desire to come home and began the process for his return.

Eighty years later, at the close of the 19th century, Albert Afraid of Hawk, Oglala Lakota Sioux, first-generation reservation Indian born in the earliest days of the Pine Ridge Agency in South Dakota, was also looking to leave his homeland. He set out with Buffalo Bill's Wild West troupe to escape the stifling colonization of the reservation system that forced him to share his childhood with starvation and ethnocide, forbidding him the fulfillment of his Lakota birthright. His grandfather rode with the undefeated Red Cloud and instilled the childhood Albert with stories of past Lakota glories and their harmony and balance with the universe before the coming of the *waschius* (white man); his father was beside Crazy Horse at Little Bighorn fighting against George Custer's Seventh Cavalry; and his older brother travelled with

Spotted Elk (aka Big Foot), surviving the massacre at Wounded Knee. Torn between two cultural worlds, he yearned to find identity, which on the reservation was being denied by a dominant, subjugating society. He wanted to be Lakota, free as his grandfather and father before him had been—warriors, buffalo hunters, men of honor—not enslaved as wards of the federal government. He left the reservation hoping to assume that life, even as a show performer. His journey would take him throughout the eastern seaboard and eventually to Danbury, Connecticut, where he died June 29, 1900, of food poisoning and was laid to rest in an unmarked grave in Wooster Cemetery. His journey suspended far from his homeland until Marlis Afraid of Hawk, Albert's grandniece, heard his yearning plea within a deep sleep and began the process of his return.

Teenagers when their journeys began, 'Ōpūkaha'ia and Afraid of Hawk had heard separate callings to leave their homelands, crossing over to inhabit the world of the cultural other. Traditional ways of life had already broken down due to contact with Western society, disrupting their Indigenous cultural systems and leading to intense warfare, depopulation, environmental destruction, and ultimately loss of lands to the American government whose imperialist goals purposely undervalued both Hawaiian and Lakota cultures by prohibiting practices, such as ceremonies, dances, traditional dress, and the speaking of their ancient languages. More than 100 years after their untimely deaths, descendant women would hear their spiritual voices and seek to repatriate their ancestors' remains, completing their long journeys home.

While the odysseys of these young Native men and the aspects of Manifest Destiny that crippled their Indigenous life ways are analogous in a remarkable fashion, they also represent distinct cultural traditions (Hawaiian and Lakota), differing time frames (Henry died fifty years before Albert was born) and legacies (Henry became celebrated while Albert remained relatively anonymous). Henry was buried under a stone monument, especially built to commemorate his memory forever; Albert was interred in an unmarked grave, its location unknown for 108 years. These two accounts were chosen for this book not only due to my personal involvement, but to highlight the disruptive commonalities of expansionism that led to massive deaths, conflicts, colonization, and conformity that continue to shape contemporary Hawaiian and Lakota communities and the resurgence of both cultures.

We know more about the life of Henry ʻŌpūkahaʻia due to the posthumous publishing of his chronicles by Rev. Edwin W. Dwight than we know of Albert Afraid of Hawk, who has no written autobiography. *The Memoirs of Henry Obookiah, A Native of Owhyhee, and a Member of the Foreign Mission School, who died at Cornwall, Connecticut, February 17, 1818, aged 26 Years*, contains a first-person account of his life in Hawaiʻi, his private New England diary, letters from the Congregational community, and Dwight's heart-rending description of Henry's death. Even 19th century authors like Mark Twain, Robert Louis Stevenson, and Jack London knew his story from Sunday school lessons. This book relies heavily on the *Memoirs* among other primary and secondary sources in relating ʻŌpūkahaʻiaʻs story and his impact on Hawaiian history.

Contrariwise, there are few primary documents referencing Albert Afraid of Hawk beyond U. S. Indian Census records, Buffalo Bill's Wild West "Route Books," and newspaper accounts of his death. The Lakota didn't have a written language then, so only Euro-American records are available for us to reconstruct his life. After death, Albert, for the most part, had become anonymous, lost even to his family who never learned why he hadn't returned home from his time with Buffalo Bill, and, except for photographs that Indian art collectors cherish in the Library of Congress, memory of him became obscured through time. As a result, we have taken more liberties with the telling of Albert's story, reading between the lines and even going so far as to suggest motives for his leaving Pine Ridge. ʻŌpūkahaʻia had a profound effect on the Euro-American culture; Afraid of Hawk barely had the opportunity to penetrate it.

The physical remains of both men were archaeologically "resurrected" from their graves and welcomed home to great acclaim from long, arduous journeys. The parallels to their stories are striking. This book is an account of their lives, the histories of their people, and our experience repatriating their physical remains, an experience that has left me with a profound respect for the importance of family, heritage, and spirituality among Native communities in response to changes in the modern world and giving rise to my own personal journey as an archaeologist. In the spirit of Indigenous oral tradition, our approach in chronicling both long journeys home is through storytelling rather than scientific treatise. The danger of this approach is unintended romanticizing. The journeys they embarked upon were rites of passage, exhibiting universal elements of "separation, initiation, and return,"[2] and, as a result, ʻŌpūkahaʻia and Afraid of Hawk have inadvertently become champions who reappeared to bestow promise, cultural continuity, and pride to their people. They are links to a cultural past that has been modified greatly by the modern world system. Their stories are inspiring and have contemporary connotations. Our challenge has been to introduce Henry and Albert to the reader in pragmatic, unsentimental ways without losing the moving experiences of their personal tragedies and the inspiration they provide to their descendants. My intent is to memorialize and celebrate Henry ʻŌpūkahaʻia and Albert Afraid of Hawk, not idealize them, though perhaps because of our personal involvement, I may fail at times.

When I began my study of, and subsequent career in, archaeology over forty years ago, contemporary Native Hawaiian/Native American communities and anthropological archaeologists rarely communicated. Archaeologists piously believed that they were the scientists, the PhDs, the experts in antiquity. What could contemporary Indigenous Peoples tell us about their unwritten past that has been so changed, so distant, and so unlike their lives today? They surely had lost too much to ever recall their unrecorded cultural history.

This view of Indigenous Peoples' ability to tell their own stories contained unintended and, at times, intended Western racist undertones. Archaeologists felt no compelling need for consultation with tribes. We analyzed pottery shards and stone points, wrote manuscripts about the cultural behavior of "prehistoric peoples" and made careers without regard to, or input from, the descendants that manufactured the objects of our study. We simply did not appreciate how our research into the distant past affected the lives of living people. Accordingly Native

Peoples viewed archaeologists as part of the exploitative system of Western society that killed millions of their ancestors, took their land, and left them impoverished on reservations of the U. S. government's making. We took, rarely gave back, and never associated with them.

I distinctly remember attending a powwow in the mid-1980s and hearing Dakota actor and activist Floyd (Red Crow) Westerman express his indignation through an audio speaker heard throughout the entire fair grounds, that Indian people had two enemies in this world: the FBI and archaeologists! I was stunned when he said that.[3] I didn't get it. How could he compare archaeologists, me, to the sometimes strong-handed tactics of the Federal Bureau of Investigation on Indian reservations? After all, weren't we working to preserve Native American heritage, to help them restore their cultural past?

"Archaeologists," Red Crow explained, "dig up the bones of our ancestors, study them in laboratories, and exhibit them for people to gawk at. Archaeologists hold our ancestors prisoners in museums! And the FBI unjustifiably arrest and hold our young Indian men in federal prisons! Prisons for our ancestors! Prisons for our youth today! They are both our enemies!"[4]

Over the years I had nurtured developing friendships within the Connecticut Native American community, and nervously I scanned the fair grounds wondering whether they looked on me as an enemy. I was confused, angry, and ashamed—all at the same time. They were infuriated; we were arrogant. Neither side understood one another or seemed to care to.

As an undergraduate student in anthropology I had read treatises by the Lakota scholar Vine DeLoria, Jr., who harshly criticized anthropologists citing our motivations as benefiting ourselves and doing nothing to respect the concerns of Native Americans who were against our actions perpetrated in the name of "science."[5] With the rise of Red Power in the 1970s, Indian activists expressed their distress by disrupting archaeological excavations, conducting "sit-ins" at museums, and organizing "The Longest Walk" from San Francisco to Washington, D.C. to bring attention to Native American anxieties about the desecration archaeologists were wreaking at burial sites across the country and the museums that housed the bones of their ancestors on hidden storage shelves. I understood these concerns intellectually, but not emotionally; after all, I was training to be a scientist and convinced myself that our work, in the long run, would benefit the Native American community. Nonetheless, Indian activism was bringing about a change within our science and a lot of soul-searching.

In the early 1980s, I was a graduate student in anthropology at the University of Connecticut entrusted with the forensic analyses of seven Indian skeletons earmarked for the first-ever Native American reburials in the state by the Connecticut Indian Affairs Council. Invited afterwards to the re-interment ceremony, I met a young Native man who seemed to have nothing but contempt for me. We launched into a long discussion, really a debate/argument, on the treatment of human skeletal remains. By handling the remains I was playing with fire, he warned me, a nuclear energy that would subsume me because of my "disrespectful work." I responded with hopes that my "forensic work" made the reburials more personal since I was able to give description to each individual—sex, age, diseases, life stress pathologies, and traumas—by letting their "bones" speak to their personal histories from hundreds of years ago. I hoped that our work made the ceremony more meaningful. The young Native man counter-argued that he didn't need science for him to hear his ancestors' stories; he heard their voices whenever he sang to them in the forest. It was all he needed to know. I countered that I heard them, too, but through the physical study of their "bones." We parted not truly comprehending each other's perspective: mine steeped in western material science, his embedded in Native spiritualism.

Five years later when I became the state archaeologist with the role and responsibility to work with Indigenous Nations over their concerns about archaeology, vandalism, and the adverse effect of construction activities on sacred sites, I began to meet regularly with tribal representatives, participating in powwows and other gatherings. Gradually, I was developing an understanding and sensitivity through dialogue and personal relationships. While I was going through this incipient transformation in the late 1980s, I met Maria Pearson (Hai-Meacha Eunka, Running Moccasins), a Yankton Sioux woman who became the "voice" for the pan-Native American reburial movement. Maria and a nationwide delegation of tribal leaders had been invited to the annual meeting of the National Association of State Archaeologists to address their concerns over the differential treatment of Indian burials by state governments.

Maria related an account that simply put the issue into perspective for me. Her husband, John, she told our gathering, worked for the Iowa Department of Transportation, and one day he came home telling a troublesome story. An unmarked pioneer cemetery had been encountered during road construction activities. All the remains were removed and reburied into another cemetery except those identified as a young Indian woman and her baby, whose skeletons were sent to the state archaeologist for study and repository. Maria was astonished. Why were the two Native burials treated differently than the white burials? Why were Indian remains considered objects of study while Euro-American remains were respectfully reburied? Under the United States' own laws this differential treatment was plain and simple discrimination. Maria spoke eloquently and persuasively, presenting a straightforward, sincere story that put a complex controversy into perfect context.

Attitudes have changed remarkably since the 1980s. Archaeologists and Native Americans and Hawaiians have since opened up dialogue to mend misunderstandings and to develop trust relationships based on communication and personal empathy. While many Indigenous Peoples remain angry and many archaeologists continue to be suspicious, both communities are working to find common ground. Many tribes see the benefit of archaeological investigations and have gone so far as to engage archaeologists to jointly work with them on their reservations.[6] Many archaeologists today are employed by Native communities and have developed equitable partnerships forging research designs benefiting both parties. Sonya Atalay's book on "Community-based Archaeology" represents, in part, a methodological paradigm shift that incorporates descendant communities into the scientific process from conception to interpretation.[7] Archaeologist Chip Colwell has examined the history of repatriation and offers model examples for what improved relationships between archaeologists/museums and Native communities should look like.[8] In the last decade, collaboration has increased and the number of college-trained Native American archaeologists has skyrocketed.

Connecticut is a marvelous example. The Mashantucket Pequot Tribal Nation has developed a world-class museum to tell their story to the public, much of it stemming from their own sponsored archaeological investigations. The Eastern Pequot Tribe has coordinated with the University of Massachusetts, Boston, in conducting archaeological surveys on its North Stonington reservation for over fifteen years. The Mohegan Tribe of Connecticut has trained tribal archaeologists overseeing cultural resource management projects and below ground historical research in their homeland. Times have changed and for the better.

Repatriation of Indian skeletal remains and tribal artifacts of cultural patrimony is now the law of the land. At the federal level, the U. S. Congress, influenced in part by the activism of Maria Pearson and others, approved the Native American Graves Protection and Repatriation Act (NAGPRA) in 1990 acknowledging that federal agencies and funded institutions, housing artifacts and human remains originating through the cultures of contemporary descendant Native peoples, have an obligation to collaborate with those communities and return human skeletons and items of cultural patrimony when requested.[9] While NAGPRA remains controversial, complicated, confusing and is not always a given, the law does represent a philosophical and legal shift in the Native and scientific/museum communities.

At the state level, the Connecticut General Assembly passed legislation creating the Native American Heritage Advisory Council (NAHAC), providing tribes (federally and non-federally recognized) input to the state archaeologist and State Historic Preservation Office (SHPO) on matters of Indian burials and sacred sites (C.G.S. 10-388, *et.seq.*). Though many states have preservation mechanisms incorporating Native voices, NAHAC is uniquely poised as a state agency with advisory responsibilities for responding to issues protecting burials and sacred sites on private lands. As a result of this consultation process, Connecticut has reburied scores of Native American skeletal remains and funerary objects, including those housed in museums and accidently discovered during construction activities.

Fearing the loss of valuable artifacts and human skeletal collections, many museums have resisted NAGPRA mandates by searching for technicalities in the law. Many cases brought by Native American tribes seemed to represent differing views of resistance or respect by museum authorities, whose stance seemed not to recognize that this land originally belonged to the tribes.[10] As a result, cogent arguments have to be made by Indigenous Peoples seeking the repatriation of their ancestors or artifacts of their heritage with the legislative burden on them to demonstrate patrimony. Museums simply did not want to give up what they felt they were preserving for all of humanity and the advancement of science regardless of whether the people who had a cultural continuity to those artifacts and skeletons objected. How were museums to educate the public to the diversity and artistic achievements of Native American cultures if their collections were returned to the tribes, who would then have the ability to keep them from the public if they deemed appropriate? How were we to advance scientific knowledge of the history of diseases and the migration of ancient peoples if Native skeletons were reburied?[11]

By the time the Native American Graves Protection and Repatriation Act (NAGPRA) was enacted by the federal government, our office had been working with the Connecticut's Indigenous Peoples for a number of years and had prepared artifact inventories for the state's two federal-recognized tribes: The Mohegan Tribe of Connecticut and the Mashantucket Pequot Tribal Nation.

In 1996, we received requests for repatriation from both tribes. At the time, the Mohegan were actively working with ten museums to recover sacred items associated with their tribal history, including nineteen objects from the Norris L. Bull Collection, which were part of the Anthropological Collections at the University of Connecticut. Based on our inventories, all of the requested objects had been removed from 17th century Mohegan burials with the exception of one artifact, a two-faced soapstone effigy pipe that belonged to the Uncas family and had originally been taken from a significant cultural site referred to as "Uncas Cabin."

Uncas was the first sachem (paramount chief) of the Mohegan Tribe and probably their most important cultural figure in the

Post-Contact Period. Mohegan oral tradition indicates that pipes of this kind had been passed down long before Europeans arrived and are still in use within the Mohegan community. Mohegan traditional religious leaders indicated that present-day adherents for the practice of traditional Mohegan religion would use this particular steatite pipe.

Of the eighteen objects found with human remains, eight were recovered from the Royal Mohegan Burial Ground along today's Elizabeth Street in Norwich, Connecticut. This well-known Mohegan cemetery had been badly disturbed through economic development and looting over the last 200 years. In the Bull Collection, grave goods from the Royal Mohegan Burial Ground consisted of a charm stone, a faceted orange glass bead, one trade axe, metal and stone pestles, a trade snuffbox, a copper kettle, a black angular stone pipe, and a paint pot with ocher staining, among other funerary objects.

Based on our inventory catalogue, there was no question that these cultural items belonged to the Mohegan Tribe and had been disrespectfully removed from graves and by unauthorized digging at Uncas' Cabin. So, based on our own information, when tribal representatives requested repatriation from the Connecticut State Museum of Natural History at UConn, there was no question regarding the cultural affinity of the funerary objects. With both parties in agreement and after posting notice in the Federal Bulletin, the formal NAGPRA repatriation occurred in April 1996.

As far as early repatriations would go, this case represents one of the least contentious returns of Native artifacts at that time. Our records were undisputable as to the shared relationships between these items and the Mohegan Tribe, so there was no reason for us to question their cultural affiliation. But, I think there was another reason for the smooth transfer of these sensitive cultural items: a trustworthy relationship that had developed for over a decade. Along the way, I made mistakes and at times circumstances between our office and the Connecticut tribes became emotional and contentious. But I like to think that through it all, a confidence developed; one that came with time, respect, and personal empathy. We came to understand each other's needs and we worked together for a common goal.

Unfortunately, in many NAGPRA cases, museum personnel and Native People may not know each other or have had the time to develop trusting relationships. In many cases, the road has been bumpy to say the least. Sometimes inventory records and cultural affiliations are not as clear; sometimes more than one tribe may make claim to cultural items. Regardless, there is no substitute for a personal rapport built on a history of communication and mutual respect. Only when we open dialogue with each other and appreciate and address concerns can we seek common ground and do what is right for everyone. Repatriation does not have to be contentious, but it does require dialogue, an understanding of motives, sensitivity, and the willingness to work together. I take heart that the repatriations of 'Ōpūkaha'ia and Afraid of Hawk are examples of that confidence and cooperation.

Through this compliant give-and-take, dialogues have opened up, forming pathways to learn from each other. I can testify that the science of archaeology has benefited from its association with Indigenous Peoples around the globe, and we hope that Native populations have also gained from the relationship. Most archaeologists have acquired a degree of sensitivity, and Native Americans have come to appreciate the contributions of archaeology to an understanding of their past.[12] We are not enemies; we all make mistakes and are constantly learning. With any change of direction, it can be a long, slippery road to mutuality, but we are working together and making remarkable advancements. The pendulum has swung from exclusive control of Native American artifacts and human remains by museums and archaeologists toward Indian communities exerting their rights to have those objects and remains returned and reburied according to their own cultural prescriptions. We can envision a day when the pendulum will settle supported by shared respect and partnership.

The repatriations of Henry 'Ōpūkaha'ia and Albert Afraid of Hawk did not fall under NAGPRA review because they represented the private actions of individual families requesting the disinterment and re-interment of a genealogical ancestor. Had the reburials of Henry and Albert come under NAGPRA jurisdiction, consent would have been required from tribal governments, including lengthy reviews and a six-month wait after publication in the Federal Register of the intent to repatriate. The process would have been more formal and protracted. Be that as it may, all families have the right to disinter and reinter the remains of their ancestors. The deaths and burials of Henry and Albert, far from their homelands, were the result of historical happenstance. In returning them home, the completion of their journeys has had significant personal meanings for their families and Native communities, and, subsequently, special and surprisingly emotional connotations for the research teams that assisted in their repatriations. Although ʻŌpūkahaʻia and Afraid of Hawk will endure in Connecticut history, Hawaiʻi and Pine Ridge will always be "home" and where their mortal remains should rightfully reside.

As I tell the story of these amazing young men and their families from a Western scientist's perspective, it unavoidably relates my own personal development as an archaeologist. Like Henry and Albert, I unconsciously set out on a profound journey which began when I started listening to, and learning from, Native Peoples over four decades ago, hearing their voices and concerns.[13] It took time, but through dialogue and development of personal relationships, I like to think that confidence was built. I was the outsider, the government official relegated with legal responsibilities and decision-making authority. Yet I assumed my duties seeking to understand a Native perspective toward my actions as a state archaeologist. Eventually, like Debbie and Marlis, I, too, would hear Henry and Albert, though not through dreams and inner feelings, but through a calling to use my training as an archaeologist in returning these young men home. From a Native perspective, I have been told, and I do believe, it was not an accident two such repatriations occurred during my tenure—they were meant to happen.

In many ways, though, this is not my story to tell, and I do not claim to speak for the families or for any Native Peoples. However, my involvement in these repatriations serves as the hinge between the two narratives, the bridge that connects Henry to Albert. My contention is that the science of archaeology does have a meaningful role assisting Indigenous communities in the return and respectful treatment of their ancestors. Our archaeological and forensic teams had to meet legal obligations defined by the State of Connecticut for the removal, identification, and return of Henry and Albert. These are secular requirements using Western state-of-the-art scientific techniques and methodologies, but we never lose sight of the fact that we are human beings handling the remains of other human beings. Hence, there are also solemn concerns demanding the ethical and sensitive approach in accordance, in these particular cases, with traditional Native Hawaiian and Lakota belief systems. Our role was to partner in the respectful excavation, sensitive analyses, and preparations for the subsequent reburial directly with the families of 'Ōpūkaha'ia and Afraid of Hawk, who have contributed in innumerable ways to this book.

The long journeys home of Henry 'Ōpūkaha'ia and Albert Afraid of Hawk are genuine American stories, embarrassingly recounting the disgraceful dealings of the government toward Native peoples in Hawai'i and the High Plains of the North American continent. The United States, soon after its forming, was not content to simply trade with Indigenous Nations. With westward expansion the government wanted their land, seeking to conquer and undermine their cultures through dominance and colonial tactics. My involvement and telling of these stories are inescapably part of this long history of oppression and subjugation, but I hope that my respect for the men whose remains were returned to their families comes through on all of these pages. The author makes no claim of being Native Hawaiian or Lakota and does not speak or read their languages, so I take on the responsibility of telling these stories with a degree of apprehension and humility, knowing that I cannot convey the complexity of their cultures or the colonial quandary they have been exposed to from a firsthand, insider's view, but only hoping that my outsider's perspective does some justice to these historical accounts and their interpretations for the general public to appreciate.

Told through the personal account of the participating archaeologist, *The Long Journeys Home* transcends historical narrative in its relationship to contemporary Native Hawaiian and Native American families dealing with culture change in the modern world, seeking respect and honor through their collective pasts. It chronicles the Polynesian discovery of Hawai'i, Kamehameha's wars of unification, the establishment of the Protestant Christian missions in the Pacific, the political coup appropriating Hawai'i from Native control, Hawaiian efforts to obtain sovereignty, Lewis and Clark's Corps of Discovery, Red Cloud's War, the Battle of the Little Bighorn, the establishment of the Sioux reservations, the horrific carnage at Wounded Knee, and the resurgence of Lakota culture.

Furthermore, the book is about modern archaeological and forensic science and the partnership created with Native families in order to find common ground in the appropriate treatment of their ancestors by bringing them "home." The assertion of this book is that archaeology and Native concerns are not mutually exclusive, not even in opposition, but strongly interrelated. Archaeologists are not "enemies" and neither are Indigenous Hawaiians and Americans. Working in partnership, scientists and Native Peoples can bring closure for families and honor to the ancestors by completing their journeys home. My goal in writing this narrative is not to enter into debates about repatriation, for others have represented both sides of the argument more effectively than I can; my hopes, though, are that the reader comes away with a better appreciation of repatriation, as well as a greater understanding of the process of "working together" through a personal account. The Lakota say, *"Mitakuye Oyasin"*—"We are all related." In many respects, it has been a journey for all of us: archaeologists have listened to Native Peoples and in return they have listened to us. This book also aspires to introduce the reader to the lives of these two remarkable Indigenous men, their individual and family struggles, and the resurgences of Hawaiian and Lakota culture that Henry and Albert have in part contributed toward.

With these factors in mind, we embrace the spirit of Maria Pearson and Native oral tradition by employing a narrative approach, storytelling, weaving the past and the present throughout the book, a hybrid of history and memoir, not necessarily in a linear, chronological order but in an informal manner that emphasizes the circular notion of time without losing sight that these are as much contemporary stories as they are also American history.

PART I

THE REPATRIATION OF
HENRY ʻŌPŪKAHAʻIA

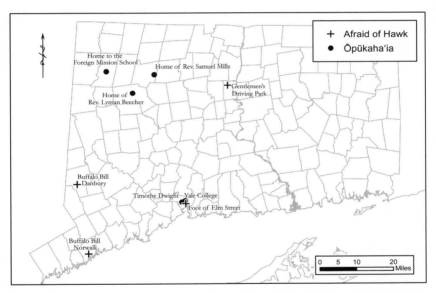

State of Connecticut highlighting places associated with Henry ʻŌpūkahaʻia and Albert Afraid of Hawk.

1 | "Oh, How I Want To See Owhyhee"

His dry, hacking cough could be heard throughout the large, two-story colonial saltbox that served as the parsonage of the Rev. Timothy Stone, pastor of the South Parish in Cornwall, Connecticut, a picturesque town tucked in the state's Litchfield Hills. The entire Stone family, along with four of his Native Hawaiian (*Kanaka Maoli*) companions, stood witnesses to the violent attack on his body, but could not feel the intense pain of his muscles or the severity of his headaches. The young Hawaiian Christian man, Henry "Obookiah," lay in bed during a cold, bitter New England February in 1818, surrendering to the ravages of typhus fever, far from his warm island birthplace. Henry had been studying at the newly formed Foreign Mission School with hopes of returning to Hawai'i with the Gospel of Jesus Christ in his hands. His early death would steal the opportunity.

Throughout his month long illness, Henry's attitude remained steadfast, patient, even cheerful at times, and above all resigned to the Will of God. Mrs. Mary Stone, who took it upon herself to care for Henry on his deathbed, read the Bible and pray with him daily, was impressed with his Christian conviction. Near the end she inquired if he thought he was dying, and Obookiah responded in the affirmative, weakly uttering, "Mrs. Stone, I thank you for your kindness."

Fighting back tears, she responded, "I wish we might meet hereafter."

Feebly, he assented, "I hope we shall."[1]

When asked if he was afraid to die, Henry cried, "No, I am not. Let God do as He pleases." Then again, he so desperately wanted to live. Live to be a powerful witness to the one, true God. Live to bring salvation to his people. Live to see Hawai'i. "Oh, mortality!" he cried out one night.[2]

Insisting that his Native companions remain close to him during his ordeal, he beseeched William Kanui, fellow-student at the Foreign Mission School, who also nursed 'Ōpūkaha'ia during his sickness, "William, if you live to go home, remember me to my uncle."[3] Bursting into tears and raising his hands heavenward, Henry lamented, "Oh, how I want to see Owhyhee!"[4]

His approaching death was peaceful. He seemed to be free of pain for the first time in weeks. With his compatriots beside his bed, he spoke in his native language, *"Aloha oʻe"*—My love be with you.[5]

Damp with perspiration, the cotton shirt clung to my back as I hunched on hands and knees over a narrow dirt base leveled at almost five feet into the earth alongside the burial. But it wasn't until the moisture gravitated onto my nose, dripping to the ground below that I

Portrait of Henry Obookiah. by Adelle Summerfield, n.d. (Courtesy of Author).

truly appreciated the July heat and humidity that had descended onto the small knoll in Cornwall Center Cemetery that summer morning in 1993. The stage from which we excavated was only a foot wide at the head area, leaving sparse room to maneuver beside the grave, necessitating balance and concentration to gently scrape away earth while not impacting the fragile skeletal remains hidden under mere inches of loose sandy soil.

The anticipated skeleton would, hopefully, be the remains of ʻŌpūkahaʻia, the first Christianized Native Hawaiian—the young man whose untimely death in 1818 inspired missionaries to venture off to the Sandwich Islands, charged with converting the "heathen" who up to that time possessed no knowledge of Christ; whose intelligence had created a phonetic Hawaiian alphabet which he applied to translate the book of Genesis from Hebrew; whose personality and cogent arguments for allowing Native men to save Native souls led to the development of the Foreign Mission School; and whose life and death story would be told in Sunday Schools to this day. His New England Calvinist patrons gave him the Christian forename of "Henry" while spelling and pronouncing his Hawaiian birth name "Obookiah." As Connecticut state archaeologist, I was given the responsibility to conduct the professional and respectful disinterment of his physical remains per the request of his genealogical relatives for repatriation home to Hawaiʻi. After almost two centuries in New England soil, the best we could hope to recover would be a decomposing skeleton.

Our archaeological field crew had already removed the heavy marble tombstone engraved with the epitaph of "Henry Obookiah" off a granite table marking the burial. The stone monument had also been systematically disassembled, as were three layers of supportive foundation, which extended well below the frost line. Thinly slicing through mixed-mottled sandy soils with the sharp edge of a mason trowel, I encountered the first evidence of the top of the coffin at fifty-two inches below ground surface when rusted metal hardware appeared. The horizontal pattern of nails revealed a hexagonal-shaped box laid in a classic Christian mortuary practice where the deceased was reposed supine with head oriented west, facing east, which means that as one reads the epitaph on a historic New England tombstone, the deceased is not in front of the stone, as most people suspect, but behind it with their feet moving away. Accordingly, on the Day of Resurrection, the dead would be able to witness the rising Christ coming up with the sun and awaken to join Him in everlasting life.

Further evidence of the wooden coffin became visible when a thin, dark, linear stain appeared, a decomposing shadow of the sideboards. Though all that remained of the wood was soil discoloration, it provided a clear outline to the coffin. Excavating within, a pattern of brass tacks with preserved wood adhering materialized along adjacent sides about the chest area. My initial impression was that the tacks secured a draped cloth or decorative linen lining the interior of the coffin. But as I carefully continued deeper into the side margins, the tack pattern changed, descending downward as we dug toward the pelvic area. A second row of brass tacks underneath the discovered row on the right side of the coffin also became visible, forming a semi-circular pattern like a half moon; on the left side, the second row tack configuration emerged but took on a dissimilar shape, horizontal.

As more of the arrangement was revealed, it became apparent that the wood and tacks were not associated with the sides of the coffin, but were actually part of the lid. When the overburdened soil collapsed into the decaying coffin interior due to weight pressure from the foundation tiers and monument above, it split the decomposing top board down the middle, filling the coffin housing with sand and compressing the lid along the sides like swinging a downward, horizontal gate. Brushing the edges revealed that the brass tacks patterned an "H" on the left side and an "O" on the right. "Henry 'Ōpūkaha'ia!" I thought to myself, smiling.

Our mandate was to remove for repatriation the remains of "Obookiah," and his remains only, so we had to be unconditionally certain that this was his grave and not that of another individual. Though we had yet to encounter skeletal remains, the brass tack pattern of initials was an optimistic first indication. We were confident now that this was his coffin, but would there be any associated remains? Acidic soils are the bane to organic preservation in New England. So we tested the sandy ground for its pH content, which fortunately yielded a relatively neutral reading (6.8), suggesting less acidity than we normally find in

Connecticut's mixed-deciduous and high precipitous environment. We remained hopeful.

Then, moving my trowel gently over the soil leveling the head region of the coffin, I heard a dulled tone. Immediately thinking I had encountered a small stone or another metal coffin nail, I put my trowel aside and grasped a small, fine-hair paintbrush among the various hand tools gathered under me. The material encountered felt hard, too hard for bone that had been in the ground for 175 years, I thought, but as my brush swept the granular soil aside, uncovering a one-inch diameter circle, I recognized the rounded structure of the forehead. My God, he is here, I realized, and his skeletal remains were firm, unusually well preserved for a grave of this time period.

An array of anxious people had aligned above me, peering down into the excavation unit, attempting to see over my shoulders, but from their perspective they could only distinguish a small, unidentifiable brownish speck where I had been excavating. I could hear the responding buzz of excitement and anticipation from the onlookers, but before resuming the process of exposing more of the cranium, I allowed myself a moment to appreciate that I would soon be the first person since his death and burial on this sandy knoll in 1818 to look upon the facial structure of Henry 'Ōpūkaha'ia. From the scant part already exposed, I realized that we would recover his intact skeleton, bequeathing his repatriation to his awaiting Hawaiian family. I remember thinking to myself, "Henry will return home." Also aware that the attending crowd stood clueless as to what had been discovered, I turned my head over my right shoulder, looked up and gave identification to the emerging speck: "He's here!"

The Hawai'i 'Ōpūkaha'ia longed to see once more rose from the depths of the Pacific Ocean thirty million years ago when vents on the ocean's floor developed a crack or hot spot through which poured molten lava from the earth's mantle. For tens of millions of years, subterranean liquid rock slowly seeped and spurted, gradually accumulating layer upon layer, until eventually emerging from the sea. Beginning from the northwest end of the rupture, small islands, beginning with Kure, reached the surface of the ocean. This continuous volcanic process created the five largest islands: Kauaʻi, Oʻahu, Molokaʻi, Maui, and Hawaiʻi (The Big Island) to the far southeast. The outgrowth is a series of 122 forming islands along a chain spreading out for almost 2,000 miles.[6] That is the western scientific explanation. Contrarily, Native Hawaiian tradition relates that the islands were born like humans, conceived by their parents Papahānaumoku, who gave birth to the archipelago with her partner, Wākea, the sky father.[7] Together, they genealogically connect the Hawaiian people to their beautiful islands, perceived as relatives, giving rise to the powerful Hawaiian love of their land (*aloha ʻāina*).[8]

These nascent islands with their barren topography would welcome hundreds of species of plants and animals that somehow found their way through wind and water. Lichen and moss grew as factors of wind and rain pulverized the lava into bits of soil. Birds came feeding on fish, depositing their digestive waste containing seeds, which germinated and grew. Insects, blown by jet streams, found the cooled lava their home. Coral and mollusk larvae as well as seaweed surfed the bounding waves from other Pacific islands reaching Hawaiʻi and setting their roots along shallow inlets. Storm swept seeds, drifting logs, and branches of wood found their way.[9] Within this emergent island ecology, life adapted and developed untouched by human hands until the first Polynesians ventured forth.[10]

Hawaiʻi's founding Polynesians sailed in large, double-hulled canoes, some seventy to eighty feet in length, lashed together affording a platform that carried sixty or more people, as well as water, household goods, animals including pigs, dogs, and chickens, and vegetables and fruits such as bananas, taro, and coconut.[11] Their seafaring crafts were floating communes, probably the swiftest ships in the world 1,000 years ago. So intrepid and warlike were the Polynesians that they have been referred to as the "Vikings of the Pacific."[12] How their flotillas ranged the great expanses of the Pacific Ocean, at least 2,000 miles from the Cook Islands and Tahiti where they had presumably journeyed from, when they had no knowledge of the lands before them, is a wonder of human history. By the time they approached Hawaiʻi, they had already inhabited almost 290 far-reaching islands, spatially the widest spread cultural population in the world.[13]

Whether these valiant voyagers came through single or multiple migrations also remains unknown. Undoubtedly in their voyage(s) they were confronted with massive storms, exposure to wind, rain, along with the harsh effects of salt water and sun. They had to take into account the doldrums, an equatorial regional phenomenon where the trade winds converge and flow upward instead of horizontal, leaving them becalmed in a windless sea, straining their self-propelled rowing energy as well as food and water supplies. Even so they persisted. Faith in their ancestors and gods, along with their vast knowledge of oceanic and island worlds, they travelled great distances without the use of navigational instruments. Rather, they closely observed the sun, nightly stars, patterns of waves, cloud formations, and the behavior of dolphins and birds to direct them to new islands. They had to be fearless and faithful and courageous.

Survival of these intrepid Polynesians depended on all family members, *'ohana,* working closely together, developing strong bonds and dedication to each other. Most likely driven to inhabit new islands by population pressures, limitations to environmental resources, and cultural tension, Polynesians, astride their "village" canoes, eventually attained the northern apex of the Pacific Triangle.[14]

Upon Polynesian arrival, Hawai'i contained no carnivorous mammals or snakes; rather, they found flightless birds with no natural predators to defend against. Fish, coral, and underwater plants abounded off shore; onshore, flowers bloomed. But other than the fish in the water and birds in the sky, there was little for humans to digest. The plants and animals they brought with them would have to bear fruit and offspring to secure their long-term survival. Serene as this Eden-like world might appear, it had immense dangers: volcanic eruptions, tsunamis, hurricanes, and earthquakes— all of which could strike unexpectedly and suddenly.

To deal with these calamitous events, the southern Polynesians brought to the northern islands concepts of their many deities, who needed to be appeased through rituals and behavioral taboos maintained by the chiefly *ali'i* class, who were supported by a social system based on genealogical rank, to ensure balance and harmony in their unpredictable world. Travelling with them were Kāne, the Creator;

Pele, the goddess of fire and volcanoes; Nāmakaokahaʻi, the goddess of the sea; Lono, the benevolent god of fertility; and Kūkāʻilimoku (Kū), the fierce god of war. The island's formation was one of fire and water (Pele and Nāmakaokahaʻi), providing cogent dichotomies of form: liquid and solid, seaweed and plants, fish and birds that enhanced their worldview.[15] These gods (*akua*) were spiritual, powerful, and dangerous—considered physical ancestors who partook in the ocean voyages and brought social stability to the newly-founded islands. The *akua* provided life, but could just as easily cause death. They were both feared and loved by the *Kanaka Maoli* (Native Hawaiians), hence worthy of worship.[16]

Deities, as all things animate and inanimate, contained *mana*, a powerful and vital life force. *Mana* could be obtained by humans through genealogical descent, through the killing and sacrifice of an enemy, as well as peacefully through personal relationships and altruistic accomplishments.[17] So sacred and powerful was *mana* that laws and restrictions, *kapu*, had to be instilled to maintain order, or evil and disaster could attach itself to the people. To maintain balance and harmony, the sacred *kapu* system provided a set of behavioral do's and don'ts. Akin to the Tahitian *tabu, kapu* encompassed many prohibitions, such as fishing out of season, walking on a chief's shadow, and the exclusion of men and women from eating together. If broken, violators could be put to death to protect the whole world; exoneration could only come from a *kahuna* or the reaching of a *puʻuhonua*, a place of refuge.[18]

Polynesian chiefdoms represented a level of political complexity based on concepts of hereditary inequality[19] with the chief representing a formal office within a ranked society including commoners and a servant class. As their populations grew, competition for limited productive farmland and other natural resources lead chiefly families to obtain, usually by force, suitable agricultural territories to which they would hold title. The common people (*makaʻāinana*) would receive rights to farm the chief's land, sanctioning the chief's authority over natural resources, wealth, and regulation of labor. The *aliʻi nui* (high chiefs) maintained social control by making judgments, resolving disputes, and punishing wrong doers as well as enforcing and creating *kapu.* While the chief's word was law with the power of life and death over commoners and servants, these social relationships benefited all the *Kanaka Maoli* by maintaining harmony and equilibrium within their world.

Since ancient Hawaiian society was an oral rather than a written culture, values and history were learned through trained storytelling, which was considered sacred. Developed hundreds of years before contact with the Western world, the *Kumulipo* consists of chants and songs that tell a creation story of the universe and the Hawaiian people from the time of darkness to that of daylight. The *Kumulipo* provide a vast cosmological genealogy that stresses the relatedness of the entire world: the land, the gods, the *ali'i,* and the *maka'āinana,* who are all closely and affectionately connected as ancestral kin, all descendants of Wākea and Papahānaumoku.[20] Only through a full understanding of their great genealogy are the *ali'i* able to assert their chiefly rank. The natural and supernatural worlds are one and the same with no distinctions. Hawaiians share a lineage with all of creation.

How to respond to this complex worldview was the role of the *kahuna.* These priests gave order and guidance; consoled and healed; advised when to plant and harvest; instructed when to fish; ordered to war or to remain at peace; conducted sacrifices and rituals; and proffered penance and forgiveness to breakers of the *kapu.* To appease the gods and maintain stability of the *ali'i, kahunas* carved the spiritual wooden *ki'i* (images) and oversaw the building of elaborate *heiaus* (temples) where offerings were issued to the divine, sometimes through human sacrifice.[21] From the practical to the spiritual, the powerful *kahuna,* holding their ceremonies on stone pyramids in private wooden enclosures, were the vital life force of the Hawaiian people.[22] The teenage 'Ōpūkaha'ia would be trained by his priestly uncle, tutored at the *Hikiau Heiau* at Kealakekua Bay, Kona, to become such a *kahuna,* translating the *Kumulipo* and other sacred legends for the *Kanaka Maoli.*

It was there, in 1778, a decade before the birth of 'Ōpūkaha'ia, that Hawaiians had greeted the British sea captain James Cook. Although other foreign populations may have made earlier contact with Hawai'i, it was Cook's encounter that brought the awareness of the islands to Western societies. The Hawaiian Islands would never again be isolated from the rest of the world; the period of being totally Native, '*Ōiwi Wale*, had ended forever.[23]

After the arrival and subsequent death of James Cook at the hands of the Hawaiians, the appearance of British and American sailing vessels was less frequent due to the Western world's concern regarding the perceived ferocity of these Native people. However, as time passed and with the recognition of the islands' strategic midway location in the vast Pacific Ocean, the sight of European and American sailing ships, whaling and merchant, became commonplace. One ruling chief who welcomed these foreigners was the tall, physically thickset, young adult *ali'i*, Kamehameha.

Kamehameha had greeted James Cook on his initial arrival to Hawai'i and even boarded the HMS *Resolution* to trade and have dinner with the British sea captain. Recognized as exceptional among the chiefs, Kamehameha appreciated the usefulness of steel weapons obtained from Western traders in military warfare, especially against his enemy's stone and wooden armaments. Employing these newly available technologies, Kamehameha launched a campaign for domination of the Big Island and, once achieved, the unification of the entire Hawaiian archipelago under his absolute rule.

According to ancient legends, a great chief would be born with the appearance of a shooting star, and that chief would unite all of the islands under his reign. In 1758, the year of Kamehameha's birth, Halley's Comet passed prophetically in the night sky. He was the son of Keōua and the grandson of Keaweikekahia-liikamoku, a former ruler of the eastern portion of the Big Island. Upon his birth, a *kahuna* of standing prophesized that one day this newborn would become a *Mō'ī, Ali'i Nui* (King, holding the highest of chiefly ranks) of the entire island.[24]

Since his family kept him isolated in the mountains during his youth out of fear that jealous chiefs might take his life, and due to his introspective behavior, Kamehameha was labeled "The Lonely One." His uncle, Kalani'ōpu'u, *Mō'ī* of the Big Island, who welcomed Captain Cook to Kealakekua Bay, brought Kamehameha back from exile and bestowed upon him the trademarks of a nobleman with a feathered helmet and cloak. The young man grew in strength and wisdom, was tutored in the arts of combat, and known for his courage in battle.

In traditional Hawaiian society, whenever an *ali'i nui* died, his successor had the right to redistribute land and other valued resources, which meant that competitive conflict would breakout between contenders for vacated, exalted positions. When Kalani'ōpu'u died in 1782, Kamehameha competed with the *ali'i nui*'s two natural sons, Kīwala'ō and Keōua, over control of the chiefdom. Kīwala'ō attempted to placate Kamehameha by naming him the caretaker of the war god, Kū, and making him the chief of the luscious and productive Waipi'o Valley. Unfortunately, this did not satiate the ambitious Kamehameha. Warfare broke out between the cousins. Kīwala'ō was killed at the Battle of Moku'ōhai, and Keōua was declared the new High Chief.[25]

With the advantage of muskets, swords, and cannon obtained from European and American trading partners, Kamehameha warred continually with Keōua for four years. Yet the steel weapons gave no immediate benefit against the aggressive son-chief who had a large following. Feigning a desire to end the continual conflict, Kamehameha invited the suspicious Keōua to a peace parlay in early 1792, which the High Chief, whose resources were being exhausted by the incessant warfare, cautiously accepted. When Keōua came ashore at Kawaihae Harbor north of Kona, Kamehameha's warriors assassinated him and his men, sacrificing his corpse to Kū in a newly constructed and massive *luakini*-type *heiau*.[26] Kamehameha forthwith possessed Keōua's powerful *mana* and was deemed the outright *Mō'ī* of the Island of Hawai'i. Now middle-aged and with both Kiwala'ō and Keōua dead, Kamehameha coveted additional islands under his personal chiefdom. We call the archipelago the Hawaiian Islands because that's the Island of Kamehameha's birth.

During his campaign, Kamehameha invited Nāmakehā, the powerful chief of Ka'ū in the southern district of the Big Island, to join forces against Maui rival chief, Kalanikūpule and his armies on O'ahu. Instead, Nāmakehā rebuffed Kamehameha and challenged his authority with power. Hostilities erupted between the two chiefs with the parents of 'Ōpūkaha'ia aligning their allegiance with Nāmakehā since his mother was a noble-born relation. Tragically, after Nāmakehā's death in a fierce battle at Hilo, Kamehameha sought revenge by attacking the fallen chief's settlements and unleashing his deadly forces against the family of 'Ōpūkaha'ia.

The name "Henry 'Ōpūkaha'ia" was completely unfamiliar when I received the phone call in the spring of 1993 from Henry L. Fuqua, whose Hartford funeral home had been contracted to remove Henry's physical remains and prepare him for repatriation to the Big Island. As a well-established funeral director in the region, Fuqua had had a good deal of experience disinterring contemporary burials using mechanical excavators to lift metal caskets out of their vaults. But fragile, decomposing wooden coffins dating to the early 19th century were far beyond his experience.[27] He needed a forensic archaeologist to conduct the sensitive exhumation and was advised to contact the state archaeologist for assistance.

Law in Connecticut is such that any time human skeletal remains are uncovered and determined by the Office of the Chief Medical Examiner to be older than fifty years and associated with an unmarked historic grave, the investigation is turned over to the state archaeologist for identification, removal if necessary, and reburial according to the cultural prescriptions of the deceased.[28] Under this legislative mandate, we had investigated a number of accidental burial discoveries as well as cemetery vandalisms, including a sand and gravel mining operation that inadvertently exposed a colonial farming family's burial ground, a house expansion project that yielded 17th century Native American graves, and a mausoleum that had been violated to obtain human skulls for satanic cult rituals. As state archaeologist, we had run the gamut from modern criminal investigations to the respectful and professional treatment of historical burials accidently uncovered during construction activities or marred by deliberate unlawful desecration. We worked closely with the state's Native American Nations, historical societies, churches, descendant families, and other associations representing the dead to facilitate respectful reburial of human remains.[29]

The unique request to disinter Henry 'Ōpūkaha'ia posed the first instance where we had been called upon to remove an undisturbed burial for purposes of repatriation. On the phone, Henry Fuqua related the Lee family's petition for the return of their ancestor; upon hearing the story, we were more than pleased to use our expertise to assist.

Pleased, but also struck by the intimidating responsibility of handling ʻŌpūkahaʻia's skeletal remains, his *iwi*, which houses his spirit (*ʻuhane*), his powerful *mana*. The archaeological treatment of the *iwi* required restraint, respect, and sanctity. We were cognizant that ʻŌpūkahaʻia's *ʻuhane* would be near, and our commitment was to handle them reverentially.

The morning broke bright and windy although the seas were unusually calm in the late summer of 1796. The playful surf splashed gently over rocks, soaking the sand of Hilo harbor. Peace and serenity gave way when Kamehameha, believed to be in Oʻahu at the time, unexpectedly appeared amid his war canoes around Pepeʻekeo Point from the north. Nāmakehā, a rival chief from the southern Ka'u district, had threatened Kamehameha's hegemony and transferred his warriors and their families to the northeastern Hilo districts, invading Kamehameha's territory. When the *aliʻi nui* heard of the threat, he quickly returned with his large *peleleu* fleet of battle-ready canoes which emerged in great numbers across the sun-swept waters.

Prepared to engage the enemy with all their strength, Nāmakehā's warriors were hopelessly outnumbered by Kamehameha's forces. The invading canoes were paddled by strong, young men bent forward, sweeping their powerful rowing strokes in unison, borne by the floodtide, moving the attackers at an amazing and deadly speed toward the beach near the mouth of the Waiākea River.[30] The Battle of Kaipalaoa had begun.

The combatants were mostly comprised of commoners—fisherman and farmers whose duty was to support their *aliʻi nui*, though some were professional soldiers, trained from their youth in the art of warfare. Once the invaders were on the beach, the attack started with a massive missile bombardment composed of javelins, followed by pikers who formed in ranks moving as an advancing wall of sharp spears. Then hand-to-hand combat ensued featuring the deadly art of *lua*, which emphasized bone breaking, wrestling, and strangulation, sometimes followed by dismemberment. To defend themselves, common warriors lathered up their bodies with oil making it difficult for their enemy to grasp them. Chiefs wore feathered cloaks which served as battledresses more than garments of opulence, used for protection from stone missiles and to hurtle their enemy onto the ground to be finished off with a spear or dagger.[31]

The warring parties fought their bloody battle along the waterfront. Defenders and attackers punished each other. Nonetheless, Nāmakehā's supporters were overpowered and horribly slaughtered by Kamehameha's invaders. As one of the last rival chiefs to oppose Kamehameha's rule, he was hunted down, killed, and sacrificed at the *Pi'ihonua Heiau*.[32] In their frenzy of revenge, the conquering forces turned on the villagers that supported Nāmakehā, continuing their reprisal on the families of the defenders. The alarm was sounded among the survivors; households fled.

When Keau, one of Nāmakehā's warriors, recognized that his fellow-defenders were being overwhelmed and the battle lost, he withdrew from the beachfront, retreating toward the village to protect his young family. Gathering up his wife, Kamoho'ula, their two sons, an infant and the adolescent 'Ōpūkaha'ia, the family fled into the mountains. Running desperately on top of and around molten flows of hardened black rock and dense vegetation, they quickly escaped inland and upland, seeking refuge from the carnage.

Finding a small lava tube cave in the higher elevations, they concealed themselves for many days until hunger and thirst sent them on a quest for water at a nearby stream. As they quenched their parched, dehydrated throats, a war party of the enemy surprised them, capturing Kamoho'ula and the young boys while Keau, hoping the warriors would chase after him, was swift enough to escape.

To entice Keau from his nearby hiding place, the warriors began torturing their captives, knowing that the cries of his wife and children would bring the father/husband/warrior out of his concealment. And it did, though his initial efforts to free his family were unsuccessful, forcing Keau to flee a second time. The torture continued; with the cries of his family unbearable and their suffering intolerable, Keau made another futile attempt to rescue them, only this time to be captured.

Huddled together on the ground, Keau attempted to protect Kamoho'ula by encompassing her with his arms and body, while a warrior's *leiomanō*, a sharp-edged, shark-toothed sword, slashed away at them.[33] 'Ōpūkaha'ia watched in horrid disbelief as the assailants cleaved unrelentingly at his parents until they were brutally dismembered; heads decapitated; arms and legs severed. Panic-stricken, in shock, the urge for survival took hold. As his parents' blood splattered his body, 'Ōpūkaha'ia gathered his infant brother, slung him over his back, and fled. His freedom was short-lived. A warrior's *pāhoa*, or two-edged spear, impaled his infant brother, killing the newborn and toppling 'Ōpūkaha'ia to the ground. He was the lone family survivor of the torture and brutal onslaught.

With the blood of his parents and brother soaking into his skin, the boy was wrestled and subdued to the ground by the warriors. Being young and posing no threat to the enemy, 'Ōpūkaha'ia was hauled away as a prisoner of war while the corpses of his mother, father, and brother lay behind, exposed on the ground for feral pigs to consume. Despondent, the abducted 'Ōpūkaha'ia was coerced into serving as the personal servant of the warrior who mutilated his parents, compelled to submit and live in the household of the murderer of his family.[34]

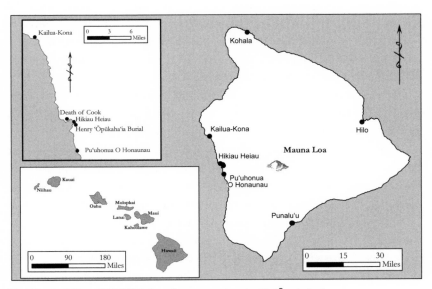

Big Island of Hawaii highlighting places associated with 'Ōpūkaha'ia.

ʻŌpūkahaʻia was born in the shoreline village of Nīnole, in the District of Kaʻū, near Punaluʻu along the southern coast of the Big Island of Hawaiʻi, circa 1787–1792, though it may have been as early as 1785.[35] "ʻOpū-kaha-ʻia" translates as "stomach cut open" and may suggest a caesarian delivery, a birthing technique that would have been unknown at that time and highly unlikely since his mother survived and had another child.[36] Some have suggested that the name may have been bestowed in the tradition of *inoa hoʻomanaʻo* to commemorate the event of a slain, dismembered royal person, maybe a chief during battle. However, ʻŌpūkahaʻia related a story to Thomas Hopu while they were sailing the Pacific Ocean onboard the *Triumph:* that he had received his name when a woman in his village died during childbirth. Her husband immediately cut open her stomach to save the infant and "ʻŌpūkahaʻia" was chosen as his namesake in honor of the event.[37]

He was descended from a family of Hilo chiefs on his mother's side, distant kin to Kamehameha.[38] He was not a commoner, though not considered royalty; his pedigree derived from noble family lines in Maui and the Big Island.[39] His childhood would have been as any traditional Hawaiian boy, predominately *ʻohana*-centered, working together and sharing all aspects of social life from the physical land, food, and shelter to the spirit of *Aloha*. He would have had a far wider range of behavioral freedom than his restricted European/American counterparts since traditional Hawaiians raised their children in a far more relaxed and less constrained manner.

ʻŌpūkahaʻia was nurtured by his parents and *kūpuna* (grandparents) residing in the same household. As he developed into boyhood, his grandfather carved a wooden bowl into which ʻŌpūkahaʻia would place a small stone as a form of confession if his behavior were not up to the family's standard. He did this voluntarily when he knew he had disobeyed or was amiss in his actions. He did not have to be told. He would not lie or deceive his *ʻohana* kinsman for they were his entire world.

ʻŌpūkahaʻia's education came from elders whom he venerated. He learned from his father how to fish, run swiftly among large lava boulders, dive, and swim strongly into the tide; his grandfather taught the cultural ways of Hawaiian traditions through storytelling, especially the family's complex genealogy which defined their place in society.

He developed into a resilient, intelligent boy with a sense of humor that was often entertaining, especially when he mimicked personal characteristics of family and village members. Great *Aloha* existed within this tightly bonded family, but dreadfully "Great *Aloha*" was broken by the warrior's sword, which yielded death and captivity.

In preparation for ʻŌpūkahaʻia's archaeological disinterment, I made arrangements to meet with Cornwall Cemetery sexton John O'Donnell to consider the logistics of the undertaking. John was a burly, muscular, no-nonsense caretaker who wanted this exhumation to be conducted properly. Meeting at the cemetery entrance, we drove to a prominent hill in the southeastern section where the earliest graves were located. I walked out ahead of John, ascending a relatively steep slope of manicured lawn, studying late 18th and early19th century tombstones delineating long-standing, prominent Anglo-Saxon names in the

ʻŌpūkahaʻia's burial monument, Cornwall Center Cemetery, Cornwall, CT. (Courtesy of Bill Keegan).

community. A small, damaged tombstone, having toppled over and lying on the ground, caught my eye. It was dedicated to Thomas Hammatah Patoo, a native of the Marquesas Islands who studied at the Foreign Mission School and died in Cornwall five years after ʻŌpūkahaʻia.[40] I continued my search for a similarly deteriorated vertical or horizontal headstone engraved with the name "Obookiah" but could find none. At last, John joined me and silently motioned to follow him further up the hill.

As we ascended the steep slope, John was advancing straight toward a rectangular stone table. The platform, composed of granite boulders, some the size of basketballs, was positioned on the incline of the hill so that the top of the table at the upper (head) end toward the west was less than a foot off the ground, but almost two feet at the downslope eastern (foot) end, leveled to balance the precipitous embankment. Lying face-up on the table was a beautifully carved, white marble tombstone with shell beads, pineapple, coins, candy, and other trinkets placed on top. Though the stone's engraving was darkened by years of acid rain, the epitaph was still legible. The sizeable lettering at the head of the stone read:

In Memory of
HENRY OBOOKIAH
A Native of
OWHYEE

When I queried John concerning the beads, food, and money, he acknowledged that visiting Hawaiians often made pilgrimage to Cornwall specifically to pay their respects to ʻŌpūkahaʻia, their countryman who never came home. In tribute they frequently placed offerings on his memorial. I was dumbstruck. Expecting a timeworn vertical fieldstone marking the grave, I was unprepared to find a raised-stone pedestal usually reserved in historic New England cemeteries for the most elite members of the community, mainly ministers, and totally unheard of for a man of color. I certainly did not anticipate a place of pilgrimage, a *shrine*.

ʻŌpūkahaʻia, now a prisoner of war, was compelled to serve and reside with the warrior who murdered his parents and brother.[41] He was taken to his captor's home at Kohala,[42] birthplace of Kamehameha and the northern point of the Island of Hawai'i, the geographic opposite from 'Opukaha'ia's home village at the southern extent. At the onset of his altered life, he suffered the constant anguish of survivor's guilt. If only the *pāhoa* that impaled his infant brother had penetrated deeper, he would have died with them. What had he done wrong? Should he have stayed and fought to the death over the bodies of Keau and Kamoho'ula? Would his brother be alive if he had not fled? Was he a coward? His remaining years on Hawai'i, and even later in New England, would be characterized by a tormented mind, subsumed in the abyss of the dark hours, sustaining periods of self-remorse and despondency, searching to find answers to questions that gave no answers, no resolution.[43]

The wife of his captor treated him kindly and even the man that killed his parents did not abuse or overwork him. Nonetheless, the face of the warrior that had tortured him and violently executed his family was a constant reminder of the horror he withstood. 'Ōpūkaha'ia existed solely with feelings of profound culpability. He suffered many nights where he cried himself to sleep while living with his captors for almost two years.[44]

In time—and quite unexpectedly—'Ōpūkaha'ia reunited with his mother's brother. This uncle, Pahua, was the praying priest (*kahuna pule*) at the *Heiau Hikiau* in Nāpo'opo'o and had arrived in Kohala while traveling around the island to collect tribute to cover the costs of the *Makahiki* festivals.[45] At these times, chiefs would confine people to their huts by virtue of *kapu*, while the *kahunas*, bearing the figure of the god Lono, would liberate them through the collection of tributes (i.e., pigs, dogs, tapa, etc.) paid to the *ali'i* in support of the *Makahiki*, which was initiated in honor of Lono's wife, Kaikilani.[46] Pahua had trained under the tutorage of Hewakewa, the high priest (*kahuna nui*) of Kamehameha, and may well have been present at Kealakekua Bay when Capt. Cook was slain.[47]

At first, Pahua did not recognize his nephew. The last time he had laid eyes on the boy 'Ōpūkaha'ia was a mere child, and he had now grown into a young teenager. Uncertain, Pahua inquired about his parents and when he heard the name of his sister, Kamoho'ula, the priest broke down in tears. He had thought 'Ōpūkaha'ia dead. Trembling, Pahua could hardly believe his fortune. His nephew was alive, saved by the gods and reunited with him.

The *kahuna* resolved that the boy should not return to the home of his captive, insisting that he must dwell with him and his maternal grandmother, Hina, in Nāpo'opo'o. Reconciled with his true family, Pahua planned to take 'Ōpūkaha'ia under his wing, tutoring the boy to follow in his footsteps and enter the priesthood, devoting his life to the gods who had saved him. Determined, Pahua instructed the young boy to return to his captor and petition for his release.[48]

The warrior who retained 'Ōpūkaha'ia did not take the request calmly. Angered at the thought of releasing the boy, the countenance and menacing voice of the man put renewed fear into 'Ōpūkaha'ia, who would never be allowed to leave until his slaver died, or the boy died first, which the warrior threatened. 'Ōpūkaha'ia wanted so desperately to go with his uncle—to be rid of the face that reminded him continually of his parents' merciless deaths. Yet he was powerless. The confrontation reopened deep emotional wounds.

After his encounter with the warrior, 'Ōpūkaha'ia sought out his uncle and told him of his captor's ire at the mere idea of yielding his freedom. Pahua fashioned an attitude, instructing 'Ōpūkaha'ia not to return to this vile man, but remain by his side. Let the warrior, his sister's murderer, come to discuss this with the priest. Pahua would handle the situation personally; as a *kahuna*, he had the power and influence to do so.

A few days later, the warrior approached Pahua to collect his property. Pahua spoke eloquently of 'Ōpūkaha'ia as his own child, making it clear that he would not let the boy leave him under any circumstance. If the warrior insisted, he must take both 'Ōpūkaha'ia and Pahua back with him as captives because the priest would never let the youth leave his house alone.[49]

In the end, there would be no confrontation, no frightening outcry. Pahua was a man who served the gods. His *mana* was far more powerful than that of the abductor. Whether out of respect or fear of the *kahuna*, who was capable of praying someone to death,[50] the warrior acquiesced and agreed to give 'Ōpūkaha'ia his freedom. He gave the uncle one curious stipulation: "You must treat him well and take care of him in a proper way, just as I have done." Pahua agreed that it would be satisfied.[51] Had this enslaver of 'Ōpūkaha'ia, murderer of his family, become fond of the boy? Or had he accepted that he was in no position to challenge the *kahuna* and, thus, attempted to make a good appearance of his predicament? Whatever his motives, 'Ōpūkaha'ia was now free to live with his uncle and train to be a *kahuna,* maybe even take his place as the praying priest at the *Heiau Hikiau.*

Under Pahua's mentorship, 'Ōpūkaha'ia matured into a bright and resourceful young man. Beginning his apprenticeship as a *kahuna,* Pahua trained him hard, demanding long tedious hours commencing at sunrise and continuing throughout the day, well into the late night. 'Ōpūkaha'ia strained to learn and memorize long litanies; repeating them daily at the *heiau,* 'Ōpūkaha'ia prayed for the life and happiness of the chiefs, for their safeguard from enemies, for beneficial weather and productive crops, for protection and appeasement of the *akuas* to prevent volcanic eruptions, tsunamis, and earthquakes. He was intelligent and quickly learned the extensive prayers and associated rituals to uphold *kapu* and to forgive violators. He committed to memory thousands of verses that were part of the significant oral histories of the Hawaiians, including *Kumulipo*, the Hawai'i creation chants. Though the long hours and intense study commanded his attention and brought on exhaustion, during the evening, thoughts of his family's deaths still haunted him into the night until welcomed sleep approached. Beginning a new life under Pahua's protection and Hina's guidance, 'Ōpūkaha'ia was being groomed to be a person of great magnitude among his people. Nonetheless, his soul remained anguished.

His seminary was the *Heiau Hikiau* in Nāpo'opo'o, by now an international deep-water seaport. *Hikiau* is translated as "moving current" which graphically describes the *heiau's* location along the lower edge of an ancient surfing beach at the inner, easternmost recess of Kealakekua Bay. *Heiaus* were special places of reverence. All Hawaiians lived to honor the gods and frequently had a small *heiau,* usually an altar or shrine in which to worship daily, within their houses. Formalized, larger *heiaus,* where 'Ōpūkaha'ia studied and institutionalized priests held ceremonies while praying for the needs of the chiefs and their people, consisted of wooden-fenced enclosures upon large stone platforms containing several houses, including massive open-air temples on top of the extensive stone podiums. Multiple carved wooden idols, *akua ki'i* who stood upright sporting grimaced faces, required appeasement. Only the chiefs, nobles, and priesthood could enter these large stone platform *heiaus* of the *luakini*-style, designated for human sacrifice. *Maka'āinana* were restricted by fear of death.[52]

The dichotomies of peace and war as well as conformity and conflict were a part of 'Ōpūkaha'ia's preparation. He became knowledgeable in the manner to pray, serve at rituals, and carve wood to symbolize religious icons. His entire existence was encompassed into a pantheon of *akuas*, spirits and other supernatural beings residing in the woods, amid volcanic boulders, in the ocean and onshore, entering into all animate and inanimate objects. There was no distinction between the natural and supernatural worlds. They were one and the same. 'Ōpūkaha'ia was trained to become the vehicle for maintaining the proper relations between these spirits and the people, the mediator between the gods and the *Kanakas Maoli*, maybe even becoming a *kahuna nui* at *Hikiau*, and presiding over all aspects of their Native religion behind the sacred wooden enclosures.

Adjacent to his seminary and along the shore, 'Ōpūkaha'ia constructed a small, personal *heiau* he named, Helehelekalani. Within, he built three small shrines to Lono, Kū, and Laka, the god of the *hula*.[53] Pahua was proud of his nephew, but he may have worried that being away from the secured enclosure on top of the *heiau* would bring 'Ōpūkaha'ia in closer proximity to the seafaring *haole* (foreigners), with their irreverent behaviors and disregard for *kapu*, posing a threat to all existence.

For more than twenty years, my right hand man on archaeological field expeditions was David G. Cooke from Rocky Hill, Connecticut. Although an amateur, Dave had a passion for history and archaeology that could not have been surpassed by any academically trained anthropologist. A retired machinist by trade, Dave was meticulous in recording data, and he remains simply the best field technician I ever worked alongside. He would be with me for the disinterment of

'Ōpūkaha'ia and was especially valuable in the systematic removal of the stone monument weighing above the burial and in organizing the volunteer field crew.

In the late spring of 1993, Dave, along with volunteers, Richard (Dick) LaRose and Gary Hottin, both avocational archaeologists, and William (Bill) Keegan, an undergraduate student of mine from the University of Connecticut, were assisting in the mitigation of sites associated with the 19th century Enfield Shaker's farming community. Lego, manufacturer of the popular plastic building blocks, was planning expansion of its offices and warehouse immediately adjacent to the Shaker South Family Farm; as state archaeologist I had raised concerns for the necessity of an archaeological survey to ensure that construction activities would have no adverse effect on any significant cultural resources associated with this National Register of Historic Places property.[54] The five of us where in the field salvaging a mid-19th century Shaker refuse deposit when I casually mentioned the "'Ōpūkaha'ia Project."

Dave consulted with a friend who serendipitously had purchased an 1819 first edition of Edwin Dwight's *"Memoirs of Henry Obookiah"* at an antique bookstore days before. Passed from hand-to-hand, the narrative would inspire all of us with the true significance of 'Ōpūkaha'ia's life and death, furnishing a much better understanding of the roles we were about to assume.

Our excavation plan provided for a systematic removal of stone and soil deep enough to expose whatever remains of Henry 'Ōpūkaha'ia were still preserved in the ground. The excavation unit was limited to a narrow forty-six inches wide by ninety-six inches long rectangle directly underneath the stone table so as to avoid the possibility of encountering other human remains, which may reside in adjacent unmarked burial plots. We anticipated evidence of soil disturbance from the original digging and refilling of the grave shaft and of encountering 'Ōpūkaha'ia anywhere between four and six feet below surface.[55]

Considering the Cornwall Cemetery Association's concerns that even with the stone table in place the exact location of Henry's remains was unknown, we were prepared to record biological characteristics of the skeleton *in situ* to determine whether the remains were that of

'Ōpūkaha'ia prior to repatriation. To assist in the osteological analysis, we invited Dr. Michael Park, physical anthropology professor at Central Connecticut State University and my first instructor in the forensic aspects of the human skeleton, to participate in the field, expediting identification and later to serve in the laboratory, providing a more thorough analysis.

With the field team assembled, we selected July 12, 1993, to commence the exhumation of Henry 'Ōpūkaha'ia. Dave Cooke would oversee the archaeological operation; Bill Keegan would be the project photographer; Dick LaRose and Gary Hottin would assist in screening soils, recording of data, and other excavation logistics; Mike Park would be prepared to examine any skeletal remains recovered, and Will Trowbridge, a local stone mason, would assist in the removal of the raised granite table and be responsible for its restoration after the disinterment was complete. Also joining us was the Rev. Carmen Wooster, United Church of Christ, who represented the Lee family, David A. Poirier, staff archaeologist at the State Historic Preservation Office, and Jeffrey Bendremer and Shelley Smith, graduate students in the Department of Anthropology at UConn. All equipment and personnel were on site early that July morning, which was forecast to be hot and humid with the possibility of thundershowers in the afternoon.

It was probably through his uncle that 'Ōpūkaha'ia would learn of an aunt, the sole surviving sister of his father, living nearby. Granted a break from his studies at the *heiau*, he travelled to her village, renewing their relationship. Regrettably, his aunt had angered a local chief by committing an infraction of the *kapu*, so when the chief sent his warriors to apprehend her, they discovered 'Ōpūkaha'ia. Both were seized and incarcerated in a guarded hut while the chief decided what to do with them. Overhearing the conversation of two sentries that he and his aunt were to be put to death, 'Ōpūkaha'ia made his escape by crawling through a small hole, absconding out the opposite side of the patrolled entrance. Unobserved, he fled into the thick, tropical vegetation and hid. Horrified, 'Ōpūkaha'ia watched from his concealment as the warriors dragged his aunt out of the hut and brought her to an elevated precipice. In executing orders from the chief, they flung her over a steep *pali* (cliff), crashing to her death hundreds of feet below.[56]

Once again ʻŌpūkahaʻia was caught up in the rivalry of competing chiefs; once again he witnessed the violent death of a family member; once again he survived and felt responsible; once again he despaired. Mental pictures of his parents' brutal murder and his brother's impalement came rushing back to him with his aunt's execution. Anger and guilt revisited. Surely he had caused the death of his aunt by escaping from the hut, just as he had his brother's when they fled from their parents' execution. What was the point of this unremitting life, filled with the death of loved ones that he, in his cowardly behavior, had caused? He could obtain no answers, elicit no sympathy, find no wooden bowl into which to place a stone to confess and seek forgiveness for his actions. Despair and self-recrimination assaulted his brain.

Confused, his mind raced and his body propelled him, the same as his flight from the sight of his parents' dismemberment. ʻŌpūkahaʻia broke from his concealment, rushing toward the same precipice from which his aunt had been hurled, hoping to replicate her death and follow her into eternity over the same *pali*, the same cliff. Death would be a welcomed relief.

Two of the chief's men saw ʻŌpūkahaʻia's charge and took chase, catching up to him before he could hurl himself off the mountain. They tackled and subdued him. He cried out to be released but was held down by the strength of the warriors and the intense weight of his suffering. After overpowering him and foiling his suicide attempt, the warriors transported their captive to the chief's quarters.[57]

Learning of ʻŌpūkahaʻia's identity and his *kahuna* training, the chief who ordered his aunt executed returned his sullen captive to Pahua so the young man could resume his priestly studies under the benevolent care of his uncle. Though free and back home, ʻŌpūkahaʻia remained reclusive and contemplative, developing an inner desire that he kept to himself—a yearning to leave the islands and break the cycle of violence, to start anew and journey to some distance place—to forget.

ʻŌpūkahaʻia wrote many years later that it was at this time in his life that he began to consider leaving Hawaiʻi. "Probably I may find some comfort, more than to live there without a father or mother. I thought it better for me to go than stay."[58] He had formulated no specific plan for his exodus until serendipitously he spied the *Triumph*, an American merchant ship out of New Haven, Connecticut, sailing into Kealakekua Bay in 1808. The *Triumph*, a rather slow, but sturdy two-mast brig, constructed of strong Connecticut oak,[59] dropped anchor in the bay and began loading water, food, and wood supplies, while 'Ōpūkaha'ia mulled over the idea of leaving the island onboard this American ship.

Should he forget this notion of abandoning his uncle and his priestly studies? If he left, where would this journey take him? Would he truly forget his personal horrors? While his mind pondered these mostly negative thoughts, he made his decision. He would go; better to do so before he was complicit in the deaths of his beloved uncle and grandmother as he had been for his brother and aunt.

Impulsively, he dove headfirst into the surfing waters, sturdily swimming against the tide toward the twin-mast sailing ship. Though he was a strong diver, his heart pounded at the thought of his impulsive plan coming closer to reality with every stroke he swam. Beside the anchored ship, he reached for the rope ladder and hoisted himself upward onto the deck. Summoning the courage to act, 'Ōpūkaha'ia looked around at the strange wind-burned European faces. He observed a Hawaiian interpreter conversing with the ship's captain. Approaching them, 'Ōpūkaha'ia asked to have his words translated and immediately petitioned Capt. Caleb Brintnall to take him on as a member of the crew.

Sailing out of New Haven just prior to the enforcement of the Embargo Act of 1807, the *Triumph* was part of the China Trade commerce of the early American Republic. The potential profits from the trading of seal furs for Chinese wares and spices were staggering for its New England investors, and worth the dangers and uncertainties of a voyage that could last two to three years. Under the watchful eye of the resourceful Capt. Brintnall, who ran a tight ship, confident investors found the risk worth taking, especially in exchange for the immense fortunes to be earned in New York City financial markets.

The *Triumph* carried twenty guns, including four and six-pound cannons for protection against Spanish vessels blockading foreign ships intent on poaching seals off Baja waters. Entering the Pacific Ocean via the tumultuous currents around Cape Horn, the *Triumph* proceeded northward toward islands off the South American and Mexican coast that offered rookeries where congregating seals could be easily procured. Leaving a small crew behind to manage the dirty work of killing, skinning, and processing fur on islands off Baja California, Brintnall headed west to Hawai'i to replenish the ship's provisions.[60]

Arriving first in Honolulu, Capt. Brintnall received permission from Kamehameha to trade and take on Hawaiian males as additional crew for their return trip to the Baja sealers. Now anchored in Kealakekua Bay, Brintnall looked over the young teenage 'Ōpūkaha'ia and felt he would fit the bill, possibly making a good seaman as Polynesians were known to be. Nevertheless, Brintnall was also cautious, wanting no trouble with the Hawaiians. Permission would have to be granted from the boy's family. When told by the interpreter that the boy's parents were dead and he was the nephew of an important *kahuna*, Brintnall invited 'Ōpūkaha'ia to have dinner and spend the night onboard ship but would make no abrupt decision.

Onboard the *Triumph* was another young Hawaiian named Nauhopo'ouah Ho'opo'o (Hopu), called Thomas by the American sailors. Born in 1795, Hopu was nine years old when his mother died. His father taught him the traditional ways of Hawaiian culture, but also instilled in the young boy that today's magic comes from the *haole* and all their iron, nails, knives, and guns. Always keep Hawaiian ways in your heart, Hopu would be taught, but acquire the new practices, for tomorrow's success and continued existence will come by knowing the customs of the light-skinned *haoles*. Accordingly, when the *Triumph* arrived, Hopu's father gave permission for his son to go aboard and travel with Brintnall; he could be educated and learn the secrets of their valuable technology.[61]

Brintnall kept his eye on 'Ōpūkaha'ia throughout supper. He noticed how the young "heathen" seemed to pick up Western gestures and comportment of consuming food at the officer's table. Though 'Ōpūkaha'ia could little understand what was being spoken among the officers, his gift of mimicry allowed him to follow their behaviors and copy their table mannerisms. In his handling of a fork and knife, 'Ōpūkaha'ia was deemed a quick learner. Brintnall asked the young Native if he would like to go to America, become a *luina kelemania e*, a sailor, on their ship. Once he understood, 'Ōpūkaha'ia replied with a positive nod of his head and was overjoyed.

After spending the night onboard the *Triumph*, 'Ōpūkaha'ia was informed that he would need his uncle's permission before he could accompany the crew on their voyage. So the young Hawaiian returned to shore seeking Pahua's acquiescence to leave the island. When they met, his uncle questioned 'Ōpūkaha'ia as to his overnight whereabouts. His nephew told the *kahuna pule* that he had spent the evening onboard the ship, and furthermore, Capt. Brintnall had invited him to join the crew and sail with them; he very much wished to do so.

Pahua flew into a rage. How ungrateful was this child after the gods had twice spared his life? He and his grandmother had been sick with worry when 'Ōpūkaha'ia did not return in the evening, and now he wanted to leave his family entirely, leave the island, leave the *heiau* and leave his studies? No, he was saved to serve the *akuas* and that was exactly what he would do! Angrily, Pahua forced 'Ōpūkaha'ia into his hut, shutting him in.

Hina implored her grandson to give up this foolish idea of leaving Hawai'i. They loved him and were frightened that if he did leave, he would never live to return. 'Ōpūkaha'ia assured her that he likewise loved them, but he needed liberation. There was an aching in his heart. He had wanted to move on for a long time and this was his opportunity. He must travel on this journey, he insisted. Maybe he didn't truly comprehend all the reasons why he had to go, but he simply did. He assured her that he would return in a matter of months. She left the hut with tears in her eyes, knowing he would never come back. He was a very foolish boy.[62]

Pahua would hear none of this pleading. There would be no discussion of deserting the island, his family, or his training. 'Ōpūkaha'ia would be confined to the house, a captive once again, until the *Triumph* left the harbor. The repeated injustices welled within him. He was incessant, more determined than ever. Defiantly, he would become a *luina kelemania e* and find the new life he was searching for among the American *haole*. Nothing would stop him.

While inspecting his latest prison, he noticed a weak spot in the back of the grass hut and crawled through it as he had when confined with his aunt. Unnoticed, he worked his way downhill to the waterfront, hiding until darkness, then silently waded into Kealakekua Bay, swimming out once again to the anchored *Triumph*. This time he climbed aboard secretly, careful not to be seen by the sailors, and concealed himself below deck among the cargo crates. With luck they would not find him until the ship was well underway, a stowaway. But his plan was foiled when he was discovered the next morning about the time Pahua's canoe appeared alongside the large sailing vessel.

With the inherent dignity of a proud and influential *kahuna*, Pahua came onboard the *Triumph*, declaring to Brintnall that 'Ōpūkaha'ia had run away, was hiding on the ship, and must be found. The captain, impressed with the presence of the *kahuna*, ordered a search for 'Ōpūkaha'ia, who was readily brought forth. Straightening himself and fighting back tears, the young man pleaded again for his release to follow the Americans, to go on his journey, appealing to his uncle that a force in his soul cried out for him to leave. He must go, and he would go.

Resigned, Pahua realized that one way or the other 'Ōpūkaha'ia was going to abandon the island, either on the *Triumph* or another sailing vessel. Pahua respected Capt. Brintnall, whom he knew to be honest and trustworthy. If 'Ōpūkaha'ia must go, this was the *haole* that would surely care for him. Nonetheless, the gods would be angry and must be appeased. Pahua would grant 'Ōpūkaha'ia his request, but first Brintnall must purchase a pig to be sacrificed to ensure the boy's protection and consent of the deities. Their parting was disagreeable, but 'Ōpūkaha'ia was willing to "leave all my relations, friends and acquaintances; (and) expected to see them no more in this world."[63]

2 | "I Have Neither A Father Nor A Mother. . . But, He"

She awoke with a start, rising up in bed while the room was still draped in eerie nightly darkness. As she later explained to me, something strange was happening to her that she did not understand. A sudden rush emerged overwhelmingly from the depths of her inner being like a swelling impulse needing to be forced out. Her heart raced, short of breath. "What is this?" she thought, unsure if health was failing her young adult body. Rather than asleep, now, at two in the morning, she was wide-awake and anxious.

Debbie Liʻikapeka Lee, thirty-two years old, a seventh generation cousin of Henry ʻŌpūkahaʻia, rose from her bed and took hold of the Bible on the nightstand, seeking comfort and reassurance. She recognized the need to let go of this feeling though she remained puzzled, "What am I to do?"

It was Sunday, Oct. 11, 1992, in Seattle, Washington, a thousand miles of ocean separating her from her devoted Hawaiian family in Hilo. Alone in the dark, she sought an explanation for this feeling that was mounting inside her. The Bible brought solace but no immediate clarification. Then from within her heart and soul, five words emerged in a voice as clear as if being spoken, *"He wants to come home."*[1]

The surfing waves of Kealakekua Bay began to fade from sight. Onboard the *Triumph,* setting sail eastward toward the Baja coast, ʻŌpūkahaʻia and Thomas Hopu occupied themselves by learning the work of a *luina kelemania e:* preparing sails, climbing yardarms, pulling and tying ropes, and doing their best to stay out of the way of experienced sailors. They were unwittingly components of a diaspora that would diffuse hundreds of Hawaiian men to ports around the globe. ʻŌpūkahaʻia loved his uncle and grandmother and he would surely miss them, but the urgency he felt was overwhelming, driving him forward on his journey. Challenged by the uncertainty, he was in pursuit of a new life, an existence rid of the violence and despondency that took its unrelenting toll on his youth. The physical journey over the vast oceans would be outward, his personal quest rooted within the depths of his psyche inward.

The sailors began calling ʻŌpūkahaʻia, Henry, a name Capt. Caleb Brintnall entered into the ship's log and, in an attempt to pronounce and spell his Hawaiian name, they contrived the phonetically sounding, "Obookiah." Accordingly, "Henry Obookiah" would become his common name onboard ship and for the rest of his life in New England.

The crew of the *Triumph* reunited with more than twenty sailors decamped off the Baja coast to procure seal furs for the China trade. One of the crewmembers culled was Russell Hubbard, a Yale College divinity student who embarked on this sea voyage to improve his health. Hubbard took a shine to the bright and engaging Hawaiian and took it upon himself to tutor "Obookiah" in the fundamentals of the English language, using the Bible as a primer to learn reading and writing. Henry felt the friendship and protection of at least two men onboard the *Triumph*, Capt. Brintnall and Hubbard, sensing himself a fortunate young man at the start of his journey.

From Baja, loaded with about 50,000 sealskins,[2] the *Triumph* sailed back to Hawaii for further provisions, providing the youths with a chance to return home, though both Hopu and ʻŌpūkahaʻia were determined to proceed on the voyage to China and America. In Macao, a well-established trading post for Europeans, Brintnall exchanged sealskins for tea, silk, cinnamon, and other commodities. The Chinese valued the under-fur of the seals to line winter clothes and were willing to exchange items of high value to New Englanders.[3] The China trade brought extraordinary profits for all parties, even to the sealers who had the bloody and rancid work of killing and curing furs. After a six-month stay and the fulfillment of all regulations and protocol, including taxes and bribes, the *Triumph* left China in March, 1809, embarking on the last leg of the voyage through the Indian Ocean, around the Cape of Good Hope, into the southern Atlantic Ocean, and finally northward toward New York City, their home destination.

The *Triumph's* arrival in New York City completed a 157-day voyage from China and two years from its New Haven departure. Formerly the budding nation's capital, New York City in 1809 was a growing metropolis, second in population only to Philadelphia, the municipality that took its place to become the temporary home of the incipient United States government. Only the southern tip of 14-mile-long Manhattan was occupied. The rest of the island was made up of scattered farms and forests. However, residential buildings were quickly advancing northward, driven by population increase and fear of yellow fever; the most desirable locations were now located beyond Canal Street. Ferry boats crossing the Hudson River between Manhattan and Staten Island were stiffs or rowboats—one of the operators, a young Cornelius Vanderbilt. The new City Hall was in various phases of construction at the cost of an astounding half a million dollars. Two years earlier, Robert Fulton and Chancellor Livingston successfully ran their steam-powered *Clermont* up the Hudson River to Albany, marking the beginning of regular ferry service between the cities without the worry of tides, currents, and winds. Mayor Clinton DeWitt established the first public school with forty students in attendance, and the city had recently christened its second playhouse, the Bowery, to accompany the venerable Park Theater.[4] The waterfront of lower Manhattan teemed with wooden sailing vessels, moored side-by-side, their masts rising like dense forests with leafless branches of yardarms jutting out from the shore. More ships, more buildings, and more people than Henry and Thomas could ever have imagined: New York overwhelmed them with culture shock and bewilderment, awed silence and mutterings in their Native language.

The timing of the *Triumph's* departure and arrival could not have been more fortuitous. The ship left port prior to President Thomas Jefferson's Embargo of 1807, designed to keep America out of the Napoleonic Wars by instigating economic hardships against England and France and as punishment to Britain for impressing U. S. sailors into the Royal Navy. The embargo halted all commercial sailing vessels going to and coming from the United Kingdom. The *Triumph* was able to obtain highly desired trade goods in China and return in time to be one of the first ships re-entering the port after the unpopular embargo was lifted. Needless to say, Brintnall found buyers to be plentiful in New York and received especially high prices for their cargo.

Once the *Triumph* docked and unloaded its valued goods, with the paid crew dispersed, the two young Hawaiians remained with Capt. Brintnall, accompanying him to his hometown of New Haven, Connecticut. Prior to setting out via Hell's Gate and Long Island Sound, the boys were entertained in the city by two local merchants who invited them to attend a performance at one of the playhouses with its candlelit stage, proscenium, and celebrated orchestra. Henry and Thomas knew little of the English language and had difficulty understanding the show's content other than interpreting the physical movements, facial expressions, and tone of the actor's voices. Probably attending the newly-built Bowery Theater, they had never seen so many people in one "hut."[5]

Their first real exposure to American culture outside life aboard the ship was overwhelming, loading them with so much information to decipher, "it seemed sometimes that it would make one almost sick."[6] The effects of culture shock heightened when the gentlemen brought the boys home for dinner. They had never seen so many rooms in one house and were especially shocked to see men and women eating at the same dinner table together,[7] a behavior that never would have gone unpunished back on the islands.

Henry and Thomas's acculturation persisted in the strangeness of New Haven where they were introduced to many new people, including young students from Yale College. They were readily accepted into Brintnall's household as servants and were treated with utmost kindness. However, as men of color, they were considered "heathens," socially defined as worshipers of pagan gods, possessors of limited intellectual potential, and containing the inherent possibility of becoming slaves. As servants, Henry and Thomas labored side-by-side with enslaved and free people of African descent, adding to their own curiosity of human biological variability. British-American New Haven society was relatively unfamiliar with Polynesians and remained challenged as where to place Hawaiians within their social hierarchy. Eventually, Thomas and Henry separated when Hopu was sent to live with the family of physician Dr. Obadiah Hotchkiss,

Brintnall's neighbor, while "Obookiah" remained within the captain's household.

It was during these early days in New Haven that Henry once again heard the Christian Word of God, recalling his initial teaching by Russell Hubbard aboard the *Triumph*. At first, his English-language skills improved slowly, but the bright and inquisitive "Obookiah" longed for more formal learning. Hopu had begun to receive instruction, attending school with other students, but 'Ōpūkaha'ia had yet to be present at these tutorials. He was obliged to sit through Sunday service, understanding little of what the minister said, no matter how much he longed to comprehend. Was the congregation listening to the memorized verses of their traditional stories, as he had learned at the *Heiau Hikiau*? If so, where were the *ki'i*, the wooden idols, and why didn't the *kahunas* conduct their rituals privately behind wooden enclosures? Strange as the behavior appeared to him, his inquisitiveness sought knowledge and understanding of the peculiar behaviors of the *haole*.

An account from Thomas Hopu's journal relates the story of young Henry weeping on the steps of Yale College. Approached by Edwin W. Dwight, a Yale divinity student and a relative of college president Rev. Timothy Dwight, concerning the cause of his distress, Henry cries, "No one will teach me."[8] *The Memoirs of Henry Obookiah* do not mention this crucial meeting in quite the same emotional manner, though 'Ōpūkaha'ia does state that Edwin approached him, inquired if he was the friend of Thomas Hopu, and asked if he also wished to learn how to read and write.[9] Henry was eager, and Dwight assumed the role of his personal tutor.

At this junction in Henry's emerging American cultural experience, Brintnall informed the boys of a ship preparing to sail out of New Haven for the Pacific Ocean, stopping at the Sandwich Islands. The captain assured both Henry and Thomas that should they wish to return home, he would provide for them to take the voyage. However, neither Hawaiian took the offer, desiring to continue in America longer to complete their education before returning home to their families. Moreover, 'Ōpūkaha'ia's personal journey, though he travelled thousands of miles, was scarcely underway.

Henry took to his studies immediately, and once again proved a hard-working and intelligent apprentice. The New Haven community slowly began to realize that this young "heathen," who in their cultural bias seemed at first so backward and uninspiring, had a huge thirst for knowledge and a heightened capacity to comprehend his teachings. He learned quickly, duplicating the arduous effort placed at the *heiau*, though many aspects of his training did not come easily.

Since there is no "R" sound in the Hawaiian language, Henry had difficulty pronouncing syllables containing the letter, which often came out like the sound of "L" when spoken in English. Edwin Dwight would repeatedly beseech him, "Try, Obookiah, it is very easy!" Henry took secretive delight whenever Dwight said this and eventually would turn the tables when Henry began teaching his mentor some of the habits and practices of his Native culture, specifically demonstrating to Edwin how to hold water and drink by cupping his hands. Adjusting the thumbs, clasping and bending the fingers together, 'Ōpūkaha'ia made an effective and natural drinking vessel with his hands. When his instructor attempted the maneuver, water dripped through his fingers onto the floor, frustrating the effort. Henry smiled, "Try, Mr. Dwight, it is very easy!"[10]

Edwin Dwight and others within the Yale community were becoming aware of Henry's singular ability to entertainingly mimic the mannerisms of people around him. He would challenge, "Who dis?" and start to walk in a distinct style that imitated one of his new-found friends. With gales of laughter, his fellow students knew all the intended victims of Henry's impersonations. When the New Englanders mimicked 'Ōpūkaha'ia's gait, he fell to the floor laughing, "Me walk so?"[11] He was becoming a favorite; his personality, humor, intelligence, and educational zeal endeared him to all he met in New Haven. His friends started to see him not simply as a curiosity from the pagan world, but an entrancing and unique individual with delightful personality characteristics previously unappreciated.

Henry's intellectual training soon advanced to the point where he requested leave of Brintnall's family to reside fulltime with the Dwight clan, accelerating his education and improving his chances of getting into an established school. The captain readily gave permission, and

Henry moved into the home of the president of Yale College as a servant, continuing his secular and religious training. In Rev. Timothy Dwight's household, he would be exposed for the first time to a true "praying family morning and evening."[12] It would mark the start of 'Ōpūkaha'ia's sojourn throughout three New England states residing within many Christian households.

The Rev. Timothy Dwight IV had succeeded Ezra Stiles as the eighth president of Yale in 1795, born into a family with many ties to the college. Jonathan Edwards, credited with flowering the First Great Awakening, was his uncle on his mother's side. Rev. Dwight was an enormous authoritarian figure in the church and college, at times derogatorily referred to as "Pope Dwight."[13] Teaching and the ministry were his vocations with 'Ōpūkaha'ia taking on the role of a rather special redemptive focus.

Although 'Ōpūkaha'ia did not fully understand all of the Dwight family's Christian prayers, he could sense that they were at times praying for him and his salvation. They mentioned God to him often in daily conversation though Henry believed "but little."[14] After all, he had been training to become a *kahuna*, the spiritual conduit of his people where preparation had been intense and instilled with the knowledge of appeasement toward the many gods that controlled existence on the islands and possibly the world, including the lives of his American friends, though they seemed not to realize it. Instead, they prayed to their all-powerful, monotheistic God, strikingly different from the pantheon of Hawaiian *akua*, who had their own individual sources of authority.

Residing among the Dwight clan, the young "Obookiah" would learn of the "Great Awakenings," religious revitalization movements that initially appeared in the American colonies during the 1730s. The "First Awakening" shook New England by storm. Powerful preachers like Jonathan Edwards convinced parishioners of their private guilt and the need to seek salvation through personal actions. To experience God in their own way required them to take responsibility for their own spiritual failures and acknowledge them through public penitence. This reduced the need for rituals, replacing the old theology with individual religious conviction.[15] The First Great Awakening split the Congregational Church between Old-Lights, who strived to maintain the traditional orthodoxy, and New-Light revivalists attempting to return the church to its "original" orthodoxy.

Then, around the year 1800, an added wave of religious revival took form. While the earlier crusade concentrated doctrine exclusively toward church adherents, the "Second Great Awakening" sought to revitalize declining church memberships by accepting those outside the congregation into the fold, bringing thousands of new parishioners together in anticipation of the Second Coming of Christ, which they believed eminent. Church membership soared throughout New England, creating new denominations and sects. Significantly to Henry, the Rev. Timothy Dwight played an enormous role in helping to create and spread the spiritual resurgence.

The sky opened, cascading a powerful deluge. Lightning pierced the humid afternoon air, sending five young men running for the shelter of a nearby barn. The thunderstorm had disrupted their twice-weekly outdoor prayer vigil by a maple grove. Samuel John Mills, Jr., Harvey Loomis, Byram Green, Frances Robbins, and James Richards sprinted for the protection of the farm building to continue their invocation. Once sheltered from the torrential rain at the lee side of a large haystack, Samuel Mills, namesake and son of a leading Connecticut clergyman and a student at Williams College in Massachusetts, confided to his colleagues his maturing thoughts on spreading the Word of Christ to foreign countries.[16]

True to the concepts of the Second Great Awakening, Mills saw the necessity for missions to exotic lands: the call to arms to save the souls of the "heathen," who would burn in hell simply for their lack of knowing the one true God. His companions instantly recognized the "truth" in Mills' words and decided to band together as "The Brethren," a secret society devoted to the promotion of the Protestant American foreign missions. Led by Samuel Mills, Jr., the "Haystack Prayer Meeting" participants would commit themselves to sharing their passion and evangelism for spreading the Word of Christ around the world.

While studying with Edwin Dwight, "Obookiah" met Samuel Mills, Jr., soon after the Haystack Prayer Meeting. On completion of his undergraduate work at Williams College, Samuel ventured to New Haven in pursuit of theological studies at Yale and, as a friend of Edwin, was poised to meet the young Hawaiian. Samuel, like many other students, became enchanted by ʻŌpūkahaʻia's charm, envisioning in Henry's intellect and resolve to learn, the validation of his emerging missionary reasoning. If this "heathen" had the mental capacity to comprehend the Bible, so could other Indigenous Peoples around the world. To Mills, this happenstance introduction to ʻŌpūkahaʻia was nothing short of Divine Intervention. If instructed and inspired properly, Mills reasoned, "Henry Obookiah" could serve as the foundation of the missions to his homeland. Samuel's dreams and aspirations were now collected in the persona of this young Native Hawaiian. To further his ambitions and oversee Obookiah's conversion, he proposed that Henry reside at his father's farm in Torringford, Connecticut, to live within the context of a loving Christian home and receive personal instruction directly from the famed Rev. Samuel Mills, Sr.[17]

Henry's friends thought the idea wise since they shared concerns that his continual presence in New Haven held the chance of his being kidnapped into the slave trade.[18] With consent from Timothy Dwight, Henry willingly moved to the rural northwestern hills of the state in 1810. In Torringford, he would no longer be a personal house servant but instead was taught the work of the farm: cutting wood, pulling flax, and mowing hay for the Rev. Mills and his family, who found ʻŌpūkahaʻia "a remarkable youth."[19] He immediately felt welcomed and loved within the Mills' household—"It seemed to me as my own home."[20]

The physical journey of ʻŌpūkahaʻia extended over three quarters of the globe, westward from Hawaiʻi to Connecticut. The spiritual journey seemed to be travelling as great a distance but remained far more uncertain. He had been exposed to a new cultural dimension, enduring some of the strange customs of these English Americans. Their clothing and food were relatively easy to adopt, yet their beliefs and worldview were alien to his *kahuna* training and were more difficult to accept. He wanted to please his new companions who treated him so warmly and took such great care of his physical needs. He certainly did not wish to disappoint them in his learning and acceptance of their ways. Rev. Timothy Dwight and Samuel Mills, Jr., seemed to have high expectations for him, making it clear that he had been purposely sent by their God to serve as the foundation for delivering the Gospel to his Hawaiian brethren. But he remained silently apprehensive and doubtful.

For a long while, 'Ōpūkaha'ia did not desire for ministers to approach him and talk about God. He hated to hear it.[21] He had a deep desire to learn intellectually, not emotionally. He left the islands to remove a stigma, to set his mind with separate thoughts and pursue an education in the *haole* world. All the same, the pain remained. The cruel and violent deaths of his family, the captivity to the warrior who murdered his parents, the heartbreak and the loneliness even after he was reunited with his uncle, and the murder of his aunt had taken a toll. He recalled his hard days devoted to *kahuna* teaching and his uncle and grandmother's disappointment at his sudden desertion. He had had enough of gods needing to be appeased.

John O'Donnell preceded our arrival at the cemetery the first morning of Henry's disinterment. He had roped off a large area around the grave to keep anticipated spectators and reporters from getting too close to the edges of the burial excavation. The Cornwall Cemetery Association and the United Church of Christ brought a beautiful, decorative wreath set on an easel at the foot of the monument and placed flowers around its borders out of respect to 'Ōpūkaha'ia and his journey home. The American national and the Hawaiian state flags were placed in the ground at the head of the memorial. The tableau was lovely and tranquil.

Laying our hand-tools on the ground, the first order of business was the careful removal of shrine offerings and the inscribed marble headstone resting on the granite table. Flowers and flags were collected and all the offerings safeguarded. We slid the dry-laid tombstone gently forward off the stone table, securing its borders as if pallbearers, carrying the heavy marble down the hill to the cemetery's storage vault to await restoration.[22]

The task of disassembling the granite table proved to be the most strenuous and time-consuming phase of the preparation. Dave Cooke had reviewed the monument the day before to determine the

necessary field tools for dismantling. He arrived prepared with crow-
bars, wooden rollers, sledgehammers, four lengths of heavy chains,
ropes, and a come-a-long.[23] Careful use of a hammer and chisel by
Will Trowbridge, our mason, loosened the mortar that bound the large
granite blocks together. Placing the edge of the chisel against a seam,
Trowbridge gently tapped the grout, crumbling enough space for a
crowbar to be inserted into the crevice, gradually prying the blocks
apart. Once released, the stones were carried downslope away from
the gravesite although a few were so substantial they required the use
of wooden rollers.

No mechanical equipment was used; every aspect of the work was
performed by hand. Prior to removal, each boulder was photographed,
sketched, and numbered to facilitate the monument's stone-by-stone
reconstruction. The interior of the table was not hollow but packed
with mortar and smaller stones that also had to be carefully removed.
The entire morning was taken with finishing this initial task.

Under the mortared granite table, we found a tier of dry-laid rectangular and rounded foundation stones supporting the aboveground
structure. The largest stones were leveled at the lower foot area,
providing greater downslope stability. These were measured, drawn,
photographed, and removed. Once the stone layer was detached, we
were surprised to find a second layer of foundation underneath, consisting of smaller flat stones with the largest supporting the upslope
head region of the monument. Assuming we had finally exhausted
foundation levels, we were astounded to encounter yet a third tier of
stones resting well below the frost line. 'Ōpūkaha'ia's memorial had
been solidly constructed with three tiers of foundation providing rein-
forcement for the structure on its steep embankment, facilitating its
survival for 175 years without shifting or pulling apart.

It was not until the mid-afternoon once all the stones were pulled
away from the gravesite that we were able to erect a portable,
aluminum-framed canopy to keep direct sunlight from contacting the
anticipated skeletal remains. We cleaned up the bottom of the excavated area, leveled the floor and sidewalls, and rid the excavation unit
of loose soil and stones that had toppled when the foundations were
cleared. After all data, including soil samples, were taken from the

exposure, a plastic tarp was laid out on the grass adjacent to the excavation unit. A hardware quarter-inch mesh screen was set up to sift excavated soils in case any funerary objects were missed during the excavation process.

Prepared for the disinterment, we commenced by slicing the soil thinly with flat, sharp-edged mason trowels to level the excavation and highlight differences in the coloration and compaction of the mottled earth. Soon a distinct outline of a hexagonal coffin appeared, confined at the head, expanding outward to the shoulders and tapering down to the narrow foot. We were at a depth of forty-two inches from the upper ground surface, and the configuration of the coffin was clear in soil coloration contrasts.

As we continued digging into the late afternoon, ominous dark clouds appeared in the west and were moving rapidly toward the cemetery. Within minutes we were engulfed by dangerous lightning strikes that preceded a violent thunderstorm. The crew hurriedly secured all the equipment into vehicles while I finished up the last level of the day under the canopy.

Amid lightening flashes, remains of the sideboards of the wooden coffin became exposed, appearing as a linear soil shadow of dark brown, decomposing wood and a pattern of hardware nails that would have held the top board in place. We were now working within the coffin and getting close to determining if Henry's remains had been preserved. At this point, I didn't want to stop though my heart pounded as lightening bolts flared overhead and thunderclaps deafened. Dave Cooke and I had made an earlier decision not to expose any skeletal remains this late in the afternoon. John O'Donnell arranged for overnight security, so I reluctantly climbed a short wooden ladder out of the burial unit, watched lightening hop-scotching the bordering hills, and anticipated tomorrow's rendezvous with Henry ʻŌpūkahaʻia.[24]

The sweat beaded upon his forehead, seeping into his burning eyes. He swung the steel axe, repeatedly cutting wood for "Mr. F," a neighbor of Rev. Mills amid the rolling hills of Torringford, stacking the logs between two small trees.[25] The morning sun was relentless; the day already seemed long, the work tiring. Yet, ʻŌpūkahaʻia maintained his pace methodically, swinging the blade as he mimicked other field workers. Then he stopped. He experienced a rushing sensation overcoming him. His heart beat heavily; he felt weak, and in his rising anxiety a fearful thought occurred, "What if I die today, what would become of my soul? Surely I would be cast off forever."[26] His apprehension was followed by a voice that seemed to encompass him, "Cut it down, why cumbereth it the ground."[27] He gazed around. No one was within sight.

He dropped his axe and fell to his knees, looking up to the heavens, seeking help from "Almighty Jehovah."[28] Realizing now that he was nothing more than a "hell-deserving sinner" and that God had the right to thrust his wretched soul into eternal damnation;[29] he deserved nothing less. He had ignored the Word though presented to him by many gracious and religious friends: Russell Hubbard onboard the *Triumph*; Edwin and the Rev. Timothy Dwight at Yale College; and now Rev. Samuel Mills and his son in Torringford—all of them had tried to save his soul. He had listened, yet refused to hear. Now he was pitiful.

'Ōpūkaha'ia lost track of the time spent on his knees in meditative reflection until removed from his revelry by another sound, the earthly voice of a boy beckoning him to lunch. At the Mills' home, 'Ōpūkaha'ia picked at his food and looked forlorn enough for people to question the source of his apparent melancholy. He kept to himself, went to bed early, and laid awake most of the night, sorting out his emotions. He rose promptly the next morning before the others to find a place where he could be alone. Morning turned into afternoon, afternoon into evening. He did no labor, remaining distant.[30]

Troubled and searching inwardly, he recalled the long days studying with his uncle at *Heiau Hikiau*; learning the traditions of his people and devotion to the island *akuas*; beseeching the deities to intervene favorably in the lives of his people; and, honoring his warrior father and priestly uncle. Was he not Hawaiian? Could he commit to this religious conversion and worship the singular God of these British Americans? Or was he simply seeking the approval of these at times arrogant and pious Calvinists by adopting their rhetoric and mores? He did aspire to get religion into his head, intellectually, as a means of learning that much he understood. But 'Ōpūkaha'ia remained uncertain about allowing this new belief, this Christianity "into his heart."[31] He had felt the same struggle learning the disciplines of Lono and Kū. He studied, memorized, recited, and sought knowledge though coveted little emotional involvement. Having been traumatized in his youth, Henry blocked any passionate responses from his mind. Now, for the first time, he would consider an alterative conviction.

The revelation in the wood lot was sandwiched between trips to Andover, Massachusetts, attending Bradford Academy where ʻŌpūkahaʻia boarded in the Abbot household, a family he considered as pious as that of Dwight and Mills. His earlier attendance in Andover was marked by his refusal to accept any solemn feelings for the Christian God, however, after the wood lot experience, his second attendance at Bradford marked more resolve in learning Scripture. He now immersed himself in the Gospels, memorizing every story, every miracle. He absorbed his spelling book so he could write and read the Bible more proficiently. He learned and made rapid progress in his religious training, exerting the concentrated work he had shown when schooled by his uncle. He remained inquisitive; his willingness to learn saw no bounds.

What endeared ʻŌpūkahaʻia to the Abbot family was not simply his growing scholarship but also his "excellence of character."[32] Mrs. Abbot confided to a friend that Henry is "always pleasant. I never saw him angry. He used to come into my chamber and kneel down by me and pray. Mr. Mills did not think he was a Christian at that time, but he appeared to be thinking of nothing else but religion. He afterwards told me that there was a time when he wanted to get religion into his head more than into his heart."[33]

With renewed diligence in his Bible study, Henry began to submit to the devotion of the Christian God. Heartfelt and sincere were his new feelings, no longer simply academic. With the fervor of a convert, he began to see his *kahuna* knowledge as irrational. He would tell a fellow Hawaiian, "O how foolish we are to worship wood and stone gods; we give them hogs and cocoa nuts and banana but they cannot eat."[34] Once ʻŌpūkahaʻia threw off the veil of his youthful training in the polytheistic religious beliefs of Polynesian Hawaiʻi, he was free to embrace Christian salvation. We can only imagine how hard it must have been to release the cultural beliefs of his ancestors; disregard what had been taught him during his childhood; denounce the pantheon of *akuas* instilled into him during his training at the *heiau*. It required a revelation, but once released, he reformed in both mind and spirit. "In my secret prayer and in serious conversation with others...I thought now with myself that I have met with a change of heart."[35]

While at Bradford, 'Ōpūkaha'ia learned that another Hawaiian lived in the vicinity of Andover. Seeking out his fellow *Kanaka Maoli*, Henry stayed a full day and evening in his company. Neither of the boys slept that night. Instead they lay awake, talking in their Native language until dawn. When asked later what he had learned from his companion concerning news from Hawai'i, 'Ōpūkaha'ia replied, "I did not think of Hawaii. I had so much to say about Jesus Christ."[36] He had truly been reborn, converting to the "one true God" and setting seeds for his actions and words as a future missionary.

In the spring of 1812, the American Board of Commissioners for Foreign Missions (ABCFM) appointed Rev. Samuel Mills, Jr., to travel through the Mississippi Valley, surveying those areas for future missionary efforts among reservation Indians and plantations of African captives.[37] Soon after Mills' departure, 'Ōpūkaha'ia would spend time in Hollis, New Hampshire, where his newly-won belief would provide its first test of faith through an ordeal of sickness.

The fever appeared to come on suddenly, leaving 'Ōpūkaha'ia frail and bedridden for five weeks. In Hollis he would live within a number of households including that of the Deacon Ephraim Burge where the sickness overcame him. Dr. Benoni Cutter presided over his young patient, praying with him many times. All in Hollis feared that the "Obookiah" they cherished in their thoughts of his complete devotion to God would be taken from them before his salvation could be secured. Mrs. Burge inquired of his willingness to die and leave a world of sin, "Do you remember the goodness and the kindness of God towards you?" 'Ōpūkaha'ia answered in the positive, "Yes, for I have neither a father nor a mother, nor a brother nor a sister in this strange country but He. But O! am (sic) I fit to call him my Father?"[38]

Often 'Ōpūkaha'ia felt alone and meaningless, affected by his survivor's guilt. "Many times I meet with the dark hour."[39]

He was able to fight off the fever and despair, regain his footing, and find a loving and forgiving "Father," one who truly cared about this "Henry Obookiah" and represented the head of his spiritual and earthly family. Within the short time he was in Hollis, he would go through the conversion for which New England had prayed. It was here that "Henry's heart was renewed by the Holy Spirit."[40] With his physical and spiritual state bettered, Henry would leave Hollis, return to Andover, and eventually go "home" to Torringford,[41] where he would take one further giant step in his transformation to realize the meaning of his journey.

When Samuel Mills, Jr., returned home from his two-year missionary tour in the early summer of 1814,[42] he inquired about the state of young 'Ōpūkaha'ia's Christian learning. He was gratified to hear that Henry was giving his life to the Lord and continuing his spiritual and academic training with friends and tutors in Litchfield, but what he found just as gratifying was the acknowledge that Henry was translating Hebrew chapters of the Bible phonetically into the Hawaiian language. In doing so, he compiled a dictionary and a grammar book, and by 1815 maintained a diary of his personal development. Henry wrote and memorized the Bible similar to his *kahuna* training, so that when Mills arrived home, he found 'Ōpūkaha'ia in the midst of an immense emission of creative intellectual energy.

With his continuing education, Henry's confidence developed. He began to speak in public, took on the learning of Latin, Hebrew, geometry, and geography while continuing to work on his English. He started to write an increasing number of letters, even beginning a personal memoir telling of his youth in Hawaii and his journey to New England. Now in his twenties, Henry's heartfelt enthusiasm for all things scriptural provided a personal joy and triumph for the Mills family.

Henry was also physically maturing into a formable young man. Edwin Dwight describes him as being above the ordinary size of young New England men, standing just less than six feet in height with limbs and body well proportioned and large. At sixteen, 'Ōpūkaha'ia had been regarded as "awkward and unshapen" (sic.), but now he appeared "erect, graceful and dignified."[43] His skin was described as olive in coloration, a mixture of dark African and "red" Native American complexions. His black hair was cut short and his clothing westernized. His nose was prominent and his chin projected.[44] There was no questioning his "otherness" when he mingled in the company of British Americans.

If Henry stood out physically, his personality and character also separated him. "In his disposition, he was amiable and affectionate. His temper was mild. Passion was not easily excited, nor long retained. Revenge or resentment, it is presumed, was never known to be cherished in his heart."[45] 'Ōpūkaha'ia was considered a good and reliable friend, always grateful for favors bestowed upon him and, most tellingly, he felt an ardent affiliation toward the various Christian families with whom he resided.

Through Henry's conversion, intellect, and personality, Samuel Mills, Jr. could now envision the formulation of "The Brethren" plan. 'Ōpūkaha'ia would be the bridge to the Hawaiian missions—a bridge

Frontispiece Portrait of Obookiah, engraver unknown, 1818, from *Memoirs of Henry Obookiah, A Native of Owyhee and A Member of the Foreign Mission School* (New Haven: Office of the Religious Intelligencer.) National Portrait Gallery, Smithsonian Institution.

that would span the oceans; a bridge over which Mills and other mis-sionaries would walk across to bring salvation to the "pagans" of the Pacific Islands. With Henry's noticeable development, Mills and Adoniram Judson took the opportunity to present a formal letter at a meeting of Congregational Church leaders seeking permission to organize a missionary effort consisting of both New England men and women accompanied by Native youths returning to their homelands in the spirit of Christ. The church leaders deliberated. The fulfillment of the "Second Great Awakening" beckoned; the timing was ripe. Sup-port was given to The Brethren plan and the Foreign Mission School was born. A powerful vision was formulated: Henry "Obookiah" would complete his journey home accompanied by Samuel Mills, Jr., and together they would replace the *kapu* system with the Gospel of a loving God.

'Ōpūkaha'ia, heartened by his new confidence in the Holy Spirit, found the courage to petition the North Consociation of Litchfield County to take him under their care and provide counsel and direc-tion into his life.[46] The Consociation voted overwhelmingly in his favor and appointed a three-person board to supervise his education. Now focused, dedicated, and resourceful, Henry was being prepared for meaningful accomplishments and, with discussions of developing for-eign missions, a possible reunion in Hawai'i as a budding Christian *kahuna*.

Though the thought of a Hawaiian homecoming had never been far from his consciousness, he had seen no earlier purpose to it, not when the meaning of his journey had no full perception. Yet returning as a Christian missionary to spread the Word of his newfound "Father" and paving a path to salvation for his brethren would be the fulfillment for which he was striving, the reason to go home. He had a message to share, a message that demanded to be heard—a message that would save Hawaiians from the pangs of hell and fold them into the arms of their benevolent protector, their Father who would love and care for them. Henry had searched for and found a family to replace the one he had violently lost. "I have neither a father nor a mother... but He."[47] Invoking his Native beliefs in the comingling of the supernatural and natural worlds, ʻŌpūkahaʻia viewed Jesus as a biological Father, as real as Keau. For years he had probed his mind for the reason why he was the lone survivor of all the ferocity forced on his family and for the agonizing guilt associated with complicity in their suffering. He now had an answer and a joyous reason for a homecoming.

ʻŌpūkahaʻia sought the strength to speak of his new desire. To a Native friend, he broached the subject, pleading with his companion to accompany him to Hawaiʻi. Getting no encouragement, he suspected that his confidant might be influenced by the fearful consequences of attempting to introduce a new religion to the *Kanaka Maoli*. "You fraid?" Henry asked. "You know our Savior say, 'He that will save his life shall lose it; and he that will lose his life for my sake, same shall save it.'"[48]

In April of 1815, ʻŌpūkahaʻia expressed his desire to become a formal member of an established church, and with the support of the senior Rev. Samuel Mills, Henry was received into the Church of Christ Congregational in Torringford.[49] However, dissatisfaction resulted among many parishioners when Mills sat Henry and other Hawaiians in his own pew in front of the New England worshipers. The church had previously remodeled slave pews located in the gallery over the stairs, an area boarded-up so high that people of color would not have to be tolerated by the white assembly below.[50] Mills rejected the idea of separation for the Hawaiians and had them seated prominently with him, much to the dismay of other church members.

By this time, "Father" Mills, as Henry called him, bestowed upon ʻŌpūkahaʻia all of the love and compassion of a true son. His powerful influence on the community gave the young Hawaiian a foothold into the congregation. Rev. Mills was a tall, well-proportioned man with a large face and round head. His eyes were bold, yet benignant. He was stately and gave his finest appearance standing at the pulpit. At times when he preached to the people attending worship, his religious themes seemed to border on the oddity, and his expressions would often solicit a smile, sometimes even provoke laughter. The great themes of Father Mills' life were "souls and salvation,"[51] and "ʻŌpūkahaʻia was his spiritual son, loved as much as Samuel Mills, Jr., his biological son.

Venturing back to Amherst, Massachusetts, at the end of 1816, Henry lived with Rev. Nathan Perkins, an agent of the ABCFM. The board was moving forward in establishing a special "Foreign Mission School," commonly referred to as the "School for Heathens,"[52] choosing Litchfield County as its home since many of the Hawaiians and other potential candidates lived in the area, and it was situated away from the temptations and dangers presented by big city life. In his association with Perkins, Henry commenced a speaking tour through New England for the purpose of soliciting donations for the benefit of the "Heathen School."[53]

The prevailing debate throughout Congregational New England and elsewhere among British Americans was whether the "heathen" possessed the mental capacity to comprehend the Bible, let alone preach it. This being unsure, previous financial and spiritual support was relatively lacking. "Obookiah," with his personality and intellect, would change many minds about the scholarly capabilities of Indigenous Peoples and, consequently, untie many conservative purse strings. Reverend Perkins noted that wherever Henry travelled, "he was much beloved."[54] Visiting many towns and speaking to church congregations, Henry addressed his conversion and his knowledge of Christianity, never failing to impress. He always presented himself appropriately, solemnly, and interestingly. He aroused New Englanders, who had no expectations for the missions, to become satisfied that conversion of the "heathen," by the "heathen," and for the "heathen," was attainable, even practicable.

Henry's narratives of his fellow Hawaiians worshiping a multitude of gods, all manufactured from wood, and of priests performing rituals involving human sacrifice, convinced Congregationalists that the need to teach Christianity there was truly great. Dollars poured in. This "Native of Owhyhee" had lifted the dispositions of these fundamentalist, "cold" New Englanders to consider the propriety of "heathen" missionaries. He changed many minds, shattering many misconceptions, and parishioners eagerly reached into their pockets to contribute. In effect, Obookiah was already a missionary, converting, in this case, Congregational New Englanders to the confidence of his cause.[55] His effect was all that the American Board of Commissioners could ever have hoped for.

With the donations Henry solicited, the Foreign Mission School became a reality. "Obookiah" would be the inspiration, the first student, the model, carrying the bursting excitement and expectation of Congregational New England on his broad shoulders. The time was approaching for ʻŌpūkahaʻia, accompanied by the leadership of Samuel Mills, Jr., to bring the Word and carry the "Cross" over the seas to deliver eternal salvation to his fellow Hawaiian islanders.

With an early start to the second day of the exhumation, I stepped onto a short wooden ladder descending more than four feet into the burial unit and balanced once again on the slender dirt platform prepared as my workspace. Ropes were tied to the handles of plastic buckets to hoist excess soil out of the grave shaft and through hardware mesh screens manned by our volunteers and students. I arranged my hand tools— primarily trowels, brushes of various sizes, bamboo picks, a small spatula, and dustpan—underneath my body as I hunched on all fours. The first task was to clean up the effects of the past evening's thunderstorm. Once I removed the tarp that covered the excavation unit from the rain, the damp, eroded earth had to be leveled and crisply cut to restore the configuration of the hexagonal coffin established the day before, allowing accurate measurement: six-and-a-half feet in length, with widths of one foot at the head board, ten inches at the foot, and twenty inches across at the shoulder.[56]

Excavating within the coffin boundary, brass tacks and black painted hardwood appeared along the sideboards in the area of the chest cavity. My initial impression was that the tacks were aligned to the sides of the coffin to secure a decorative cloth lining the interior; however, it soon became apparent that they had been hammered into the coffin lid, which had split down the middle, compressed to the sides by earth pressure. The coffin was hardwood, painted black, and except for where the brass tacks neutralized adjacent soils, no other wood survived other than as soil shadows. When the reconstructed coffin lid was mended, the brass tack pattern yielded "**H. O. AE 26**" enclosed in a heart-shaped motif which are interpreted as the initials of the person lying in the coffin, the Latin "*A.E.*" for "age of," followed by the age at death with the heart signifying a sign of Christian endearment.

Even without knowing the story of "Henry Obookiah" in New England, the physical evidence of the coffin strongly suggested that the person lying here was very much loved by his contemporaries.

Small, broken fragments of window glass, some twenty in all, were encountered in the region of the cranio-facial complex, establishing that Henry's coffin contained a viewing glass, allowing mourners to observe his face during the 1818 funeral without having to lift the entire lid. The glass also prevented mourners from cutting pieces of clothing or hair as memorial artifacts. The painted hardwood, brass tacks on the lid providing the deceased's initials, and a viewing glass over the face represented innovative mortuary designs for early 19th century coffins and reflected state-of-the-art funerary technology for its time. The entire burial complex suggested the high status and importance given to the deceased; little expense[57] was spared to give Henry a monument that would perpetuate his memory for a long time after his death.[58]

The first evidence of skeletal remains was the frontal bone of the forehead, the highest elevated area when the body is supine, which exhibited limited cortical loss for its age and suggested that the rest of the skeleton should possess excellent organic preservation. Excavation proceeded at the superior portion of the skeletal anatomy, concentrating on exposing the high points and maintaining horizontal control. Delicately I brushed around the broken pieces of glass to maintain their positions and reveal the face. Henry slowly emerged before me, the very image of his portrait.

Concentrating on the subtle work at hand, I had not noticed or heard the increasing assembly of bystanders that had accumulated in the cemetery to observe the disinterment until I rose to stretch my legs, giving myself a moment's reprieve, eager to avoid carelessness through fatigue. As I stood, my shoulders were level to the ground surface where I could see more people gathered than had been there on the previous day, many more, possibly forty or so. While our crew was busy with the responsibilities of the archaeological excavation, I placed a damp cloth over Henry's face to keep the fragile bones from drying out in the heat, but also out of respect, so public eyes could not gaze upon him.

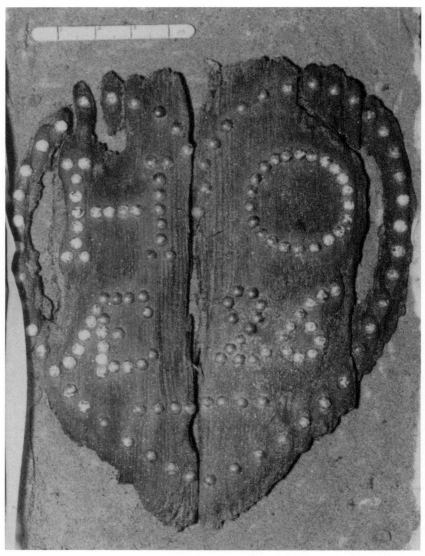

Wooden coffin lid of Henry Obookiah, exhibiting brass tack patterns of his initials and age of death, outlined in a heart-motif. (Courtesy Bill Keegan.)

Ascending the ladder, I was immediately met by reporters covering the story for Connecticut newspapers. I emphasized immediately that no published photographs of Henry's remains would be tolerated. Also present at the cemetery were members of the repatriation team including Henry Fuqua and Rev. Carmen Wooster. My reprise from excavation was spent satisfying the role of public relations director and educator, repeatedly explaining our procedures, methodologies, and findings to the various communities present.

Content to descend the ladder and resume work, I would remain in the burial unit uncovering Henry ʻŌpūkahaʻia's *iwi* into the early evening. Since the skeletal remains were well-preserved and the surrounding subsoil matrix a fine-grained beach sand, excavation proceeded far more expeditiously than I would have anticipated; by the end of the second day, the burial was completely exposed. Revealed was a primary interment of a single individual, fully articulated in a supine position with the legs extended and the hands placed on the pelvis with fingers interlocked as if in prayer, the head tilted slightly forward to his right. The organic preservation of the skeletal remains was astonishing.

Green stains were noted on the bones of the lower right arm indicating positions of two-piece copper-headed straight pins, which held a sheet or shroud together during the funeral process.[59] The copper heads had dissolved with soil acidity, leaching its cuprous minerals into the bone, leaving green discolorations where the shroud pins had been located. We found no evidence of clothing; Henry had been buried naked with a winding sheet pinned to blanket his body. The textile of the shroud had completely decomposed, leaving no trace other than the green-stains as clues to its presence.

As I continued to bring to light the skeletal elements of Henry's face and body, I could overhear the background sound of people conversing above me. I consciously blocked out their voices so my concentration remained on ʻŌpūkahaʻia and the task at hand. Try as I may, my attention did wander as I considered the significance of this young man slowly emerging before me: his Hawaiian origin, the trauma of his early life, his journey to New England, his conversion to Christianity, and the melancholy of his deathbed scene. Forensic archaeologists generally investigate the skeletal remains of unidentified victims, many lost in history due to the lack of written records. Yet in this case we were well acquainted with the enormous impact Henry had on both New England and Hawai'i. I was fully cognizant of being involved with something very special. Savoring the moment, it became intensely personal.

The skeleton was surprisingly complete. The only elements missing were the hyoid, a horseshoe-shaped bone in the throat commonly referred to as an "Adam's Apple" in men, and five phalanges of the finger bones. The coccyx, or tailbone, and the xyphoid process (the pointy projection at the bottom of the breastbone) were badly decomposed. However, the only other damage was some deterioration of the back and underside (occipital and basilar) of the skull and to some of the posterior neural arches of the cervical (neck) vertebrae. Henry's head had laid on a pillow, possibly sewn by girls from Miss Pierce's Academy in Litchfield who attended the funeral and burial in 1818.[60] The pillow's subsequent decomposition retained moisture from the soil that enhanced skeletal breakdown to those specific anatomical areas. Nonetheless, Henry 'Ōpūkaha'ia endures to this day as the most remarkably preserved historical skeleton I have ever removed from Connecticut's typically acidic soil.

Though it was getting late in the day, Dave Cooke and I made a command decision not to leave Henry's remains exposed through the night, but taking advantage of the longer summer light, continued working into the evening to remove 'Ōpūkaha'ia before sunset. Though overnight security measures were still in place, we felt it was best to disinter the remains as expeditiously as possible due to concerns of publicity generated by the press and the possibility of unwelcomed overnight visitors.

After every skeletal element was carefully and individually freed from the soil, I handed each bone up to Mike Park, working with Dick LaRose to record onsite forensic data.[61] Volunteers and students wrapped the remains in acid-free tissue and placed them ever so gently into a zinc box to prevent any surface damage. After removal of the complete skeleton, I continued to excavate through the bottom of the burial feature until encountering sterile, glacial soils in order to be sure the burial feature did not extend deeper and possibly contain another body under 'Ōpūkaha'ia. Stacked burials were not uncommon in historic New England, so we had to verify that Henry was alone in his grave shaft.

In the field, we were able to determine the remains were of a young adult male of good stature and, coupled with the recovery of the initials "H. O." on the coffin lid, our team was more than comfortable with the preliminary identification of 'Ōpūkaha'ia so as to permit removal of the skeleton for further forensic verification in a controlled laboratory setting.

As the sun descended over the western verdant hills of Cornwall, Henry was prepared to leave the ground he had resided beneath for almost two centuries. Henry Fuqua took official custody of the remains and transported them in a hearse to his Hartford funeral home. As I drank quenching water from a thermos, I remember hoping that the disinterment was handled respectfully and would meet the approval of Henry's family. I also remember thinking with enormous satisfaction that it was such a great honor to be a part of this repatriation.

The American Board began to draw its attention to the small, rural community of Cornwall in Litchfield County as a permanent home for the Foreign Mission School. Settled in 1740 by thirteen families from throughout the Connecticut Colony, Cornwall's western boundary touched the Housatonic River, yet remained relatively secluded.[62] The populace consisted mostly of farmers, though there was a small woolen factory and mills processing grain, lumber, and carding of wool, providing an ideal community that the board commissioners sought as an excellent example of hardworking Christian habits and relative isolation.[63]

In May of 1817, the "School for Heathens" transferred officially to Cornwall, and Henry moved there on his return from Amherst. While the board contributed $3,300 toward the founding of the school, the people of Cornwall showed their support of the institution by allotting $1,400, the use of an old school building, and fourteen acres of land,[64] outbidding other towns in their desire to have the Foreign Mission School in their community. 'Ōpūkaha'ia's original tutor, Rev. Edwin

Wells Dwight, was named its first interim principal.[65] The student body expanded to twelve students, half of whom were Hawaiian along with Native Americans, primarily Cherokees and Choctaw.[66]

Among these young Native men, 'Ōpūkaha'ia continued to be the model evangelical student. By accepting whole-heartedly and uncriti-

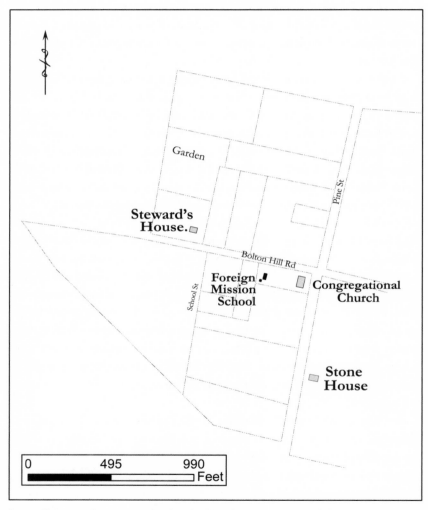

Cornwall Center, Connecticut, in 1817 highlighting places associated with Henry Obookiah.

cally the Christianity of his tutors, he earned their high trust and admiration. These parochial New England Calvinists with their concepts of racial distinctions, their ethnocentric view of Indigenous barbarism, and their profound belief in their superiority among peoples of the world, recognized in their "Obookiah" the transformational revivalism that would mark their generation.[67] He was their marvelous example of God's mercy, their promise of Christian conversion throughout the entire world. While the other Hawaiians, especially Thomas Hopu, would also inspire hope in their work for Christ, it was 'Ōpūkaha'ia who set a new paradigm for all Indigenous Peoples in the minds of these British Americans that would see fruition in the rising movement of 19th-century abolitionism.

One of the founders of the American Board, Rev. Lyman Beecher of nearby Litchfield, was the father of Harriet Beecher Stowe and Henry Ward Beecher. Both young Harriet and Henry, who may have been named after 'Ōpūkaha'ia,[68] would remember for all their lives the visits of this celebrated Hawaiian to the Litchfield household of their childhood. The presence of this intelligent, charismatic man of color shaped their adulthood zeal in the righteousness of the abolitionist cause, sowing the seeds for "Uncle Tom's Cabin" and powerful Sunday sermons emitting from the pulpit of Plymouth Church in Brooklyn during the Civil War, calling out for the abrogation of slavery. 'Ōpūkaha'ia was the fulfillment of the argument that "all men are created equal" in the eyes of God and humanity, and it has been argued that his long journey from Hawai'i to America fostered the course of 19th-century American abolitionism.[69]

Henry Obookiah prepared himself for the rigors of advanced training in Cornwall with the "principle studies (being). . . English Grammar, Morse's Geography and Dabald's Arithmetic."[70] Lessons would commence every morning from 9 a.m. to noon, again from two to five and finally from eight to nine in the evening. No visitors were allowed during study hours and no one was permitted to leave the school unless authorized. Along with academic training, each student was required to work outdoors in the school's agricultural farm two days a week. It was a rigorous schedule, but Henry basked in the learning. He had experienced intense scholarship before at the *Heiau Hikiau* under the tutorage of his uncle, Pahua, so he had developed the capability to devote his energy and passion when the opportunity was presented to him. He loved his fellow Hawaiian companions and spoke encouragingly to them during meals taken at the Steward's home across the road from the school.[71] "His counsel was sought and regarded as decisive."[72] He would lead by example with industry and a thorough commitment to his education.

Arising out of the Haystack Prayer Meeting, Samuel Mills, Jr., continued to be at the forefront of missionary activity as a verbal proponent and by traveling into the field performing missionary work in the Mississippi Valley. He was now considered the "Father of Foreign Missions."[73] In late 1817, he embarked on a trip to Africa searching for a

Foreign Mission School, ca. 1873, photographer unknown. Classrooms were on the lower level with student sleeping quarters on the upper. (Courtesy Cornwall Historical Society.)

place along the west coast to establish a republic of liberated African Americans. Samuel Mills Jr. was one of the leading proponents for the annexation of enslaved and free Africans back to their homeland and became one of the founders of the American Colonization Society.[74] His abolitionist goals were two-fold: 1. Deal with the troubling emancipation issue by the misguided strategy of sending Africans back to Africa, and 2. Bring Christianity and civilization to the Dark Continent.[75] His long oceanic voyage was embarked upon to purchase land in Liberia with the goal of establishing a Christian missionary colony. On Mills' return, it was anticipated that 'Ōpūkahaʻiaʻs training would have advanced to the point where the ABCFM would consider designs for sending the Hawaiian mission abroad with Henry and Samuel Jr. serving together as trailblazers.

The Foreign Mission students were returning from 1817 Christmas celebrations spent among sponsoring families when they learned that 'Ōpūkahaʻia was gravely ill. Initially manifesting as a minor headache, the sickness was soon followed by chills and an accompanying high fever. The discomfort started gradually but within a couple of days developed into something far more serious. Dr. John Calhoun, his attending physician, diagnosed the malady as typhus fever.

A notorious disorder in early history, epidemic typhus is an obligate disease caused and spread by body lice, usually transmitted by field mice and other rodents. When the resultant itch from the arthropod's bite is scratched, the wound opens and disperses bacteria into the bloodstream where they grow and increase over time. With its origins little understood in Henry's era, typhus begins with a loss of appetite accompanied by general aches and pains, eventually graduating to profound prostration, backache, severe fever, bronchial disturbances, and, in severe cases, secondary infection and renal failure.[76]

Rare in colonial New England, a typhus epidemic spread during "The Year Without a Summer" in 1816. That April, Mount Tambora in the Dutch East Indies exploded, spewing volcanic ash into the atmosphere and spreading a cloud of debris that encircled the globe, blocking out the sun for months. Without sunlight, the summer of 1816 brought freezing temperatures and snowfall to New England. Crops were destroyed, resulting in hunger for people, their domestic animals, and unwanted rats and mice, who carried the infected lice from the barren agricultural fields and into New England houses searching for food. Typhus epidemic was the result.[77]

Henry may have been susceptible to foreign infections, contracting the disease when traveling around New England and speaking before various congregations in support of the Foreign Mission School.[78] However, lice could easily have become embedded in 'Ōpūkaha'ia's clothing, feasting on his blood and transmitting the bacterial disease while he was studying in Cornwall. From whatever source, 'Ōpūkaha'ia was in a dangerous condition.

As his illness worsened, Henry was transferred from the mission school to the nearby residence of Rev. Timothy Stone in Cornwall Center. With the Stone family's attention and Dr. Calhoun's prescribed medicines, Henry appeared to be making progress against the ailment. Regrettably, the reprise was only temporary, and before long the Hawaiian youth, with hopes for his work in Christ, had fallen into a terminal state.

His sickbed became a sanctuary where a parade of supporters and his Hawaiian compatriots visited and maintained vigil. "Father" Mills was among those in attendance to pray with Henry and ensure that his "son" was prepared to face God and final judgment. 'Ōpūkaha'ia insisted that at least one of his fellow Hawaiians be with him at all times, especially Thomas Hopu, who was a constant companion at his deathbed, praying with him in their Native language.

Through these visitations, Henry always appeared composed, even upbeat. His patience, cheerfulness, and resignation to the will of God were on exhibit for all to observe. Dr. Calhoun testified, "He ('Ōpūka-ha'ia) was the first patient whom he ever attended through a long course of fever, that had not in some instances manifested a greater or less degree of peevishness and impatience."[79]

Mrs. Stone exclusively devoted all her attention to the care of her beloved patient. Witnessing the fortitude, faith, and grace 'Ōpūkaha'ia exhibited in the face of such a "violent disease" made her feel that this time of nursing was "one of the happiest and most profitable periods of her life."[80] When told by Mrs. Stone that the doctor thought his condition uncertain, Henry replied, "God will take care of me."[81] His strength and tender devotion to Jesus Christ was the underlining theme on his deathbed. After a long sleep, he awoke and immediately prayed, "O Lord, have mercy on my soul–Thou knowest all my secret sins– Save me for the sake of Jesus Christ our Lord and Savior--Amen."[82]

The day before he died, after a particularly distressing night, ʻŌpūka-haʻia summoned his Hawaiian companions around his bed and addressed them in their Native language. He had something important to tell them: his obligation to them and his thanks for their prayers and comradeship, but, more importantly, to remind them that they "will follow. . .make your peace with God, make Jesus your friend, God has done great deal for you and for me, you must love God, or you will perish."[83] Holding off tears, they all pledged to continue training in the new faith and committed to bring the Gospel to their home islands. ʻŌpūkahaʻia had more to tell them, but his strength failed; all he could do was utter inaudible sounds. The intensity had completely exhausted him, and he fell into lethargy. The gathered Hawaiians could barely contain themselves; uncontrolla-ble sobbing was heard throughout the house.

Tomb of Henry Obookiah, Cornwall Center Cemetery, Connecticut, date and photographer unknown. (Courtesy Cornwall Historical Society.)

Death approached the following day, February 17, 1818. He was told that he "must die soon," and he acknowledged it without signs of emotion or distress. To the assembled students, he spoke once again in Hawaiian, "*Aloha o'e.*" He professed to be free of pain, and his countenance was that of perfect peace. He even seemed to have rebounded from his suffering. Then when everyone seemed least prepared, Thomas Hopu, who was standing by Henry's bed, saw that his breathing had stopped and announced, "Obookiah is gone!" Everyone raced to the bedside. He was dead, though a smile "such as none present had ever beheld" remained on his youthful face.[84] 'Ōpūkaha'ia, the former pagan, the "heathen" who in his youth had worshiped and studied a pantheon of demanding gods, would teach generations of Christians how to die a Christian death.

The funeral and burial, as was the custom in the days before embalming, would be held the following day at the First Church of Christ Congregational in Cornwall Center next door to the Foreign Mission School and less than half a mile away from the town cemetery. Rev. Lyman Beecher, travelling from nearby Litchfield, gave the eulogy, mourning to all those assembled that "We bury with his dust all our high hopes of his future activity in the cause of Christ." Yet he admonished the congregation, "Let there be no despondency!" The "darkness" of the moment should give way to being "cheered," he proposed, "forasmuch as we know that our labor is not in vain in the Lord."[85] The Foreign Mission School and the Congregational missionary movement had acquired a martyr, an inspiration and call to arms, vowing that "Obookiah's" life and death would not be futile and that his revelation and name would live well beyond his mortal lifespan.

The people of Cornwall took up a collection and raised $28 to meet the cost of an appropriate tomb fitting for such an extraordinary and beloved person. Though some denounced the expenditure, arguing that it could have gone to establishing the missions,[86] the table-topped fieldstone monument would be the largest and most elaborate shrine in Cornwall Cemetery at the time. The carved marble tombstone covering the extent of the memorial told his redemptive story for all who pilgrimage to this day.

Memory of
Henry Obookiah
A native of
OWHYHEE
His arival (sic) in this country gave rise
To the Foreign mission school,
of which he was a worthy member.
He was once an Idolater, and was
designed for a Pagan Priest; but by
the grace of God, and by the prayers
and instructions of pious friends,
he became a Christian.
He was eminent for piety and
Missionary Zeal. When almost prepared
to return to his native Isle to preach the
Gospel, God took to himself. In his last
sickness he wept and prayed for Owyhee,
but was submissive. He died without fear
With a heavenly smile on his
countenance and glory in his soul.
Feb. 17, 1818
Aged 26.

In June, Samuel J. Mills, Jr., returning from his missionary and colonization work in Africa, became ill onboard the brig *Success*. He would die, probably of consumption, shortly after the schooner set sail and was buried at sea. "Father" Mills broke down when he received the news, his personal pain unbearable. He had lost two "sons" within four months of each other, sons who together were to have chartered a new course in missionary work. He never questioned God's will. He persevered, dying five days short of his 90th birthday in 1833.[87] Julia Mills, granddaughter of Samuel, Sr., would carry on the family's missionary fervor by accompanying her husband to Hawai'i in 1842 in fulfillment of the legacy of her uncle and Henry "Obookiah."

Edwin Dwight compiled 'Ōpūkaha'ia's writings on his early life in Hawaii as well as his letters and diary, publishing them in the form of a short autobiography. *The Memoirs of Henry Obookiah*, released by a missionary press in New Haven in 1819, became a best-selling book in New England.[88] Translated into three languages, all proceeds contributed to the first Christian delegations to be sent to Hawaii as well as subsequent missionary activities around the world. Catapulted by hundreds of donations that came into the coffers of the Foreign Mission School in ʻŌpūkahaʻia's memory, the American Board prepared to fulfill Henry's legacy.

With Congregationalist's voices regaling spiritual hymns all through Boston harbor, the brig *Thaddeus* sailed away from its pier on Oct. 23, 1819, carrying a company of two ministers (Revs. Hiram Bingham and Asa Thurston), two teachers, a doctor, printer, farmer, and all their wives, some newly married, plus five children and four Hawaiian youths, including Thomas Hopu, who was returning home for the first time since leaving the islands with ʻŌpūkahaʻia a decade earlier.

Though his mortal remains reposed beneath a hilltop cemetery in Cornwall, Henry "Obookiah" was in all respects onboard the *Thaddeus* as much as the pioneering passengers were. His martyrdom launched that ship; his consuming spirit powered the winds that billowed the sails transporting it forward over the swelling Atlantic seas just as Samuel J. Mills, Jr. had envisioned; his faith bridged the oceans that the *Thaddeus* glided upon. While ʻŌpūkahaʻia's corporeal journey home would take another 175 years, his formidable influence was well under way, transforming Hawaiʻi forever.

3 | After ʻŌpūkahaʻia

Were these the remains of Henry ʻŌpūkahaʻia? We had to be certain before they could be repatriated to Hawaiʻi. So, our team reassembled a few days after the disinterment at Fuqua's Funeral Home on North Main Street, Hartford, to conduct a more thorough forensic examination. We unwrapped individual skeletal elements from the zinc box and placed them anatomically on a gurney so that Mike Park could begin the bone-by-bone observation. We cleaned, photographed, measured, and described each element. In respect of the Native Hawaiian sacredness of the *iwi*, we employed no destructive techniques and limited our work to gross morphological analyses.

The human skeleton is more than the hard tissue foundation for our bodies that sustains us in an upright posture and protects our vital organs. It does that, but bones are also living tissue, connected in complex ways to muscles, blood vessels, nerves and skin, which modify constantly during the life of each individual. Forensic anthropologists can estimate age, sex, nutritional levels, degrees of muscularity, bone density, stature, disease, trauma, and at times cause of death. With the right diagnostic biomarkers, handedness, episodes of childbirth, and life stress pathologies associated with occupation can also be discerned. These life history reconstructions have long been used in modern criminal investigations to profile missing persons or homicide victims when only skeletal remains are retrieved. The same process is regularly used in historical reconstructions. Dead men do tell tales.

Written descriptions of Henry's physical characteristics and the single engraved portrait were available to establish important diagnostic features. The following account by Edwin W. Dwight, published in the *Memoirs*, offers just one example:

> "He was considerably above the ordinary size; but little less than six feet in height and in his limbs and body proportionally large. His form, which at 16 was awkward and unshapen, had become erect, graceful and dignified. His countenance had lost every mark

of dullness; and was, in an unusual degree, sprightly and intelligent. His features were strongly marked. They were expressive of a sound and penetrating mind. [H]e had a piercing eye, a prominent Roman nose and a projecting chin. His complexion was olive, varied equally from the blackness of the African; and the redness of the indian. His hair was black: worn short and dressed after the manner of the Americans."[1]

The remains before us corresponded to both written descriptions and the original etched portrait of Henry 'Ōpūkaha'ia.[2] The pelvis is the best sexually diagnostic skeletal element in the human body because of structural differences associated with childbirth: females are wide, males narrow. The constricted sciatic notch and subpubic angle of the skeleton we observed were classically male. The cranium was large and exhibited moderate brow ridges, a sloped forehead, a protruding, squared chin and rounded superior eye orbit borders—all male skeletal characteristics. However, the gonial angle of the jaw was relatively more flared (120 degrees) than expected for a male and the mastoid processes, though slightly deteriorated, appeared to have been atypically small. Despite these two generally feminine features, there was no doubt as to the male sexual estimation of the skeleton.

Length measurements from the well-preserved long bones of the lower and upper limbs were applied to mathematical formulae to determine stature, providing projections ranging between 5' 7" and 5' 9", consistent with Henry's height description as "less than six feet."[3]

Assessments of age were a bit more ambiguous. The ends of all the long bones (epiphyses) were fully fused and adult in size and form. Active fusion was still evident on the iliac crest of the pelvis, which usually fuses between 18 and 23 years of age, and the medial clavicle (collarbone), between 23 to 30 years of age. The pubic symphyseal surfaces were comparable to Todd Stage 4 (25–26 years)[4] and Brooks-Suchy Stage III (21–46 years; mean 28 years).[5] Sternal rib ends best matched Iscan, Loth and Wright Phase 3 indicating an age of 19 to 33 with a mean of 25.9 years.[6] All of these maturation characteristics were fairly consistent with our expectations of a 26-year-old adult male; however, the one age factor that did not correspond to expectancies was the unanticipated closure of all cranial sutures. Cranial sutures are the jigsaw pattern of lines separating the various bones of the cranial vault that fuse together with growth and development. These lines eventually obliterate with advanced age. Finding these fibrous joints closed in such a young man could be a factor of the wide range in biological variability in suture closure. However, Henry's closure may have occurred prematurely or may suggest that Henry was older than most historical records suggest. Nonetheless, taken together the overall age indicators are consistent with an individual in their mid-to-late 20s and possibly early 30s.

All dentition had erupted except the four third molars and the upper second right premolar. The third molars evidently had never erupted; the premolar had been lost during Henry's life exhibited by the complete re-sorption of the tooth socket. There was no noticeable tooth wear and no caries though some plaque development was present, particularly on the lower right side teeth. In all, 'Ōpūkaha'ia had good dental health, exhibiting no cavities or signs of periodontal disease, and his tooth row was straight and even.

With a single exception, there was no evidence for major pathological condition or trauma. That departure was demonstrated on the medial surface of the right ribs 3 through 10, which exhibited an ashy, porous surface between the head and the neck angle. Henry 'Ōpūkaha'ia is reported to have died of typhus fever; however, such lesions have typically been identified in tuberculosis victims.[7] Nonetheless, typhus is occasionally associated with pulmonary distress.[8] When osteomyelitis results, lesions may appear on several surfaces adhering to the lungs, including the ribs, usually near the neck angle, suggesting that Henry's illness registered on the hard tissue of his bones.

Mike Park also identified a few minor skeletal abnormalities. The temporal-mandibular joint (where the jaw articulates with the skull) was oddly shaped and noticeably worn. As a result, Henry may have experienced some discomfort when chewing hard food substances though this malady is never mentioned in historical accounts. Also the joint where the head of the femur (thigh bone) sockets into the pelvis was likewise oddly shaped though there is no indication that this condition caused him any pain or malfunction.

Cranial and facial measurements were taken to compare with numerous human populations to determine if 'Ōpūkaha'ia's ancestry was consistent with Polynesian samples.[9] However, these results proved inconclusive in specifying biological insights into ancestry, and again, in compliance with using no destructive scientific techniques on the skeleton, we chose not to process for DNA sequencing.

What we did not find in the forensic examination, and might have anticipated, was evidence of the *pāhoa* (spear) that impaled his infant brother to Henry's back when they fled Kamehameha's warriors after the ruthless murder of their parents. We predicted that scar tissue and/or remodeling of the posterior rib surfaces or vertebrae might indicate if the spear penetrated Henry's back. Yet no trauma or remodeling were recorded anywhere in the suspected area; hence, we could not verify the account through forensic examination. We suggest, however, that the *pāhoa* was thrown with sufficient force to kill his younger brother but only stunned and toppled Henry without penetration.

Mike Park's skeletal analysis of 'Ōpūkaha'ia introduced us to him in ways that written records fail to document. We appreciate that Henry may have experienced some physical joint discomfort never mentioned in historical accounts. He, obviously, never complained. These were not incapacitating irregularities but would have caused periods of discomfort as he reached adulthood; by that time Henry had found new purpose for his life.

The brig *Thaddeus* had been anchored for several days in the harbor of Kailua-Kona on the western shore of the Big Island of Hawai'i before the Christian missionaries were allowed an audience with King Liholiho and Queen Ka'ahumanu, the son and favorite wife of Kamehameha, respectively, who served as co-rulers since the death of the Great One. These founding missionaries had traveled for more than 160 days overtop the rough waters of the Atlantic Ocean, through the tumultuous currents of the Straits of Magellan, and northwestward across the vast Pacific, arriving at their Hawaiian destination on April 4, 1820.

Permission was being sought of the king and queen to bring the Word of Christ to the Hawaiian people by establishing mission stations throughout the archipelago and by "covering these islands with fruit-ful fields and pleasant dwellings, and schools and churches; of raising up the whole people to an elevated state of Christian civilization."[10] After days of deliberation and some convincing that the royal hierar-chy would not be threatened by the development of the missions and that British authorities would not be displeased, the Hawaiian mon-archs gave their consent and the pioneer company of seventeen people came ashore. Though greeted hospitably, trepidation in the great work ahead filled their hearts.

None of these Congregational ministers or laity could have imag-ined that the religious "idolatry" they sought to replace with the doc-trines of Christianity had already undergone drastic changes. Massive death rates, the result of disease epidemics brought on by contact with Capt. Cook and other Western sailors, weakened the *Kanaka Maoli*. Measles, whooping cough, tuberculosis, and influenza had drastically reduced the Hawaiian population before the missionaries ever set foot on the Big Island.[11] Estimated at almost a million people when Cook arrived, only 84,000 *Kanaka Maoli* survived the epidemics by 1853, a devastating 90% population reduction.[12] Although Kamehameha, the *aliʻi nui*, and the *kahunas* tried to stop the evil sicknesses by strictly enforcing *kapu*, none of their attempts were successful. As traditional ways were proving unreliable in stemming the mortalities, Hawai-ians were beginning to doubt their ancient beliefs. Once her husband, Kamehameha the Great, was dead, Queen Kaʻahumanu sought to defy the existing *kapu*. Six months prior to their arrival, Lihohiho and the strong-willed Kaʻahumanu, in an act of defiance, abolished the prohi-bition of males and females eating together (*ʻal kapu*).

During a great feast attended by hundreds of *aliʻi*, *kahuna*, and *makaʻāinana*, the multitude of wide-eyed onlookers watched in hor-ror when Liholiho sat down by Kaʻahumanu's side and not only joined with the women in sustenance but ate from the same serving vessels. All awaited the expectant retribution from the gods, though none came. Volcanoes did not erupt, tsunamis did not shallow the shore, royal vio-lators of the *ʻal kapu*, were not struck dead. Cautiously, the conviction arose among the multitude that the *ʻal kapu* had ended. However, in their attempts to stop the massive deaths, Kaʻahumanu and Liholiho mired Hawai'i in a transcendent void. The people were primed and ready for a new spiritual voice that would be powerful enough to offer stability to their disintegrating world.

Dismantling of the sacred *kapu* system was in direct response to the horrific epidemics that brought uncertainty and attempted revolution amongst the Hawaiian people. Unrest involving rival chiefs and *kahunas*, who were shocked by the abolishment of behaviors that would further entice the wrath of the gods, brought an attempted coup, but the powerful armies Liholiho inherited from his father restored peace; opposition soon ceased.[13] Though the act seemed to be sudden—even revolutionary in its scope—in reality, the elimination of *kapu* was the outgrowth of a continual process of culture change that began when James Cook dropped anchor in Kealakekua Bay.

With the frequent arrival of Western ships, Hawaiians scrutinized the behavior of these bizarre Western sailors who showed no regard for *kapu*, breaking its formal prohibitions regularly with no apparent ill effect. The transition was not immediate but noticeable. The Protestant missionaries attempted to persuade the people that the old ways were evil and were responsible for the mass fatalities. However, long-held religious beliefs could not be ordered to cease with the wave of a royal hand. The final breakdown of the *kapu* system with the associated destruction of the stone *heiaus* merely drove many traditional Hawaiians to continue their worship within clandestine shrines. Nonetheless, "idolatry" had been officially removed and could only have been interpreted by the missionaries as they stepped off the *Thaddeus* as Divine Intervention, a sign for the future success of their cause—"the Lord hath gone before us."[14]

Liholiho was prepared now to grant the missionaries permission to proselytize among his people, though cautiously restricted them to a one-year probationary period. Disembarking with Rev. Asa Thurston and his wife, Lucy, to begin the Kailua mission were Thomas Hopu and William Kanui,[15] prodigies of the Foreign Mission School, whose principal thoughts were to emulate the character and resolve of their martyred brother and compatriot, the dearly departed Henry "Obookiah." 'Ōpūkaha'ia was their motivation, model, and spiritual guide; as difficult as it would be, they ached to live up to his high expectations.

In this they were not alone, for all of the New Englanders who came ashore, even the stoic and racist Calvinists, taking their first steps onto the volcanic stone of the Big Island, sustained "Obookiah," the "heathen" Hawaiian as their inspiration, their paragon in spreading the Word of Christ.

Even with Christian baptism, the horror of deadly epidemics continued to reduce the *Kanaka Maoli* population, hampering the initial attempts of the missionaries to convert Hawaiians. While numerous theories were put forth by the *ali'i* and *kahunas* to explain the unimaginable dying, it became apparent that these new Americans were unaffected from the same diseases. Without an understanding of germ theory and the spread of Old World pathogens introduced into Native populations having no built-up immunity, the upheaval experienced by the Hawaiians has been compared to post-traumatic stress disorder.[16] Hawaiian faith in traditional healing powers started to wane, shaking the very foundation of their indigenous worldview, their sense of identity. Some began to conceive that the Christian God must be more powerful than the Hawaiian deities (of which there were thousands), protecting the *haole* from the diseases and death. Unlike previous Westerners who impacted the islands with alcohol, rape, and exploitive economic practices, the missionaries were seen as offering something different, something spiritual.[17]

By 1824, a second company of missionaries arrived creating another major mission station on the Big Island's east coast at Hilo;[18] a decade later they could count 18,000 Hawaiian converts, almost twenty per cent of the Native population.[19] New missions spread throughout the main islands with varying success, and their efforts received a most important lift when the queen mother, Keōpūolani, converted to Christianity on her deathbed. With her health fading, she charged her son, King Liholiho, to "walk the straight path... observe the Sabbath... serve God" and to "kindly protect the missionaries."[20]

Since the deaths continued after baptism, there remained active voices against the missions, especially among the *kahunas*, though many of the *ali'i* were now turning toward the Christian God, setting examples for the rest of their communities. Commoners looked to the *ali'i nui* to protect them through proper ritual and behavior, whose responsibility it was to prevent famines and sickness. The massive number of deaths seemed to break this reciprocal relationship.[21] Soon keeping the Sabbath became public law with its restrictions on Sunday travel and work; the wooden *ki'i* were being systematically destroyed, and stone and thatch *heiau* were dismantled. In Hilo, high priestess Kapi'olani became the first *ali'i* to sponsor a church, and Queen Ka'ahumanu embraced the missionaries, calling upon her subjects to receive the Word of God.[22] Still, it was difficult for all of the *ali'i* to give up their old traditions and embrace the new behaviors of self-denial that the Calvinist preachers espoused for eternal salvation.[23] Among many of the *Kanaka Maoli*, it appeared that the old *kapu* was simply being replaced with a new *kapu* comprising Christian concepts of sin and self-denial, still restricting and prohibiting certain behaviors.

The American Board Commissioners for Foreign Missions (ABCFM) recruited a third ship to Hawai'i, arriving in March of 1828. Within ten years of 'Ōpūkaha'ia's untimely death, Congregational New England realized that something progressive, well beyond their immediate expectations, was happening in those distant "pagan" islands, and they rushed to meet the demand for books, Bibles, and other resources required for the mission's continued success. During these years, Hawaiians demonstrated a profound enthusiasm for education, an enthusiasm that preceded European intervention. By 1832, there were more than 50,000 students learning in more than 900 church schools. Over the next twenty years, the ABCFM would send out eleven companies, totaling more than 120 individuals, to complete the work launched by the *Thaddeus*.[24] Funding for these expeditions was primarily generated by the sales of the *Memoirs*, reflecting 'Ōpūkaha'ia's spiritual and financial contribution well beyond death.

Before long, competition arose for Hawaiian souls. Within seven years of the founding of the Kailua-Kona Congregational mission station, Roman Catholic missionaries disembarked. The Protestants appealed to Queen Ka'ahumanu, imploring her to refuse the interlopers permission to practice their papal superstitions. She granted their request, but the governor of O'ahu was agreeable to Catholicism and issued temporary permission. Mormons soon followed Catholics, and both were highly successful, especially Catholicism with its belief in the Virgin Mary and its bounty of revered saints that appeared a modification of the traditional pantheon of Hawaiian *akua*. The Protestant missions also had to deal with the persistent veneration of traditional gods and goddesses, especially Pele who controlled the fiery flames of Kilauea. Fearful of retribution for accepting Christian behaviors, Hawaiian traditionalists still held sway among the *Kanaka Maoli*, maintaining covert rituals and prayers to appease the vanquished deities.

Rivalry among these religious philosophies occurred amid changes in the royal family. Liholiho and his wife Kamamalu made a decision to visit their fellow monarch King George IV in England, setting sail in November of 1824, reaching the United Kingdom in May. While abroad, both husband and wife contracted measles and died in London within days of each other. Word of their deaths would not reach Hawaiʻi until May of 1826.

Liholiho's adolescent brother, Kauikeaouli, was elevated as King Kamehameha III, but the real power still lay with his mother and regent, the Christian convert, Kaʻahumanu. By 1829, she outlawed cohabitation without marriage among the sexually uninhibited Hawaiians, and by 1830 she forbid the *hula* that the missionaries decried as possessing carnal connotations. Completely misunderstood by Westerners, *hula* is a sacred dance that tells of revered deities and ancient legends, and maintains oral traditions. Prohibiting *hula* was not merely restricting a form of dance but striking at the heart of traditional Hawaiian culture.[25]

Of all these political and religious intrigues, the main avenue to the Protestant mission's success lay in what ʻŌpūkahaʻia had inaugurated in New England: the development of the written grammar of the "Owhyhee" language which could be converted to printed pages and taught to the children of the *Kanaka Maoli*.[26] *Piʻaʻpa* were the basic elements of the alphabet, numbers, and simple readings that the elite's young learned. With the sharing of the printed word, the *aliʻi* found a new way to communicate with each other that could be used to teach the sacred texts and prayers secretly held by the *kahunas*. The long passages memorized by ʻŌpūkahaʻia at the *Heiau Hikiau* could be shared now by reading among the *Kanaka Maoli*, resulting in a covert means of resistance to outside domination.[27]

Once the "autopsy" of Henry ʻŌpūkahaʻia was completed and the physical remains exhumed from Cornwall Cemetery confirmed as his, we began the process of securing him in a casket for transportation back to Hawaiʻi. At the request of the family, Winkler Products, LLC, of Honolulu built a coffin of native *koa* wood to accommodate and transport Henry's physical remains.[28] Fuqua provided six-inch thick sheets of rubbery, sponge foam, which we cut and tightly fitted to the interior of the coffin, creating a bed and cover to secure the remains for transport. Mike Park measured all the skeletal elements while Dick LaRose and Dave Cooke carved out the appropriate-sized cavities into the foam with pocket knives, cradling each bone separately in anatomical position. Before long, Henry reemerged before us as he had in the ground, laid out head-to-foot and secured within the *koa*-grained coffin.

As we were completing the layout of the skeletal remains at the funeral home, the door swung open and Henry Fuqua escorted Deborah Liʻikapeka Lee and her parents, Elizabeth Kapeka Hoʻomanawanui and Kwai Wah, to view ʻŌpūkahaʻia for the first time and be introduced to our team. We were well aware of Debbie's spiritual call to bring Henry home less than a year earlier, and of her parents who supported her repatriation efforts, but this was the first time we had met. Representing Ahahui O ʻŌpūkahaʻia, they had made the long trip from Hilo and were overjoyed to encounter their beloved ancestor. Alohas, introductions, and gratitude abounded, generating many smiles; even Henry was perceived to be smiling back at his ʻohana.

Debbie recited in detail her midnight experience and the inner voice appealing to return Henry to Hawaiʻi, as well as their efforts to raise money and solicit government officials, contacting the airlines for the logistics of bringing Henry's casket home, and telling of their trip to Connecticut and involvement with the United Church of Christ Congregational. Debbie acknowledged that it was simply time for Henry to come home, and she was seeing to it.

We, in turn, told of the excavation process and the forensic analysis. There was little doubt in our minds that they would be returning the remains of their ancestor in fulfillment of his desire to see Hawai'i once again and, hopefully, to inspire new generations of Hawaiians with his Christian message.

The Lee family had brought sacred *ti*-leaves to be placed inside the coffin to protect Henry in death. The broad, long, green foliage was positioned on both sides of Henry's remains. Originally, the family wished to have the leaves placed with the stems positioned down along the insides of the coffin. But being lengthy, they had to be placed horizontally parallel to the upper body and lower legs. Early Polynesians believed the *ti* plant, found around the houses of contemporary Native Hawaiians, was sacred to the god Lono and used to ward off evil and beckon good spirits; it has many medicinal properties and is used in religious ceremonies even today.[29] Although devoutly Christian, the Lee family, proud of their heritage, adhere to many *Kanaka Maoli* traditions.

We presented the family with the reconstructed viewing glass and mended coffin lid with its pattern of heart-shaped brass tacks. Their consensus was that these artifacts of Henry's first coffin should be interred with him into his final casket. Our work completed, the casket lid closed, we were all invited to attend the planned farewell service at the Cornwall's United Congregational Church as guests of the family.

Four days after giving birth to her third son, Emily Dole died of complications during a demanding delivery. She had come to Hawai'i in 1842 with her husband, Daniel, in the Ninth Company to educate the developing second generation of missionary children born on the islands. When Emily became pregnant, husband and wife had been teaching for a year at the new Punahou School established by Hiram Bingham on O'ahu. Her surviving son, Sanford Ballard Dole, born April 23, 1844,[30] would personify his generation, not so much interested in sowing Native souls as their parents had been summoned to do but rather sowing the economic potential of the islands for cash crops.

While in his early twenties, Sanford Dole traveled to his parents' New England origins and attended Williams College in Massachusetts where Samuel Mills, Jr. had founded the Haystack Meeting's "Brethren" a half-a-century earlier. Dole would become a law clerk in Boston before returning to Honolulu in 1868 where he soon married. Business was slow for a young lawyer, so in his spare time he wrote articles for a local newspaper, climbed mountains, descended into valleys bird watching, and developed a veneration of the Hawaiian landscape that would soon put him and other missionary offspring in direct conflict with bona fide Native Hawaiians over control of the land they both coveted.[31]

In efforts to maintain sovereignty and recognition in their ever-changing global world, Hawaiian leadership increasingly modified their government to conform to Euro-American conventions. The Kingdom developed a constitution, enacted laws in accordance with the western world's legal systems, and defined the islands as a single nation in hopes of gaining recognition in the modern world system of governments.[32] To assist entry into this international political fraternity, Hawaiian royalty bade the missionaries to serve as advisors in governing the country. However, the American Board of Commissioners had warned against interfering with the Hawaiian political system and the "private and transient interests of chiefs and rulers."[33] Yet, in reality, no matter how much they hoped to adhere to this counsel, by proselytizing the *ali'i* the missionaries had become politicized.[34]

As the Hawaiian missions sought to find their appropriate balance within the quickening pace of culture change on the islands, New England church leaders back home were formulating new missionary policies. A senior secretary for the ABCFM, Rev. Rufus Anderson, delivered an 1845 ordination sermon titled "The Theory of Missions to the Heathen" in which he espoused that once the missionary effort planted the seeds of Christianity among Natives, it was up to God to determine if there would be a harvest or not. Subsequently, the Hawaiian missions should withdraw and let "His will be done," allowing the development of independent Indigenous churches with Native ministers to instruct the true religion without interference of foreign cultures; do this or else there was the danger of imposing Western principles into the evangelical process. Rev. Anderson's appeal for a methodology that served "Christ Only" to create Christians not Americans was often criticized by detractors who felt that the work of civilizing the "heathen" should include the promotion of Western technology and culture.[35] Nonetheless, Rev. Anderson saw that the Hawaiian missions had already converted an Indigenous People and developed churches; it was now time to "let go" and move on to new fields, like migrant workers harvesting souls of unbelievers in favor of Native ministries and a self-propagating Christianity.[36]

Attitudes toward the Foreign Mission School's assimilative approach had also changed in Cornwall. The American Board espoused a policy of teaching the English language to the mission students in hopes of saving them from extinction by becoming more civilized in their habits and Christian in their religion. The ability to read, write, and speak English, they hoped, would merge these men of color into the greater white New England society and "be of one blood with us."[37] However, disagreement with this policy was fierce, especially when two Cherokee students married local white women. Lyman Beecher, father of the abolitionist Harriet Beecher Stowe and "Obookiah's" eulogizer, believed in the importance of converting and civilizing the "heathen," but he could not bring himself to conceive of them as equals. These unresolved diametric viewpoints led to the closure of the Foreign Mission School in 1826, only nine years after opening its doors to Henry ʻŌpūkahaʻia.[38]

The first sugar cane plantation was developed on Kauaʻi in 1835. Although the originators of the growing and selling of sugar were not missionaries, the evangelists supported foreign entrepreneurs in their efforts to acquire vast areas of land from the *aliʻi* for cash crops, and they benefited from the association.[39] One missionary, Rev. Amos Starr Cooke, a trusted advisor to Kamehameha III, developed a method of land division that allowed foreigners to acquire large tracts to sustain the emerging plantation system. The 1848 *Māhele*, (to portion) shifted traditional Hawaiian land tenure from an ordered system of reciprocal accountability between the *aliʻi* and the *makaʻāinana* to concepts of Western private property, blurring the symbolic meaning of *ʻāina* and landownership.[40] The thin line between "Christ Only" and involvement in the political and economic affairs of the islands was becoming distinctively blurred as colonial capitalism began to dictate land tenure and political leadership.

Soon silk production followed sugar, as did pineapple, cotton, coffee, and cattle husbandry, all of which were successful. Cash crops began to dominate the economy, leaving less land for Natives to cultivate subsistence crops. The *Kanaka Maoli* was being reduced to plantation laborers, working the fields for practically nonexistent wages. By 1890, *haole*, primarily Americans, owned one quarter of all Hawaiian lands and controlled an additional 750,000 acres under low-cost leases provided by the government.[41]

The flourishing plantation system soon led to dramatic changes in the political realm as European and American authorities vied for influence and outright control of the islands. In 1839, when the Protestant missionaries convinced Kamehameha III to extradite Roman Catholic priests and imprison all Catholic converts, French Capt. Cyrille Laplace sailed into Honolulu harbor with fifty-two cannons ready to level the city if Catholicism was not restored. To avoid bloodshed, King Kamehameha III capitulated and reinstated the Catholic Church on the islands.[42]

Taking a page out of Laplace's playbook, the British attempted a similar coup in 1843 when Lord George Paulet demanded, again under threat of artillery bombardment of Honolulu, that the Royal Government yield control over to the British Crown. Without a protective army or navy, Kamehameha III once again submitted, though the monarchy was restored when Adm. Richard Thomas, Paulet's superior, overruled and reprimanded him for his actions.[43]

Concerned about political interference from other colonial powers, the U. S. government entangled itself with the Hawaiian Kingdom by facilitating the Tyler Doctrine in 1842, which recognized Hawaiian sovereignty and independence by affirming that no government had the right to take over or colonize the islands.[44] Still, American actions continually sought to control Kamehameha III through the influence of the New England missionaries and political intrigues at court. The French and British had similar dispositions for the islands so that by the 1840s warships from various Western nations were a constant, powerful, and threatening presence in Honolulu harbor. The monarchy seemed to be a minor obstacle in the wake of Western imperialism.

In the end, it was the U. S., with its early influence of Protestant missions, economic development of the plantation system, and apparent recognition of royal sovereignty that had the greatest impact on the Hawaiian government. In 1874 the monarchy signed an alliance providing the U. S. with exclusive trading rights. Ratified two years later as the Reciprocity Treaty, the American government was now poised to advance the economic production of the plantation system to its advantage by extending duty-free imports of sugar into the U. S. in return for the same duty-free privilege for American businesses entering Hawaiʻi.[45]

Of even more long-term significance, the treaty conveyed to the United States use rights to Pearl Harbor, Ford Island, and five miles interior from their shorelines free of charge, though no territory or sovereignty were ever ceded. An amendment also allowed the U. S. to build and maintain a deep-water naval base. The Reciprocity Treaty was shrewdly negotiated by the American government as a means of securing political and military control of the islands through reinvention of Hawaiʻi as a part of the United States[46] and providing the American government with an exclusive role in the international affairs of the Island Kingdom.[47] *Kanaka Maoli* displeasure at the treaty resulted in a civil rebellion that was promptly put down by U. S. Marines.[48] Native Hawaiians were rapidly losing control of their islands to a white minority who attempted to manipulate the monarchy to do its economic and political bidding. The devastating epidemics and low birthrates presented a problem in managing land, and the switch to private property controlled by foreign investors was viewed as a possible solution, even though the concept of land as a commodity was alien to Hawaiian beliefs in their genealogical connections to their *ʻaina*.[49]

With the death of Kamehameha V in 1872, political power was transmuted to the Kalākaua family.[50] Establishing the Reform (Missionary) Party with its strong-armed, Honolulu Rifles, American capitalists wrested control of the government from the Kalākaua family in 1887 when they impressed King David Kalākaua to support a new constitution that would limit the powers of the monarchy in favor of a white minority-dominated cabinet responsible to the legislature. It was termed the "Bayonet Constitution" by Hawaiians who believed that

Kalākaua was forced to sign at point of a bayonet.[51] To keep the *Kanaka Maoli* from influencing policy, voting requirements were changed to favor white property owners who, by now, held all the major political offices with the ability to appoint legislators and develop policy.

When King David Kalākaua, known as the Merry Monarch, died in San Francisco of Blight's disease in early 1891, the American minority found themselves up against a formable opponent: the King's sister, Princess Lili'uokalani, rose to the throne and began to push the limits of her queenly authority to challenge the "Bayonet Constitution." Lili'uokalani, as her brother David Kalakaua before her, resented the American minority and encouraged resistance through the *KaHoku o KaPakipika*, a Hawaiian language newspaper whose editorials highlighted the unethical activity of the plantation owners and their attempts to subjugate the *Kanaka Maoli*.[52] The newly vested queen was antagonistic toward American imperialism and was a strong advocate on behalf of "Hawai'i for the Hawaiians."[53]

Two years after her ascendancy to the throne, a consortium of sugar planters known as the Annexation Club overthrew Queen Lili'uokalani's government. Led by Sanford Dole, the coup, supported by Hawai'i's American Minister, established the Provisional Government as a stepping-stone to full annexation by the U. S. Rationalizing that there was a threat to American lives, U. S. Marines once again came ashore in Honolulu to support the annexationists with their show of military might. The queen had no choice but to temporarily yield her authority under protest to avoid bloodshed.[54] She found herself between the proverbial "rock and hard place." Without a single shot fired, the Stars and Stripes flew over all government buildings by the evening of the Marines' landing.

Lili'uokalani immediately wrote to Benjamin Harrison, who had recently lost his U. S. presidential reelection bid to Grover Cleveland, to protest the actions of the American businessmen and their provisional government. Two months later, President-elect Cleveland authorized a congressional investigation into the new Hawaiian government, finding that the great majority of *Kanaka Maolis* were against annexation to the U. S. while emphasizing that the queen truly had the support of her people.

The American president considered reinstating Queen Liliʻuoka-lani if she were willing to grant amnesty to those responsible for the coup. She was ill disposed to comply, wanting instead to deport Dole and his conspirators from the islands.[55] Although President Cleveland admitted the wrong done to the monarchy,[56] stressing that the "Provisional Government owes its existence to an armed invasion by the United States,"[57] he refused to remove Sanford Dole and his allies, who in turn refused to relinquish control or reinstate Queen Liliʻuokalani. Dole's provisional government held on. Nonetheless, due to Grover Cleveland's sympathies, growing concern developed among American landowners that the U. S. government would soon no longer support the coup and might restore the monarchy. Before that could happen, Dole and his compatriots called for an immediate "Constitutional Convention," announcing the formation of the "Republic of Hawaiʻi" on American Independence Day, July 4, 1894. Dole was elected the first president.

By 1895 rumors of a planned revolt, a "counter revolution" led by *Kanaka Maoli* to regain control of the Hawaiian government emerged, forcing Dole to declare martial law over the islands. The following year, the "Republic" passed a law banning the teaching of the Hawaiian language in all public and private schools. Queen Liliʻuokalani was arrested, falsely accused of hiding guns and ammunition for the rebels, tried for treason, and convicted. Sentenced to five years house imprisonment, the queen had no choice but to pledge allegiance to the new Republic of Hawaiʻi or once again risk the lives of her followers.[58]

Although the Queen was not through with her active opposition to this illegal government, her support in Washington waned as recognition of the strategic importance of the Hawaiian Islands became increasingly obvious to the new President William McKinley and Congress, which favored the concept of annexation. While large quantities of food and water supplies could be stored onboard military steamships, replenishing coaling stations were essential for trans-oceanic voyages. Whoever controlled Hawaiʻi controlled the Pacific, so by the turn of the 20th century, the U. S., already engaged in a war against Spain which included naval battles in the Philippines, was not prepared to allow another Western power to assuage its hegemony. McKinley made the case, "We need Hawai'i just as much and a good deal more than California. It is Manifest Destiny."[59]

Without a single vote from Native Hawaiians, who expressed their vehement opposition, the U. S. went ahead and authorized a treaty of annexation with the Republic of Hawai'i, creating the new "Territory of Hawai'i," appointing Dole as Territorial Governor. Queen Lili'uokalani traveled to Washington and presented the "Ku'e Petition," which consisted of two separate solicitations, the men's *Hui Aloha 'Āina* and the women's *Hui Kalae 'Āina* and signed by over 38,000, or 95 per cent, of all *Kanaka Maoli*. The men's petition opposed annexation, while the woman's petition concurred, but went further by appealing for a restoration of the monarchy. Both petitions challenged the U. S. to adhere to its own principles of government of the people, by the people, and for the people.[60] These combined efforts defeated annexation in 1897 when the U. S. Senate could not come up with a two-thirds majority to pass the treaty, thus acknowledging that the takeover had no legitimacy.[61] Regardless, Congress contrived an end-around by passing a joint resolution (Newland) requiring a simple majority of votes to accept the treaty, allowing President McKinley to sign the annexation on July 7, 1898. The United States had formally seized Hawai'i.[62]

Surely the subjugation of the Hawaiian monarchy and appropriation of the islands is one of the most disconcerting and troublesome episodes in American governmental history.[63] During annexation to the U. S., the Territory of Hawai'i underwent vast outside population increases from Japan, China, Philippines, Samoa, Korea, Portugal, and other countries emigrating to work the expanding pineapple, coffee, and sugar plantations. As their land base shrunk and employment given over to foreigners, *Kanaka Maoli* found themselves in the minority, living amid rapidly deteriorating economic and social surroundings. They solicited the U. S. Congress to release lands for Native Hawaiian homesteading, which the threatened plantation owners with their powerful economic and political influence lobbied strenuously against.

With land issues becoming a major concern among Native Hawaiians, Lili'uokalani was not through sparring with the U. S. government. In 1910 she brought a lawsuit to reclaim land lost in the overthrow of her government. She was denied by the U. S. Court of Claims, which argued that the Hawaiian monarchy and not the queen owned the land seized by the provisional government. Hence, the new government had every legal right to the land as a result of the overthrow. Of course, the claims court did not consider that there was no legal right for the coup in the first place. American intervention in Hawaiʻi not only stripped Native control of the land but also their right of self-determination.[64] Liliʻuokalani died at age 79, Nov. 11, 1917.[65] As the last queen of Hawaiʻi she fought for her people's rights to the very end of her life.

Sunday morning, December 7, 1941, "a date which will live in infamy"— the Empire of Japan conducted a surprise aerial attack on the U. S. Naval Base at Pearl Harbor, west of Honolulu, killing more than 2,000 Americans in less than two hours.[66] Probably no other day in world history has caused the disruption of so many lives, initiating a global nightmare and plunging humankind into a devastating World War for the next four years. To many Americans who had never heard of Pearl Harbor or had only a fleeting notion as to where Hawaiʻi was located in the Pacific Ocean, the name and place would be maintained as a battle cry and remembrance for the rest of their lives.

For the *Kanaka Maoli*, World War II changed their relationship with the outside world as dramatically as Capt. Cook's landfall. America declared martial law for the duration of the war, including curfews, blackouts, and the abeyance of civil rights, while the island's residents lived with the constant threat of a Japanese invasion. Only after the war did the U. S. Supreme Court rule martial law in Hawaiʻi as unconstitutional. Many from Hawaiʻi's large Japanese population were sent to detention camps on the mainland, crippling the sugar plantations since they represented the majority of field workers, compelling many American businesses to close their operations.

The influx of soldiers and sailors and the buildup of industrial military installations greatly increased the *haole* population of the islands that had been primarily a farm-based commerce. Native Hawaiians lost further control over traditional claims, such as decreased use of land taken over by the military, prohibition on areas in which to hunt, fish, and even walk, and restrictions from space considered as sacred sites.[67] The post-war period brought polarized factions competing, on the one hand, for the territorial government to heighten interest in statehood while on the other *Kanaka Maoli* resurgence towards political sovereignty. As both parties pulled in opposite directions, the rise of the post-war tourist industry served to reorient Hawaiʻi's economy.

Several of the vast pineapple plantations owned by the Dole family, started by Sanford's cousin's son James in 1898, saw conversion into sizeable seaside resorts for the wealthy. Sugar plantations were transformed into hotels and residential housing to accommodate tourists and foreign citizens seeking their piece of paradise. With tourism, the cost of living rose dramatically while economic prospects for Native Hawaiians diminished, resulting in many relocating to the mainland in search of jobs and educational opportunities.

Resistance to statehood in Washington, D. C. originated from fears of including a territory with a non-white majority, but events of World War II and questions surrounding the constitutional rights of Hawaiians soon changed opinions in Congress. Backed by an effective lobbying effort, President Dwight D. Eisenhower signed the Hawaiʻi statehood bill in March and introduced the Aloha State as the fiftieth state in the union on August 21,1959. In less than two hundred years, the political organization of Hawaiʻi transformed from powerful chiefdoms to monarchy to republic to territory to statehood, an unprecedented sequence of governmental change in world history. Nevertheless, many Indigenous Hawaiians were, and remain, adamantly against statehood, testifying that they had never relinquished their claims to sovereignty as a separate independent nation.[68] Today, Native Hawaiian sovereignty and civil rights movements envision an independent Hawaiʻi and are revisiting the concept of statehood, hoping to reclaim self-determination.[69]

Stemming from the success of the Civil Rights Movement on the continent for African Americans and the Red Power campaign among Native Americans, there was a rise in resistance[70] to outside authority among the *Kanaka Maoli*, which was brought to the forefront by the Bishop Estate's attempt to remove Native vegetable farmers from their land in the Kalama Valley of Oʻahu in 1970. The rural *Kanaka Maoli* were given a month's notice to evacuate their farms and make way for upper-income housing. They resisted and their cause received international attention. Unfortunately, the Native community leased the land and possessed no legal rights to it; ultimately, they were forced off their small farms. Still, the sovereignty movement had a cause and heightened awareness, which has resonated to the present.[71] Advocates for independence have framed their arguments on the illegal overthrow of the monarchy and the fact that of the five treaties signed between the United States and the Kingdom of Hawai'i, none were treaties of cession, that is, no land was ever turned over to the American government.

One offshoot of this resistance is a resuscitation of traditional Hawaiian culture, including the teaching of the language which the younger generation had never spoken.[72] Radical movement leaders want full independence from the U. S. and a return of all land taken with the overthrow of the Kingdom of Hawai'i.

Following a hotly debated contest, a joint resolution of Congress was passed, and President Bill Clinton signed a public apology in 1993 on behalf of the entire U. S. for the takeover of the Hawaiian government on the 100th anniversary of the coup.[73] While some Native critics contend that the government's apology was "merely symbolic," the United Church of Christ Congregational offered a more heartfelt atonement:

> **"Whereas, the Eighteenth General Synod of the**
> **United Church of Christ in recognition of the**
> **denomination's historical complicity in the illegal**
> **overthrow of the Kingdom of Hawai'i**
> **in 1893 directed the Office of the President of the**
> **United Church of Christ to offer public apology**
> **to the Native Hawaiian people and to initiate**
> **the process of reconciliation between the**
> **United Church of Christ and the Native Hawaiians."**[74]

While some contemporary Native Hawaiians wish the missionaries had never come to their islands, Henry 'Ōpūkaha'ia was not complicit

in the overthrow of the monarchy. He had lived the life of both traditional Hawai'i and Congregational New England, where he discovered
the teachings of Jesus Christ. There was only Great Aloha in Henry
'Ōpūkaha'ia's heart for his people and his beloved 'aina. Although
there were unintended negative consequences, the positives that the
missionaries brought were education and the Gospel to the Hawaiian
people, and many today rejoice in that achievement.

Amid this rise in Native Hawaiian resistance and movements
toward sovereignty, Deborah Li'ikapeka Lee, far away from her homeland, working for a bank in Seattle, Washington, heard the voice and
a very spiritual feeling within herself during the wee small hours of
a Sunday morning. Henry 'Ōpūkaha'ia desired to come home, and
if this was God's plan, she knew doors would be opened. She flew
home to tell her parents that she had heard Henry's call. They could
hardly believe what was happening. Her mother, Elizabeth Kapeka
Ho'omanawanui Lee, confessed that when she listened to Debbie's
story, she was scared.[75] They were not rich people— how could they
ever bring something like this about?

Acting upon her inspiration that was "so overwhelming, it could
not be ignored,"[76] Debbie committed herself totally toward Henry's
repatriation. She worked for ten months polling family members gaining their consent to exhume Henry's remains in Cornwall and bring
him home to Hawai'i. At first, there was little enthusiasm, but that
soon changed as Debbie's passion became evident. That winter she
attended a meeting of the United Church of Christ for which Rev. Paul
Sherry came to Hawai'i to formally apologize for his denomination's
role in the overthrow of the monarchy and to initiate the process of
reconciliation between the Church and Native Hawaiians. Socializing
after the official expression of regret, Debbie queried several people
on her proposal to bring Henry home with all in attendance supporting
her intention.

Debbie's aspiration in returning 'Ōpūkaha'ia to his 'aina was that
he could serve the same inspirational role he provided the missionaries in the nineteenth century for young Native men and women of
present-day Hawai'i, who were striving to maintain cultural identity

within their rapidly changing social world. She became empowered and strengthened, resolving to give Henry's life contemporary spiritual meaning by the return of his physical remains, his *iwi*, to Hawaiʻi in compliance with his deathbed wish.

The idea of bringing ʻŌpūkahaʻia home had been circulating for many decades. In the 1920s, Hawaiian Territorial Governor Lawrence M. Judd proposed the plan, but the people of Cornwall, Connecticut, objected so strenuously to losing such a beloved person from their community that Judd backed down.[77] However, this time, it was Henry's family who were requesting his return.

In view of her daughter's determination, Elizabeth Kapeka Lee started to come around to the feasibility of the repatriation. "It was no small thing she (Debbie) wanted to do. If this is God's Will then, I said, we will work together on this project."[78] Mutually they formed the non-

Frontispiece Portrait of Henry Obookiah, engraving, Daggett, Hinman & Co., from *Memoirs of Henry Obookiah, A Native of Owyhee and A Member of the Foreign Mission School*, (New York: American Tract Society, n.d., [1832]). Note the Anglicized features with each subsequent engraving.

profit, "Ahahui O ʻŌpūkahaʻia" (ʻŌpūkahaʻia Association) with Elizabeth as president and Debbie as project coordinator. They commenced discussions with church leaders and made contacts with Cornwall officials. They gathered support from ʻohana and explored fund-raising opportunities. The citizens of Cornwall, once adamantly opposed to Henry's removal, had undergone a cultural sensitivity, acknowledging their "'Obookiah'"'s dying wish "to see Owhyee." Though not overjoyed, Cornwall no longer stood in the way of his repatriation.

Debbie did not want to hurt the people of Cornwall, but the time had come to bring Henry home. ʻŌpūkahaʻia was poised to inspire a new generation of Hawaiians as the final wheels were placed in motion to complete his journey homeward. The ball was rolling and would roll much faster than either mother or daughter could have ever imagined.

4 | "He Wants To Come Home"

Two outrigger canoes, lashed together with a narrow platform stretching across their hulls, surged forward into the clear water off the beach at *Pu'uhonua o Honaunau*, the Place of Refuge where the royal *ali'i* had established an important stonewalled residence and built the *Hale o Keawe Heiau* more than 100 years before Capt. James Cook debarked on the island. With long sweeps of the oars projected by Keoua Canoe Club paddlers, powerfully bent forward, the linked double-hull canoes negotiated the surfing waves off the south Kona shore, carrying a precious cargo: the casket housing the mortal remains of Henry 'Ōpūkaha'ia, returned to the Big Island of Hawai'i 185 years after he embarked on his journey to New England. The canoes charted a course along the coast advancing to Kealakekua Bay four miles to the north.

Debbie Li'ikepeka Lee and her parents, Elizabeth and Kwai Wah Lee, as well as assorted cousins and supporters, watched from the beach as the canoes swept into the sea. Though reassured by club members, she and her parents shared anxieties that the narrow platform sustaining the outer box with the cherished casket within could bear the weight. While concern was clearly on their collective minds, they were also struck by the beauty and energy of the occasion. Henry 'Ōpūkaha'ia, their ancestor who had expressed on his deathbed the desire to see Hawai'i once more, was on the final leg of fulfilling that passion. Kealakekua Bay was where his long journey had begun and where it would be completed.

The canoeists paddled into the bay cradling the coastline escorted by a flotilla of other club boats. Just that morning, August 5, 1993, Henry 'Ōpūkaha'ia had arrived at the Big Island's Keahole Kona Airport courtesy of Aloha Airlines and was transported by hearse to Honaunau where the casket was attached to the canoes for the symbolic return trip to Kealakekua Bay. The afternoon weather was overcast with heavy clouds generating a dusky sky that made the day seem later. The darkness accentuated the family's apprehension.

Within minutes the swift canoes disappeared around Palemano Point.

On board the lashed canoes containing 'Ōpūkaha'ia's remains was a first cousin to Debbie Lee, Henry Ho'omanawanui, descendant and namesake of the Christian martyr he was accompanying home. When the outrigger sped by the small town of Ke'ei and rounded the southern point into Kealakekua Bay, Ho'omanawanui searched the wooded hills above the harbor for the white spire of Kahikolu Congregational Church, soon to be the site of 'Ōpūkaha'ia's final resting place overlooking Nāpo'opo'o harbor. Debbie had instructed Ho'omanuawanui to swim toward the shore once the steeple came within sight. Finally, spying the church, he dove into the cool waters, recreating in reverse 'Ōpūkaha'ia's outward swim to the anchored *Triumph,* metaphorically completing Henry's return home.

When Henry Ho'omanawanui submerged into the bay for the final leg of his ancestor's journey, the sun for the first time that afternoon broke away from dark clouds only minutes before it would disappear under the western ocean. The low angle of the late post meridian sunrays bounced off the sparkling waves of Kealakekua Bay, creating the illusion of a floodlit pathway guiding Ho'omanawanui's forceful swimming strokes to the rocky shore. The Lee family anxiously awaited him and 'Ōpūkaha'ia's canoe at the recess of the bay, having travelled by car from Honaunau.

As the canoes pulled along side a concrete wharf, Ho'omanawanui's glistening husky frame rose from the illuminated waters and scaled the rocky shore. The canoeists secured their vessel and with finesse raised the box encasing the casket safely up to friends who had assembled to welcome their returning *Kanaka Maoli.* 'Ōpūkaha'ia's long journey had come to completion. Henry was home.

For the 150th anniversary of the death of Henry 'Ōpūkaha'ia, February 17, 1968, two services were held the following day to commemorate his memory: at Congregational Churches in Cornwall, Connecticut, and also in Honolulu, Hawai'i. An additional service was held that same day at Nāpo'opo'o on the beach of Kealakekua Bay, Kona, where 'Ōpūkaha'ia had studied with his uncle in hopes of becoming a *kahuna.* Ministers and invited speakers from Yale University and other institutions articulated on "Obookiah" the "Island Boy," the "Student," the

"New Christian," the "Zealous Apostle," and the inspiration for the "Missions to the Sandwich Islands."[1]

Twenty-five years later, a second series of services would be held in Cornwall and soon in Hawai'i as farewell and welcoming home ceremonies. On Sunday, July 25, 1993, more than 200 people, including six family members of 'Ōpūkaha'ia and more than two dozen Hawaiians, filled Cornwall's United Church of Christ Congregational to attend his farewell memorial service. A blue sheet with large, bright red lettering hung over the main entrance of the church, greeting all who entered with "Aloha." *Leis* were hung around the necks of each guest. As I crossed the church's threshold, Debbie Lee honored me by placing a long, flowing string of the versatile *ti*-leaves and *leis* of pink and white flowers over my shoulders.

The simplicity of the church's interior was contrasted by the exotic Hawaiian floral designs and bright colors. Exhibited in front of the altar, 'Ōpūkaha'ia's skillfully grained *koa*-casket was covered with orange

Deborah Li'ikapeka Lee speaks at the Farewell Service for Henry Obookiah, United Church of Christ Congregational, Cornwall Center, August 1993, Cornwall, CT. (Courtesy of Bill Keegan.)

feather *leis* and strands of *maile*, a fragrant Hawaiian leaf. His framed portrait rested on an easel besides the lectern, also surrounded by leis, while *ti*-leaves, orchids, and anthuriums enhanced the altar, all brought and arranged by the Lee family from Hawai'i. The aromatic and visual effect may have presented the most colorful and fragrant display ever to grace the interior in a New England Congregational Church.

The service started with a loud cry of "Aloha," setting the tone for a combined Hawaiian-New England Congregational ceremony, which included a litany of remembrances and readings from the Bible in both English and Hawaiian.[2] 'Ōpūkaha'ia relative, Rev. Thomas Walter, who had assisted the family in making arrangements in Connecticut, delivered the Prayer of Invocation. Adorned in a red, black, and white *mu'umu'u*, Deborah Li'ikapeka Lee recited a Hawaiian prayer.[3] Rev. David Hirano, also a Native of Hawai'i, spoke about his father who often told him the inspirational story of "Henry Obookiah," a story that had a profound influence on his desire to enter the ministry. Hirano raised the question of what Hawai'i would be today if Henry had lived to return and preach the Gospel on the Islands. Debbie had the last word, anticipating that Henry's return will help to heal an old controversy in Hawai'i where resentment still swells over the role of missionaries in the overthrow of the Hawaiian monarchy. Lee told the congregation that Henry had nothing to do with the overthrow and subsequent annexation by the U. S. "He only had good intentions for his people," she said. "He is a Hawaiian. He has every right to be coming home to be buried in his homeland, his *'aina*." With God's permission, she was seeing to the fulfillment of Henry's deathbed wish to see Hawai'i once again.[4]

When the church service concluded, family and friends circled Henry's casket for a final prayer. With a responding "Amen," the sun pierced through the church windows radiating a beam of light that fell directly on the casket symbolizing that all was good. Overwhelmed by the moment, Aletha Kaohi, representing the UCC of Hawai'i, placed her five-strand Ni'ihau Shell *lei* around Debbie's neck in gratitude of her achievement.

Dave Cooke, Dick LaRose, Bill Keegan, and I were given the honor of serving as pallbearers, carrying 'Ōpūkaha'ia's casket from the church out to Henry Fuqua's waiting hearse for transport to Bradley International Airport. We had lifted him from the earth and now we were privileged to convey him on the first leg of his journey home.

During the traditional Hawaiian *luau* following the service, members of the Cornwall community approached me to express their sorrow in Henry's departure, reiterating that he was an important part of their town and they truly hated to see him go. Clearly, however, they understood the need to fulfill his deathbed desire and were happy for his family. We all agreed that the most important thing was the perpetuation of ʻŌpūkahaʻia's memory and his message of love that could serve to inspire today's young men and women in continuing his vision of sharing the Gospel with the people of Hawaiʻi and the Pacific.

Before we left Cornwall late in the afternoon, members of the archaeology team returned to the cemetery to revisit ʻŌpūkahaʻia's grave. Will Trowbridge had worked expeditiously restoring the granite monument in time for the farewell service. We were all truly amazed to see the memorial table erected so promptly with such care and exactitude, stone by stone. Unless you had been with us on that hill for the two-day disinterment, you would have never imagined that the monument had been completely dismantled and the ground underneath excavated. The wreath, flags, and stunning new flowers were once more in place at the head and foot of the grave. The only element missing was Henry himself, who was already on his way home. Serenity restored, it was impossible not have a warm feeling for all that had transpired.

The morning following the farewell service, Henry's casket, secured within an outer wooden box, was placed on board a United Airlines flight leaving Bradley International Airport north of Hartford with a final destination of Honolulu, Hawaiʻi. Exhausted but elated, the Lee family chaperoned their beloved ancestor home. It had been ten months since the night Debbie experienced the intimate realization that moved her to act—ten months of hard work and uncertainty for the family; of coordinating, raising money, and making cogent arguments for Henry's return. Together they had accomplished so much in such a short period of time. Debbie Lee, wanting the very best for ʻŌpūkahaʻia's return to Hawaiʻi, "reached for the moon" to arrange an itinerary that would be a lasting tribute. The two-week two-island circuits would be replete with welcoming honors, religious ceremonies, and *luaus*. The reality of the homecoming set in as they watched the casket box loaded onto a ramp from an airport window, ascending by conveyor belt and disappearing into the belly of the aircraft. At each stopover in Chicago and San Francisco, Debbie disembarked the plane and ran to the cargo space to watch and ensure that the casket box came out and was reloaded on the next plane.

The final flight carrying the Lee family and Henry 'Ōpūkaha'ia arrived in Honolulu August 26, 1993. The skeletal remains had landed without any damage, though two upper incisor teeth had loosened and slipped out of their sockets, needing to be replaced. The wooden coffin lid with the embracing heart-motif of brass tacks surrounding Henry's initials and age of death did not fare as well. Slowly decomposing since it had been removed from the moisture of the ground and drying en route, it was starting to break apart.[5] Fearing the loss of this precious funerary object before the final reburial, Debbie had a fiberglass frame made to protect the coffin lid from further disintegration before the final re-interment.

From Honolulu Airport, the casket was brought to the Hawai'i Conference of the United Church of Christ (UCC) where 'Ōpūkaha'ia laid in state at the Royal Mausoleum Monument on July 28, 1993, permitting members of the general public a two-day opportunity to pay their respects. Henry was descended from a noble family in Maui and the Royal Mausoleum treated him like royalty. UCC became the special stewards of Henry's remains while on O'ahu, offering appropriate respect and reverence to the man who had inspired the Christian missions and established their church in Hawai'i in the early nineteenth century.

The opening religious service in honor of 'Ōpūkaha'ia's return was held at Kawaiaha'o Church in downtown Honolulu and was attended by a throng of well-wishers. The church, established in 1838, was constructed from rocks hand-quarried by divers, mined from underwater coral reefs, and canoed to shore. Some of the building blocks weighed more than 1,000 pounds.[6] The Kawaiaha'o congregation had requested an opportunity to demonstrate its joy in Henry's arrival back to Hawai'i by holding a homecoming service in their chapel on the first Sunday of his return.

This observance was followed by another two-day public respect at the Kamehameha School's Bernice Pauahi Bishop Memorial Chapel where services allowed students to call on Henry's casket. When school administrators expressed a desire to host Henry overnight, Debbie was initially concerned about security issues, but she also may have been struck by the irony--it had been warriors of the school's namesake who slew ʻŌpūkahaʻia's family, driving Henry away from Hawaiʻi. However, once security issues were satisfactorily addressed, the Lee family granted permission for ʻŌpūkahaʻia's visitation.

The last service on Oʻahu was held at Kaumakapili Church where an afternoon ceremony was filled to capacity and extended into the evening. The Lee family, energized by the outpouring of love for Henry, was grateful that every one of the facilities hosting him had funded and arranged for fresh flowers, *leis*, and decorations in his honor. The logistics of providing floral arrangements and displays for every event were daunting, not to mention expensive. For one week, the people of Oʻahu proclaimed ʻŌpūkahaʻia as their own.

The following morning, the remains of Henry ʻŌpūkahaʻia were conveyed to Aloha Airlines, Flight 94, and scheduled to depart Honolulu for Kona in the early afternoon. Aloha Airlines generously donated its services free of charge for the honor of transporting ʻŌpūkahaʻia back to his home island. Upon landing, representatives of Dodo Mortuary took custody of the casket, draped with the Connecticut state flag, at Keahole Airport and transported it south to Honaunau Bay for the anticipated canoe passage and return to Kealakekua Bay.

When the canoes arrived at the Nāpoʻopoʻo wharf, a brief ceremony was held and ʻŌpūkahaʻia was conveyed up the hill for an evening service at Kahikolu Congregational Church, whose cemetery would host his re-interment. At the service Debbie Lee spoke of her inspiration in bringing cousin Henry home in fulfillment of his dying wishes. Kahikolu, however, was only a temporary stop as there were many more honors and observances to be rendered to ʻŌpūkahaʻia on his birth island before he would be placed in permanent repose overlooking Kealakekua Bay. The Henry ʻŌpūkahaʻia Memorial Chapel, constructed in 1957 at Punalu'u, Ka'u, site of his birthplace, hosted a welcome home service followed by a traditional *luau* sponsored at the Kauaha'o Congregational Church Hall in Waiohinu.

On Sunday, August 8th, Henry arrived in Hilo where he was honored at the Haili Congregational Church with public respect and services for two days. Haili is the church of Debbie Lee, and it has a long history of honoring Henry 'Ōpūkaha'ia as the zeal behind the missionary efforts to bring the Gospel of Jesus Christ to Hawai'i. The historic response to the Christian message on the east side of the Big Island was especially strong because of the charismatic personality and preaching of Rev. Titus Coan, a Connecticut native who oversaw construction of the present church in 1859. The first Christian house of worship was a large grass canoe shed owned by the local *ali'i* in 1824. The present building is the fifth in Haili Church history.

On August 11, 1993, Henry circumnavigated the Big Island when he returned to Kailua-Kona for an evening service at Mokuaikaua Church, the earliest Christian church in Hawai'i and the site where the *Thaddeus* missionaries anchored and requested permission of King Liholiho (Kamehameha II) and Queen Ka'ahumanu to come ashore to initiate their proselytizing efforts under a temporary thatched-roofed structure. Construction for the present building began in 1835 and was dedicated two years later.[7] Today Mokuaikaua houses a small museum with exhibits including a model of the brig *Thaddeus* and plaques honoring Henry "Obookiah."

A further day of public respect and services was held at the Lanakila Congregational Church, just north of Kealakekua, before the entourage returned to Kahikolu for the final interment. Lanakila was Debbie's mother Elizabeth's church, and the service was held there as a tribute to all her hard work, her leadership of Ahahui O 'Ōpūkaha'ia, and her willingness to use personal funds to offset the final costs of bringing Henry home. Without Elizabeth and Debbie's father, Kwai Wah, the repatriation would never have happened as expeditiously as it had. To honor their commitment, Debbie organized the Lanikila service, which was attended by family of 'Ōpūkaha'ia.

Though no written genealogical records were kept when Henry left the Big Island almost two centuries earlier, extensive oral traditions maintained complex genealogical relationships serving as the paramount of Hawaiian social organization. The Lee family and others trace their descent through 'Ōpūkaha'ia's first cousin, Tutu Kauwe. 'Ōpūkaha'ia and Kauwe shared common grandparents in Kainakuawau and Oheieluaikamoku, who came to the Big Island from Lahaina, Maui, and settled at Manuka, Kona Mea Ka'u sometime in the eighteenth century. After 'Ōpūkaha'ia had left the island for New England, Tutu Kauwe married a *haole* named Davis[8] and had two children. Davis apparently died, and Kauwe married Kuhea, with whom he had one child. Elizabeth Kepeka Lee is the great-great-granddaughter of Tutu Kauwe and Kuhea.

As the final segment of the welcoming home tour revisited Kahikolu Congregational Church and Cemetery in Napo'opo'o, Debbie Lee was experiencing emotional difficulties in letting Henry go. Kahikolu's current site rests on the lower west-facing slope of Mauna Loa overlooking the *Hikiau Heiau* and Kealakekua Bay where canoes had disembarked him a week earlier. The church is one of Hawai'i's early stone, lime, and timber structures, erected in 1840, and appropriately named Kahikolu, meaning "third church" or "trinity" because it was the third church constructed in the "land of the chiefs." Established by Queen Kapiolani, one of the earliest *ali'i* to convert to Christianity, Kahikolu would be the final resting place of Henry 'Ōpūkaha'ia. Debbie was grieving as the time approached. Bringing Henry home had been the goal of her life for almost a year and now he had arrived. She missed him already.

In excess of 200 descendants and friends crowded into Kahikolu Congregational Church in the late afternoon of August 15, 1993, as the final service and re-interment of Henry 'Ōpūkaha'ia took place. The *koa* casket was surrounded with colorful native plants and flowers set next to an easel with 'Ōpūkaha'ia's portrait enfolded by plumeria *leis*. In attendance from Connecticut were the Reverends Drs. David Hirano and Carmen Wooster representing the Missionary Society of Connecticut and the Connecticut Conference of the United Congregational Churches, respectively. Both had attended and spoken at the Cornwall farewell ceremony and had come full circle to witness

'Ōpūkaha'ia's homecoming and reburial. Hawaiian Sen. Daniel Akaka, whose shoulders were draped with a long string of *ti*-leaves resembling the one I was privileged to wear at the Cornwall service, represented the federal and state governments. To all assembled, the occasion was joyful and yet solemn.

Dr. David Hirano spoke at the lectern, bringing greetings from the State of Connecticut. He expressed the feeling of the people of Cornwall that while they will miss having Henry in their community, they agreed it was, and is, the right thing to return him to Hawai'i. A century after 'Ōpūkaha'ia died, Dr. Hirano's immigrant father, who worked the sugarcane fields in Hamakua, was invited to attend the Hilo Boarding School established by the Congregational missionaries. There, as a boy, he learned of the life and death of "Obookiah." Henry's inspiring message was passed on to his son David, who would make missions his life work.

Rev. Carmen Wooster spoke as a witness to the disinterment of Henry 'Ōpūkaha'ia, stressing that the archaeological excavation had been executed with great respect. She concluded, saying that God had answered Henry's prayer to see Hawai'i and his message today is still as relevant as it was 175 years ago—"be faithful, remember God, and love one another."[9]

Sen. Akaka gave thanks and welcomed home a son of Hawai'i, *a keiki o ka aina*, who "positively altered the course of history for a people, a nation, and a state." He also paid tribute to the Lee family: Kwai Wah, Elizabeth, and Deborah who were "endowed with the strength of their spiritual bond and the commitment of kinship" to bring their ancestor, Henry 'Ōpūkaha'ia, home. He summed up Henry's journey as leaving us all a legacy of triumph: "the victory of faith over wrenching heartache, the achievement of untold success after severe despondency, and the realization of full and true identity despite the passage of nearly two centuries."[10]

Upon conclusion of the church service, family members privately viewed the remains of Henry 'Ōpūkaha'ia for the last time, placing personal mementos and assorted *leis* into the casket to accompany him into eternity, while friends and well-wishers filed out of the church forming two parallel lines for the casket to be carried between in passage to the monument and final resting place, which had taken two weeks to build. Soil taken from Cornwall Cemetery, drawings made by children of his *'ohana,* and a bright Hawaiian shirt were placed inside the casket where the *ti*-leaves, viewing glass, and coffin lid resided. Debbie prayed over Henry and tearfully whispered her final good-byes.

Insistent on joining her male cousins serving as pallbearers, Debbie Lee donned white gloves and carried the *koa* casket bearing the beloved remains of Henry ʻŌpūkahaʻia out of the church and towards the cemetery, holding on to him as long as she could. Voices sang *"Aloha oʻe"* as they made their way to the open monument overlooking the harbor from which he had set out on his journey to find peace and self-fulfillment. The casket was lowered by ropes amid a ceremony called *"Kao he olahou"*— the bamboo lives again.

In Cornwall Cemetery, a bronze plaque was placed at the foot of the reconstructed monument of ʻŌpūkahaʻiaʻs initial resting place. It reads:

"OH! HOW I WANT TO SEE HAWAIʻI!"
In July of 1993, the family of Henry ʻŌpūkahaʻia
took him home to Hawaiʻi for interment at
Kahikolu Congregational Church Cemetery,
Napoʻopoʻo, Kona, Island of Hawaiʻi.
Henry's family express gratitude, appreciation
and love to all who cared for and loved him
throughout the past years.
- Ahahui O ʻŌpūkahaʻia

I would have loved to take part in Henry's reburial in Napoʻopoʻo. After all, we disinterred his remains and felt it only proper that we should be a part of the re-interment. However, the State of Connecticut did not see the expediency in funding its archaeologist's trip to Hawaiʻi, and at the time we couldn't personally afford the travel. So, twenty years would pass before my wife and I had the opportunity to pay our personal respects at ʻŌpūkahaʻiaʻs final resting place.

Our initial attempt to find Henry's monument failed when I drove downhill, passing the small marker on Nāpoʻopoʻo Road proclaiming Kahikolu Congregational Church as an official Hawaiian historical landmark. Only after retracing our drive did the sign become apparent, and then it was quite obvious. My confusion stemmed from the fact that the driveway where the sign stood led to some exquisite houses overlooking Kealakekua Bay. We worried about trespassing on private property but sucked up the courage to enter what appeared to be a private estate. Happily, the driveway diverted from the houses and lead downhill through an open grassy field. The paved drive turned sharply to the left before a clump of trees and ended in front of a locked gate extending off a low stonewall barring any entrance of motor vehicles. Between the grates of the gate, we could see numerous tombstones emerging above black volcanic rock and in the distance the prominent steeple of Kahikolu Church.

Determined to see Henry's burial place, my wife and I left the car, climbed around the gate, and carefully scaled over the stonewall. Debbie Lee had sent us photographs of the monument, and we knew it was

Final Resting Place of Henry ʻŌpūkahaʻia, Kahikolu Congregational Church, Napoʻopoʻo, Kona, Hawaii, April 2013. (Courtesy of Author.)

in an open area by the parking lot. However, planted vegetation and high trees blocked our view until we made our way up the road past assorted tombstones to the church where the landscape opened up and a beautiful volcanic stone monument, Henry's burial, appeared before us.

The memorial enclosure consists of two low-mortared stonewalls, constructed into half-circles, opening toward the visitor. Within the inner circle at the foot of the monument stands a chest-high stone podium with a bronze plaque telling the story of Henry 'Ōpūkaha'ia and his return home. Within the larger, outer half-circle resides the raised table of his burial monument. The elevated stone platform was designed to replicate in Hawaiian black volcanic rock Henry's original burial table of New England granite. The entire gravesite has been built up leveling the steep downslope with the churchyard grade. Encased within the stone base under the raised table is the vault housing Henry's koa casket. Two tall flower vases set at the foot end of the monument contained fresh fragrant flowers and *ti* leaves standing as guardians to protect Henry. At the head of the podium was a smaller, raised platform upon which the tombstone epitaph reads:

Henry 'Ōpūkaha'ia
Aloha ke Akua
Hanau: 1792
Make: Pepeluali 17, 1818–Cornwall, CT
Hu'e: Iulai 13, 1993
Kanu Pa'a: 'Aukake 15, 1993–Kepulu, HI

As I walked over the stone floor to the head of the monument, I was flooded with memories of twenty years ago at Cornwall Cemetery. It all came back, even the heat and the lightening. But mostly, I saw the face of 'Ōpūkaha'ia looking up at me, prepared to arise for his final journey home. I held my wife as both of us were overwhelmed by the sacred and peaceful ambiance. We were finally here. The contrast in burial settings is readily apparent: Cornwall offered a beautiful, rural New England landscape while Hawai'i provided an exotic paradise. Both were home to Henry. He now looks out over the far-reaching waters off Kealakekua Bay, the connection between his two worlds.

The "Island Boy" who had left Hawai'i searching for peace and purpose; who settled in Connecticut and received a scholar's education and converted to Christianity; who had found love in God and translated the Book of Genesis into the Hawaiian language; and whose martyrdom inspired Protestant missions throughout the world had finally come home, the long journey complete.

As I stood over his burial, I expressed silent gratitude for the opportunity to have played a small part in his return. Through the Lee family, I could feel Henry's touch reaching across 200 years; through 'Ōpūkaha'ia, I witnessed first hand the allegiance and dedication of a Hawaiian family, strengthened by their love of God and their heritage, emulating their strong faith and revered kinship through the power of his repatriation.

Mahalo, Hoahanau Henry. Thank you, Cousin Henry.

PART II

THE REPATRIATION OF
ALBERT AFRAID OF HAWK

5 | The Buffalo Nation

The fist-sized stone deflected along the parade ground after accidently encountering the toe boot of Johnny Baker, sharpshooter and manager for Buffalo Bill's Wild West.[1] The evening performance in Danbury, Connecticut, had ended, and the ground crew was busy dismantling the tents, arranging wagons, and herding horses to the railroad station, providing Baker a moment's reprieve to inspect the condition of troupe members who had been ill with food poisoning since arriving in Connecticut on June 25, 1900. In his rush, he didn't see the stone before he sent it bounding in front of him, almost tripping.

Johnny Baker was irritated and the stone did nothing to ameliorate his disposition. A violent windstorm had blown through the arena around 6 p.m. knocking down several tents and their backings. His staff worked rigorously to rectify the damage before the evening's performance, and considering the unexpected gale, the show functioned reasonably well. Nonetheless, Baker retained his anxiety, worrying about sick cast members and their availability for the next day's performance in Pittsfield, Massachusetts.

The consensus of local doctors was that the intestinal agony affecting more than fifty performers stemmed from toxic tins of corn served in Hartford or the bad water they drank two days later in South Norwalk.[2] Since the show must go on, the New Haven pageant was staged with a skeleton crew of those few remaining performers unaffected by food poisoning. Now in Danbury, Baker especially wanted to examine the "Show Indians," composed primarily of Oglala Lakota from the Pine Ridge Reservation in South Dakota. Though the last group in the company to contract the malady, the manager was particularly troubled over two young Indian men who had not responded well to the distress, and he hurried on his way to the Lakota campground.

J. J. Ryan,[3] watchman for the Indian camp, pulled the entrance flap to the tipi aside as Baker entered, his eyes adjusting to the darkness. On the ground, he saw the figure of a young Lakota male, Albert Afraid of Hawk, lying on his side wrapped in blankets with his legs and arms drawn into a fetal position. Though the twenty-year-old Native American was tall, solidly built, and a strong rider in the show, he now appeared small and fragile. Without uttering a sound, Afraid of Hawk's face displayed the immensity of his suffering. Abdominal cramps caused by constipation, vomiting, and muscle fatigue confirmed the severity of his crippling pain. Baker was immediately alarmed.

Addressing tribal leaders, including the celebrated Chief Black Hawk, Baker strongly urged a physician's presence, and Dr. A. P. MacDonald was summoned. Through interpreter David Bull Bear,[4] a childhood friend of Afraid of Hawk, MacDonald made it clear to the chiefs that Albert was dying and insisted that the only possible way to save the young Lakota's life was to transport him to the "white man's hospital" where he could get immediate and continual care. The chiefs were unsure. Two Lakota women started singing Albert's death song but were quickly silenced by Black Hawk's pointed glance. Reluctantly, the chiefs consented, and several cowboys lifted Albert's fragile, agonizing body out of the tipi and into a horse-drawn wagon. He was convulsed in pain but calmly held his composure. Helpless, though grateful for the efforts to save him, Albert gazed into the faces gathered around the wagon. The Lakota stood beside him, silently, watching the cart until it disappeared from sight.

Albert Afraid of Hawk died on June 29, 1900, at Danbury Hospital amid white-coated strangers, immersed in a strange society and succumbing to a strange disease of "civilization." His was not the glorious death of a Lakota warrior defending his people or a buffalo hunter amid the danger of providing food for his family. His body would not be placed upon a scaffold above the High Plains; rather, he would be buried in an unmarked grave beneath a white man's cemetery far from home, soon to be forgotten by all but his family.

The Lakota have no word for "good-bye," so before being conveyed to the hospital, with his tribal community assembled beside the wagon and with difficulty swallowing or speaking, he may have whispered weakly in his ancestral language, perhaps personifying Lakota warriors advancing into battle in the manner of his father and grandfather, *"Le anpetu kin mat'e kin waste ktelo!"* This day—I die—it will be good!

Albert Afraid of Hawk, three-quarter length portrait, seated, taken in Omaha 1899, Heyn Photographer. (Courtesy Library of Congress, LC-USZ62-94932.)

"Please be here, Albert!" I pleaded, looking up from the below ground burial excavation to see if I had embarrassingly spoken out loud. No one overhead seemed to notice so I continued, almost in supplication, "Your family has come a long way from South Dakota to bring you home, to honor you. Please, be here," I begged.

When unearthing burials, I hardly made a habit of talking to the dead and certainly not aloud, but my concerns for finding any skeletal remains were due to the acidic composition of the soils at Wooster Cemetery in Danbury, Connecticut. The results of the soil pH tests indicated a range from 5.3 to 5.8[5], low in the pH scale, and hence, highly acidic; too acidic for the likelihood of organic remains like bone and wood to last for more than 100 years in the ground.[6] Thus, our attempts to disinter the remains of Albert Afraid of Hawk, Oglala Lakota, who died of food poisoning here in June, 1900, while performing with Buffalo Bill's Wild West, for repatriation to his family at the Pine Ridge Reservation in South Dakota, could be threatened.

Owing to these fears of heightened organic decomposition, I had alerted the Afraid of Hawk family, under whose authority the repatriation was being conducted, that there was a distinct chance nothing remained of Albert but decomposed soils. Ashes to ashes, I supposed. Based on a three-dimensional model of the coffin recreated from the positions of hardware recovered during the archaeological excavation, I could return to them the organic soils that were once Albert but could not ensure that any tangible human remains would be present for them to rebury at Pine Ridge.

Nineteen years after the disinterment and repatriation of Henry 'Ōpūkaha'ia, another Indigenous family had requested the archaeological recovery of a young male ancestor who had died in Connecticut, so he, too, could be returned to his homeland. However, unlike the well-preserved skeletal remains of 'Ōpūkaha'ia, we could not be certain that Albert Afraid of Hawk still existed in any physical form other than as darkened organic earth.

We located the coffin, which had been laid down at a depth of six feet, and exposed six elaborate coffin handles, attesting that Buffalo Bill afforded a respectable wooden casket for his "Rough Rider." Excavating the interior of the coffin, my heart sank when no skeletal remains emerged, so we made a conscious decision to concentrate our efforts toward the head portion of the grave. Typically, we would excavate the complete burial, head to toe, horizontally, but that would take time, and I desperately desired to know if any skeletal remains had survived the acidity. Recognizing that the crania would be the highest point coming down on a supine burial position, and that of all the organic compounds, the enamel of the teeth, the hardest substance in our bodies, had the best chances of surviving, I directed my efforts to locate the skull as our first possibility of encountering any physical evidence of Albert Afraid of Hawk. If his remains had persisted in the corrosive soil for more than a century, we would know before long.

Despite this change in excavation strategy, rusting coffin hardware were the only materials uncovered. Extending to a depth of five inches inside the funerary box, there were still no human remains; at this point I anticipated the recovery of the bottom board row of nails and the terminus of the burial feature, the boundary of our chances of ever recovering Albert.

I glanced up over my shoulder from my position on all fours straddled beside the coffin, searching for the Afraid of Hawk family: Marlis, whose dream of Albert initiated the repatriation process; her father, Daniel, patriarch and keeper of the family history; John, her brother, who maintained the smoldering, sacred sage and sweet grass; and Richard Red Elk, a relative who drove the family across the vast prairie and eastern woodland so they could personally bring Albert home. Together they sat patiently at the foot of the excavation, steadfast for two days as our team descended deeper into the ground with the hopes and anticipation of retrieving their ancestor. But as I looked above me, they were nowhere to be seen.

When I inquired, someone called down that the mayor was hosting a luncheon for the Afraid of Hawk family at Danbury Hospital, and that Robert (Bob) Young, the genealogist/historian whose persistent research had located Albert's unmarked grave, his wife Mary-Jo, and Tania Porta, the funeral director overseeing the exhumation, had escorted them. They would return soon, I was assured.

It hardly mattered considering that as I excavated deeper into the head of the coffin with no discovery, there would only be disappointing news to share with them anyway. It would break my heart to tell them that there where no physical remains of Albert left, but at this point, that was all I could anticipate. That's when I started talking to him. "You know, Albert, it would mean so much for your family and people back at the reservation to return you home, to complete your long journey. Just give me one bone. C'mon, be here!"

Prior to the luncheon and while I disheartenly worked the gravesite, the Afraid of Hawk family requested to be shown the section of the hospital where Albert had died, wanting to perform a ceremony there. The hospital wing that once comprised the men's ward in 1900 had long been dismantled and was currently the location of an outdoor Victorian garden. The hospital chaplain ushered the family into the courtyard and indicated the general area where Albert would have succumbed to the ravages of botulism. Requesting privacy, Bob, Tania, and Mary-Jo removed themselves so the family could be alone. Sage was burnt and tobacco spread while Daniel Jay Afraid of Hawk recited traditional prayers over the locale of grandfather Albert's death.

While the Afraid of Hawk family were conducting their prayers, my trowel dislodged a patch of soil about the size of a fifty-cent piece. At first, I wasn't quite sure what I was looking at, but I was encouraged. Brushing the area gently to inspect more closely, I recognized the curvature of the frontal bone at the high peak of the forehead. Poorly preserved, decomposing, fragile, but there!

At the hospital reception, Danbury Mayor Mark Boughton formally greeted the Afraid of Hawk family on behalf of the city and promised logistical support for their repatriation effort. Hospital staff presented the family with a photo book showing doctors and nurses that would have been present to care for Albert in 1900, including Dr. MacDonald, who signed his death certificate. In turn, Marlis told the narrative of her dream, and Daniel spoke of the family's desire to bring Albert home. These Lakota visitors and their story of Buffalo Bill's Sioux Rough Rider who perished in their hospital over one hundred years ago mesmerized the hospital staff.

While the family enjoyed the luncheon, a phone call was placed to Tania Porta, alerting her: "Nick has found Albert." Incredibly, I had uncovered the first physical evidence of Albert Afraid of Hawk while his family, high upon the hill above us, were privately presiding over a sacred Lakota ritual, perhaps the Keeping of the Soul[7] ceremony in honor of his spirit at the site of his death. All along the family had been confident that Albert would be there, regardless of my scientific concerns. They somehow knew. Just as twenty years ago when we first located the remains of 'Ōpūkaha'ia, I rose up on my knees deep within the burial shaft and looked upward to those standing above me. Cutting the widest grin possible, I cried out in relief, "He's here!"

The Black Hills (*Paha Sapa*) is where it all began, high on the forested peaks, deep within Wind Cave. According to Lakota oral tradition, they were the first people to exist, emerging from the heart of the earth beneath *Paha Sapa*, the physical and spiritual epicenter of the universe. These first Lakota arose through the innermost caverns of Wind Cave, one of the lengthiest in the world, passing out of its narrow opening onto the exterior of the earth. *Tatanka*, the buffalo, would also emerge, creating the nearby swale of Buffalo Gap through the pounding from millions of stampeding hooves reaching the earth's surface simultaneously.

The Lakota venerate these hills that stand out distinctly from the surrounding rolling prairie. *Paha Sapa* is sacred, spiritual land, as well as a place abundant in natural resources. Though promised by treaty to be theirs forever, the Lakota fought to keep the Black Hills until they were eventually forced to relinquish their place of origin to the United States government after George Armstrong Custer trespassed and found gold. The ensuing "rush" brought illegal miners into the hills and when the federal government did little to halt the trespassing, the incited Lakota went on the warpath. Two years later, Custer paid dearly for his intrusion when the Lakota and their northern Cheyenne allies annihilated his cavalry at the Battle of Little Bighorn. But it was too late by then; hordes of gold prospectors and unruly types like Wild Bill Hickok were already blasting and shooting up *Paha Sapa*. Within sixty years presidential faces would be carved onto its peaks. Yet to the Lakota, then and today, the land remains sacrosanct, and the tribes have refused money rather than give up to their rights to the Black Hills.

My graduate school studies in archaeology taught that the Siouan speakers originated in the Mississippian or Ohio Valleys[8] and may have been associated with the political chiefdoms of the mound-building cultures whose extensive agricultural fields and prominent earthen hillocks dominated the central continent prior to European settlement. By the 1600s and the abandonment of Mississippian Culture, the people had moved into the upper regions of the river into Minnesota near the Great Lakes,[9] where they lived in villages hunting and growing corn, beans, and squash amid tended fields. There they initially encountered French fur traders, who bestowed upon them the combined French and Ojibwa word, *Nadouuessioux*, derogatorily meaning "little snakes" and more commonly shortened to "Sioux." The people themselves prefer to be called Dakota, Nakota, and Lakota, which represents the cultural differences in dialect, economy, and territory among them, but basically means, "allies," "friends."[10]

Together they are *Oceti Sakowin Kin*, the Seven Council Fires, specifying that they are a single nation divided into seven tribes. Six of the Council Fires speak the closely related dialects Nakota and Dakota and reside near the upper Mississippi and lower Missouri Rivers, but the westernmost of the tribes, the *Titonwan*, or Tetons, known as Lakota, live farther west near the upper Missouri River.

The Lakota are further separated into seven subdivisions referred to as bands—Sicangu or Brules (Burnt Thighs), Oohenuunpa (Two Kettles), Itazipcola or Sans Arcs (Without Bows), Miniconjou (Planters By The Water), Sihasapa (Black Feet), Hunkpapa (End of the Horn or Entrance), and Oglala (Scatter One's Own). Collectively the Lakota are known as the People of the Prairie or the Buffalo Nation (*Pte Oyate*).[11] The only binding force of the Seven Fires was that none of the bands would make war against or ever be considered enemies of each other.[12]

Sometime around the turn of the eighteenth century, the Lakota moved westward toward the Missouri River. Conflict with enemy tribes like the Ojibwa and Cree forced the Sioux onto the High Plains. Ironically, this worked to their advantage as the fur trade also moved westward with the increasing scarcity of beaver in the east, providing them with many untapped streams and rivers that still contained fur-bearing mammals.[13] Trading furs for guns with the French, the Lakota were able to remove the Omaha, Iowa, Missouri, and other tribes out of the territory. By mid-century, the Lakota were encamped along the Missouri River, and as they proceeded west, the buffalo would play an intensifying role in their settlement/subsistence patterns.

The Lakota acquired their uniqueness among the tribes with the appearance of the most revered personage in their ancestry, White Buffalo Calf Woman (*Pte Ska Win*). The way it is told,[14] in the days before the horse, two young braves were instructed by their chief[15] to go out and search for game in the area of the Black Hills. A great drought brought on hard times among the people, and the hunters had to stray far from their village on foot in search of food. Hungry and discouraged, the trackers combed the land in their pursuit of game day after day with no realization of their quest.

As they awoke one morning, a floating white mist could be seen upon a distant hill. Cautious, though curious, they slowly approached the vapor where the image of a beautiful young woman dressed in white buckskin appeared to them. One hunter imagined the vision as a carnal opportunity and approached the woman, while the other hunter stood still, deeming the woman as a sacred presence. Without warning, a black cloud rolled down and intercepted the licentious hunter.[16] When the cloud receded, the reverential young man was horrified to witness his amorous companion reduced to a skeleton with snakes crawling among his bones. Humbling himself before the woman, the hunter realized he was in the company of a powerful force. The woman was pleased with his humility and instructed him to return to his village, have the people prepare a great medicine lodge, and await her next appearance. The young man obeyed, spreading the word of the compelling and beautiful woman in the mist while the lodge was prepared.

Within four days she reappeared for all to see, descending from a cloud in the sky as a female white buffalo calf. Reaching the earth, the white buffalo calf proceeded to roll on the ground and turned into the beautiful woman seen on the hill. She carried a bundle folded in her arms and requested that the elders be assembled in the prepared lodge, where White Buffalo Calf Woman taught them the seven sacred rituals[17] that must faithfully be performed for the people to be powerful again. She imparted holy songs and dances and encouraged traditional ways. She unwrapped her bundle revealing the sacred stone pipe, *chanunpa*, carved with seven circles for each of the given rituals, as a gift from their relatives, *Tatanka*. Smoking the pipe with them, White

Buffalo Calf Woman instructed that if they kept and protected it forever, they would flourish.[18]

Her teachings concluded, she informed them that she would be gone for a long, long time, and they must maintain the rituals until her return. Satisfied, she walked up a nearby hill and again began to roll on the earth changing colors each time until finally transformed back into a white buffalo calf.[19] And then from out of the hills a great herd of buffalo appeared surrounding her, and the Lakota understood that all the good life-sustaining elements were once again in place and plentiful.

The people were obedient and flourished. White Buffalo Calf Woman bestowed upon the Lakota their social organization and spiritual bearings. The sacred pipe became linked to the buffalo, perceived as gracious relatives, offering themselves as food, clothing, shelter, fuel, and tools to sustain the lives of their Lakota kin. *Tatanka* would be the banquet, the giver of life. The people would be hungry no more. And ever since, among the Lakota, the birth of a white buffalo calf has come to signify the purification of the world with harmony, balance, and peace.

A white buffalo calf was born on Peter Fay's Mohawk Bison Farm in Goshen, Connecticut, two months before the archaeological disinterment of Albert Afraid of Hawk in the early summer of 2012. The rare and sacred event brought four Oglala Lakota elders from as far as California to visit and pray beside the newly-born calf. Joined by members of the eastern tribes, the Lakota elders conducted a Naming Ceremony amid rain and thunder and introduced Yellow Medicine Dancing Boy to the world. Lakota medicine man Steve Stonearrow told the assembled participants they didn't need the birth of a white buffalo calf for White Buffalo Calf Woman to return, for "she comes back all the time."[20]

Later that summer, while the Afraid of Hawk family was in Danbury for Albert's disinterment, Ed Sarabia, Native Tlingit and Connecticut's Indian Affairs Coordinator, escorted the family to Mohawk Bison Farm so they could personally see Yellow Medicine Dancing Boy. Even from a distance the white calf stood out among the herd of dark brown bison grazing inside acres enclosed by wooden fences. The calf's uniqueness was undeniable from a genetic, scientific viewpoint, but its cultural significance superseded the biological. Smiles abounded. Daniel Afraid of Hawk prayed, and all were in awe of the birth and its important symbolism. Astonishingly, within weeks of each other, a white buffalo calf was born and Albert was repatriated to Pine Ridge, linking Connecticut and the Lakota Nation in unique, unexpected, and blessed ways.

In 1700, the French missionary Le Sueur encountered Lakota camps somewhere between the upper Mississippi and Missouri Rivers. His account tells us that they practiced limited horticulture, did not eat wild rice, had no fixed villages, and having no need for canoes on the prairie they traveled by foot.[21] Initially the Oglala Lakota attempted to settle in with their stronger Arikara neighbors. However, conflicts led them to abandon their horticultural practices, continue westward crossing the Missouri around the mouth of the White River and live by the hunt. Buffalo were in great abundance. The Lakota were afoot.[22] The move proved prudent since European diseases, especially plagues of smallpox and cholera, lead to the decimation of the Arikara villages they had occupied.[23]

Originally the Lakota traveled by placing their bundles attached on two poles lashed to their dog's shoulders, dragging behind them along the ground. Termed *travois* by the French, it provided a very practical mode of travel across the treeless expanse of the plains.[24] However, due to the small size of the dogs, short poles and few possessions could be transported. Hence only small shelters could be constructed, and the women were charged with the burden of carrying whatever the dogs could not manage. Material comforts had to be kept to a minimum.

Life was harder on the plains than in the woodland. Game was scattered farther, patchier and difficult to obtain. Hunters, wrapping themselves in buffalo robes, crawled on hands and knees to get close to their prey. Concealing bows and arrows, stalkers had to make their kill without stampeding the entire buffalo herd, which could mean sudden death. Sheer survival was a day-in, day-out challenge. Then around 1730 from the west and neighboring Cheyenne Indians,[25] came a strange and wonderful beast—a Spirit Dog.[26]

The horse roamed the North American continent for more than forty-five million years, lasting until the end of the Ice Age, becoming extinct around 12,000 years ago.[27] Not until Spanish Conquistadors entered Mexico in the 16th-century was the horse reintroduced to the mainland of the Western Hemisphere, and once Plains Indians took possession of the "Spirit Dog" they never looked back.

Direct diffusion of firearms came into the High Plains from the Northeast through barter with European fur-traders while the horse advanced out of the Southwest from Native American partners; together they would make the Plains Indian the swiftest, most feared and mobile cultures on the continent. "Pedestrians became equestrians."[28] Some tribes gave up farming completely to become nomadic horse-mounted game hunters and warriors. Stealing herds from traditional enemies was more productive than capturing wild horses or obtaining new ponies through trade. Social prestige and economic benefit arose from successful horse raiding and counting coup from traditional tribal enemies, providing a key to social and political advancement through ritual combat.[29] Technology never reverses itself; they were now buffalo hunters on horseback, growing into the hallmark of Lakota society for the next century and a half, the epitome of the American Indian in most contemporary perceptions.

It wasn't so much that the horse dramatically changed their lives, as it enhanced pre-existing economic patterns.[30] Increased mobility through the great expanses of the plains was now possible, as was the ability to carry more belongings. The horse drawn *travois* could drag eight times the load placed on the smaller dog-pulled poles. Longer poles allowed house structures to become larger, and tipis could now reach as high as 20 feet, enabling more living space for the occupying families. Successful buffalo hunts by men on horseback provided enough hides, food, and tools that kept the women busy skinning and preparing more elaborate clothing and personal items. Their populations increased and the buffalo were in such abundance the mere thought of their disappearance was inconceivable, especially with support of ritual. This feedback mechanism of increased dependence on horses and bison was all that White Buffalo Calf Woman proclaimed it would be, and true to her instruction the Lakota remained faithful to the ceremonial life, growing strong as a nation and feared among their enemies.

Although *Tatanka* graciously gave themselves to their Lakota relatives, the buffalo hunt was a dangerous and demanding affair involving the entire tribe. Highly choreographed, the buffalo hunt required precise timing and enormous amounts of technical skill, courage, and appropriate ritual, combining the secular and the solemn. Beginning with the excitement that a herd had been sighted, ceremonies, normally the buffalo dance, were conducted as the entire encampment prepared for the hunt. Women would assemble the needed tools to butcher the meat and process the hides, dismantle the tepees, and organize the *travois*; men would prepare their highly trained buffalo ponies and gather their weapons; the village police, the *akicita*, would assign appropriate places for each family within the marching order to the killing fields; the older spiritual leaders prepared the pipe and conducted ceremonies. Young braves would seek the opportunity to show themselves in action and prove their worth within the society.

With encouragement from the chiefs, the horse-mounted hunters approached from the back of the stampeding herd. Their bow and arrows, the weapon of choice for the buffalo hunt, were at the ready. Guns whose powder and ammunition were expensive required time to reload while multiple arrows, each marked with the design and color patterns to identify individual warriors, could be launched far more accurately within the time it took to spend two musket balls. The buffalo pony was keen to the sound of a snapping bowstring. Charging with little guidance along the backside of the stampeding buffalo so not to be gored by the horns, the ponies kept pace. Buffalo were not easily brought down. If the arrow hit too forward in the body, the animal could escape. The hunters sought the area just behind the last ribs where the piercing projectile could penetrate the liver and other essential organs. Written accounts describe arrows shot with such force they would drive completely through the large beast and have even recorded an event where a single arrow brought down two buffaloes.[31]

Carcasses spread out over the countryside. The liver was cut out and ceremonially consumed by the hunters while the women and children commenced the skinning and butchering process. Within forty-five minutes no trace of the animal would remain. Nothing went to waste and except for ground disturbance little evidence was left of the hunt. The aftermath was celebratory, eliciting jubilant singing and dancing while the exhausted and hungry people were soothed and sated by great feasts, rejoicing into the early morning, giving thanks to *Tatanka*. Families without males were provided for so that no one went hungry.

Buffalo hunting required nomadic movement through large expanses of land and gave rise to close-knit families working together under the leadership of patriarchal leaders. These groups, *tiospaye*, were extended family like the *'ohana* of the Hawaiians and had their origins in Lakota economy. Members of the *tiospaye* lived, travelled, and worked together, developing strong social and familial bonds. Loyalty and honor were significant attributes. *Tiospaye* protected and defended one another. Individual cooperation and conformity were rewarded with sustenance and protection.[32] Likewise leadership demanded the ability to provide people's daily requirements for food and shelter. Leaders were nominal in authority and gained supporters through their generosity, hard work, and trust. The *tiospaye* and their munificent chiefs, both warrior and spiritual, represented the main social order of the Lakota, an order that united the people and separated them from all others.

The world of the Lakota is animistic, full of living spirits. Buttes are not mere geological formations; they are alive and have meaning. Plants, animals, the wind, and the seasons are endowed with supernatural powers, sometimes good, sometimes bad, within the realm of the natural world. Rituals and dances that celebrate this relationship maintain harmony and balance. Vision quests, through self-sacrifice, are sought to gain insights into this spirit world and are crystalized in the Sun Dance.[33] The two-legged do not take "dominium" over the four-legged animals. All animate and inanimate objects, all visible and invisible forces, have a place and hold the right to be in the world. *Wakan Tanka*, the Great Mysteries, are in all of them.[34]

With the technological advent of Internet communication, the number of telephone calls coming into the Office of State Archaeology decreased dramatically into the 21st century. So, in late June of

2012, rather than the phone ringing, an email flashed across my computer screen from Dan Cruson, a long-time friend and president of the Archaeological Society of Connecticut. His message told of the request by genealogist and historian, Robert (Bob) Young, in seeking the aid of an archaeologist to disinter a Sioux Indian named "Man-Afraid-of Hawks," (sic) who died in Danbury in 1900. Although I had known Bob Young for many years as president of the Friends of Danbury Cemeteries, assisting their volunteer organization in locating and unearthing tombstones obscured beneath their ancient burying grounds, I was unaware of his discovery of Albert Afraid of Hawk's grave and the subsequent request of the family to bring his physical remains home. Reading Dan's message was reminiscent of my initial conversation with Henry Fuqua and the repatriation of Henry 'Ōpūkaha'ia. I immediately offered my assistance.

Initially, Bob Young remained skeptical about having a state official involved with the disinterment, fearing the project might get convoluted in bureaucratic red tape, but he acknowledged the necessity. A meeting was coordinated at the Cornell Memorial Funeral Home in Danbury to discuss the logistical and legal requirements of the exhumation. Ironically, I had worked with Rodney L. Bourdeau, former director of Cornell Memorial, many years earlier when a historic 1870 cast-iron coffin was accidently unearthed during construction activities downtown. As state archaeologist, I coordinated with the Danbury Police Department and the Office of the Chief State's Medical Examiner for the archaeological recovery, historical research, autopsy, and re-interment of the discovered corpse. Cornell Memorial, under Rodney's direction, provided a new casket and oversaw reinterring the anonymous individual at Wooster Cemetery, unwittingly one row away from Albert Afraid of Hawk's grave.

We convened with Bob and Dan at the office of Tania L. (Bourdeau) Porta, Rodney's daughter and in mid-July current director at Cornell. Tania assumed the role that Henry Fuqua had performed in the 'Ōpūkaha'ia exhumation, handling the remains for the family, seeing to their wishes, and acquiring legal disinterment permits. She would be present every day at the cemetery providing a legal presence, logistical support, and considerately assisting to the family's needs. Also in attendance was Wendell Deer With Horns, Oohenonpa (Two Kettles) Lakota, who had been living in Connecticut for more than twenty-five years. Wendell is the uncle of Marlis's brother-in-law and was chosen to represent the Afraid of Hawk family at the cemetery, ensuring that proper Lakota purification rituals were appropriately observed. We discussed with Wendell our proposed methods and procedures, trusting they would be acceptable from his culture's standpoint. In return, Wendell taught Lakota principles and the appropriate handling of the dead. A starting date of mid-August was agreed on, and we all prepared our calendars.

Dave Cooke, who had assisted me so ably during the 'Ōpūkaha'ia repatriation passed away in January 2009. We missed him dearly as a friend and field companion, and with this new repatriation request, I became especially aware of how much I had relied on his technical skills and longed to have him by my side. Fortunately, we had Bruce Greene, a retired engineer from Wethersfield who trained under Dave for decades. Bruce and I met during excavations at a Late Woodland Indian village site in the mid-1980s; now he assumed Dave's role, personally assisting in the excavation, organizing the Friends of the Office of State Archaeology (FOSA) volunteers, a non-profit organization created by Dave's wife, June, and maintaining field records. Along with Dan Cruson, we also enlisted FOSA members Ken Beatrice, longtime field/laboratory volunteer, and Jeremy Pilver, teacher and historical archaeologist, as experienced field assistants; Dan DeLuca, noted Old Leatherman historian, served as field photographer; former FOSA president Gary Nolf and William (Bill) Morlock, chair of the Connecticut State Museum of Natural History, managed the metal detectors; Ed Sarabia, Native Alaskan and Connecticut Indian Affairs Coordinator, represented the local Native community; and Dr. Gary Aronsen, director of the Biological Anthropology Laboratories at Yale University, conducted the forensic analysis. Our team was assembled and prepared to archaeologically resurrect Albert Afraid of Hawk.

The Lakota have a strong understanding of their past and historical chronology due to oral traditions and records transcribed as *waniyetu yawapi* "counting the winters,"[35] which are pictographic calendars highlighting the exploits of warriors and hunters, as well as other momentous occasions encompassing the preceding year. Originally drawn in color on buffalo hides and later on muslin and paper, "Winter Counts" were compiled from year-to-year and traced the Lakota cultural past in the tradition of oral history and storytelling. Pictographs, arranged in spirals and read from the center outward, served as mnemonic devices, triggering specific information from the minds of the Winter Count "Keeper," who interprets the symbols for the *tiospaye*.[36] Named Winter Counts because the Lakota calculated their year beginning with the first significant snowfall, they provide an extraordinary window into Lakota cultural history and into the nineteenth century, documenting the increasing appearance of the "*Wasichus*," He-who-takes-the-fat, the White Man.[37]

American Horse Count, Oglala Lakota, 1805-1806, Lakota "had a Council with the Whites on the Missouri River."[38]

After the successful political and military revolution against the British monarchy, Americans began to see their destiny in the West. Once venturing over the Alleghenies, they literally sprinted to the Mississippi River, fighting a series of wars and displacing many Indian Nations along the way. Discontented with remaining east of the Mississippi River, President Thomas Jefferson executed one of the greatest real estate deals of all time by obtaining the Louisiana Purchase from France in 1803 and authorizing Captains Meriwether Lewis and William Clark's expedition into the Western interior to explore the newly-acquired land of the United States and venture to the Pacific Ocean. The Purchase, granted by "Rights of Discovery"[39] among European-Christian nations, doubled the territorial size of the U. S., claiming all the tributaries flowing into the Mississippi River from the Rocky Mountains. With an ever-expanding eastern populace, Jefferson saw the possession of Western lands as securing America's imperialist expansion through the nineteenth century. Scant regard was given to the point that the United States was declaring possession of land already occupied and defended by Native American societies, who were considered pagans and savages, thus having no God-given rights to the continent.

By the early nineteenth century, the Lakota had developed a powerful and fearful reputation. They controlled trade on the Missouri River near present day Pierre, South Dakota, where the Oglala and Brule had two large villages at the confluence of the Bad River. With their populations expanding and the need for continual food supplies, fur traders, merchants, and other Native American tribes traveling along the river were expected to advance the Lakota tribute for permission to pass through their territory. Lewis and Clark would be no exception, though they attempted to disregard Lakota sovereignty, apparently unconcerned that Jefferson had made it clear to his captains he wished "most particularly to make a favorable impression, because of their immense power, and because we learn they are very desirous of being on the most friendly terms with us."[40]

The "favorable impression" Thomas Jefferson hoped to achieve with the Lakota remained unrealized when Lewis and Clark failed to grasp the indigenous political and economic balance of trade and transport along the Missouri River by not extending appropriate compensation to the Lakota. Inadequate gifts were offered, and diplomatic relations became strained between the Americans, who viewed the Lakota as marauders, and the insulted Lakota, who thought the Americans miserly. Tempers escalated to the point where firearms were leveled and bows notched. Remarkably, no arrows flew and no musket balls fired. Tension was resolved and bloodshed avoided, primarily because of the conciliatory efforts of Chief Black Buffalo, without whom the Corps of Discovery would have advanced no farther on their trek to the Pacific Ocean.[41] The captains failed in their diplomacy, and their resultant hatred of the Teton would influence United States/Lakota relationships throughout the remaining nineteenth century. Meriwether Lewis described the Lakota as "the vilest miscreants of the savage race, and must ever remain the pirates of the Missouri,"[42] casting their image into the American mindset and serving as a backdrop for race wars and the colonization of the West.

To the Lakota these were a new kind of *wasichus,* unlike the French fur traders whose exchange of economic goods were teemed beneficial to both cultural groups. Americans, on the other hand, showed no respect to the country's rightful occupants, affording unappreciable acknowledgement of Lakota sovereignty. If anything, the Americans acted like it was *their* river and *their* land, presenting a new threat to the Lakota, who based on this initial encounter, were determined to be prepared when these disrespectful people revisited the High Plains.

American Horse Count, Oglala Lakota, 1849-1850, "Many die of the cramps."[43]

The fatal "cramps" were the result of cholera, which had reached epidemic proportions in the eastern U. S. in the 1840s and was carried westward through the Great Plains by immigrants en route to Oregon and California. The flow of travelers started as a dribble through the 1830s, hardly noticeable within the vastness of the land. But in less than a decade, Conestoga wagons and their accompanying herds of cattle, sheep, oxen, and horses gathered a momentum that was changing the ecology of the plains. Swelling to at least 50,000 a year when the California gold rush and the Mormon migrations were launched, the total number of immigrants travelling the Oregon Trail

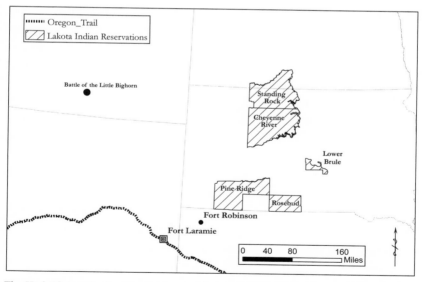

The High Plains showing places associated with the Afraid of Hawk family and the six Lakota Reservations established in 1889.

would reach 350,000 before the development of the transcontinental railroad in 1869.[44]

We assume that the western film genre's classic depiction of wagon trains as single-filed formations of linear cloth-covered schooners pulled by teams of horses is historically accurate. However, like much of filmdom's "Cowboy and Indian" fare, it is mainly mythology. While many of the prairie schooners followed the rutted tracks of former wagons, others drove side-by-side with their herds of cattle, sheep, and horses stretched broadly across the corridor. Oxen, not horses, were the preferred animals to pull the wagons since they had additional staying power, sure-footedness, and were more docile.[45] The Trail was not so much a single-lane road as a slow moving, multi-lane interstate highway cutting a swath through the Great Plains.[46] They felled what sparse trees were available for firewood, killed buffalo for food,[47] and littered the High Plains with abandoned wagons, wheelbarrows, trunks, furniture, and other supplies they could not sustain on the crossing.[48] Cattle, sheep, oxen, and horses ate up valuable grass, denuding whole areas that were essential for indigenous herds of buffalo to survive. Domestic cattle carried bovine diseases that sickened bison; immigrants brought pathogens such as cholera, smallpox, and measles, weakening Native populations. Rather than a harmless group of pioneers traversing the plains to seek a better life in Oregon and California, they were the carriers of an ecological devastation that affected both human and natural inhabitants.

The Lakota and other Plains Indians recognized the havoc and attempted to halt the flow of *waschius* wagons through their territory, at first diplomatically, then by force. Initially, the Lakota complained to U. S. representatives, testifying to the changes in the land and their inability to find buffalo in the vicinity of the Oregon Trail. Though government officials well understood the deleterious transformations occurring on the plains, their response was basically unsympathetic.[49] The issue was not so much stopping the flow of emigrants but how to keep them safe from Plains Indian retaliation.

A peace conference was needed before events grew out of control. Accordingly, U. S. government agents fanned out across the plains inviting tribes to meet in an effort to resolve their grievances. The result was the Fort Laramie Treaty of 1851, which limited tribal territories, prohibited intertribal warfare, and allowed the federal government to build way stations (really forts) along the Oregon Trail in lieu of gifts for the next fifty years. It was the beginning of the end for the horse-backed, buffalo-hunting societies.[50] The Oglala Lakota, the fiercest and strongest tribe in the region, never "touched the pen," that is, they were not signatories to the treaty, making it clear that they had no intention to live by *wasichus* regulations.[51]

Driving to Wooster Cemetery on the morning of August 12, 2012, I strived to focus on the work ahead, but my thoughts kept revisiting the disinterment of Henry 'Ōpūkaha'ia. Could it already have been twenty years since we repatriated Henry to Hawai'i? How was it possible that a similar request would happen again? Two ancestral, young Native men, journeying far from their homelands die prematurely and are buried in Connecticut; independently, descendant women have visitations/dreams that their ancestors desired to come home and pursued repatriation with state and local officials. In both cases, I was given the responsibility for the professional and respectful removal of their skeletal remains. Should such an opportunity occur once in a career would be remarkable, but having two such repatriations within my tenure was unimaginable. As we advanced toward the rediscovered burial plot of Albert Afraid of Hawk in Wooster Cemetery along an old historic dirt road by a small pond, my thoughts returned to the task at hand.

On arrival, we renewed our developing friendships and working relationships with Bob Young, Tania Porta, and Wendell Deer With Horns. Also on hand to support the recovery of Afraid of Hawk were Wendell's wife, Nancy; Norma Audette Vinchkoski, sexton of Wooster Cemetery; Christine Rose of Changing Winds, a Fairfield County-based Native American civil rights group and reporter for the Danbury Patch; and Bob Young's wife, Mary-Jo, who was given permission by the family to photo-document the proceedings. They all would play substantial roles in the removal and return of Albert Afraid of Hawk. As our team unloaded field equipment from the truck and set up for the archaeological undertaking, we had a most unexpected and very pleasant surprise.

Walking slowly from a high-wheeled white SUV parked along the dirt road were Marlis and her father, Daniel Jay Afraid of Hawk. I had no idea the family was traveling from South Dakota to attend personally to Albert's repatriation. Marlis grasped her father's arm as the 82-year-old Daniel, youngest child of Albert's older brother Richard Afraid of Hawk, supported by a cane, strolled to the gravesite followed by his son John Afraid of Hawk and tribal member Richard Red Elk. Relations and tribal members on the Cheyenne River Sioux Reservation sponsored a fund-raiser so the Afraid of Hawk family could travel to Connecticut and personally accompany Albert home. I couldn't have been more pleased, remembering that Debbie Lee had always regretted her family's inability to come to Connecticut in time to witness the archaeological unearthing of ʻŌpūkahaʻia. To have the contemporary family with us in the field made our work especially personal and meaningful.

The Afraid of Hawk family members must have felt a major cultural disparity at the cemetery. In Danbury, they were confronted by a host of people, including archaeologists, historians, volunteers, general public, and media, among others. Nevertheless, they appreciated all who made the repatriation possible and graciously provided the time to impart their gratitude—sharing family history, teaching Lakota language and cultural values along the way.

Prior to breaking ground, Daniel, John, and Richard performed the opening pipe ceremony. The Cheyenne River Sioux Reservation banner was unfurled. A medicine wheel, representing the Sacred Circle of Life, adorned with eagle feathers, was set on a pole and secured into the ground at the foot of the burial plot. The round shape of the wheel represents the never-ending circle of life and death; the cross symbolizes the four directions and the four Lakota Virtues of generosity, courage, respect, and wisdom. *Tatanka*, giver of life, present at all Lakota rituals, was embodied at the foot of the medicine wheel pole by a buffalo skull with projecting horns. An abalone shell containing burning sage infused a delicious, sacred fragrance into the air around us. A photograph of Albert taken in Omaha in 1899 was positioned behind *Tatanka*, lying against the base of the pole.

Marlis assumed many of the family responsibilities for the repatriation and explained, "He came to my dream and I had to go and bring him home."[52] In her youth she had seen a picture of Albert that relatives brought back from a visit to the Library of Congress. For years she looked curiously at the portrait, but no one ever mentioned the young man from long ago. She always wondered who he was and what had happened to him. Now, with her dream being realized, she cherished the story of her lost ancestor and wanted Albert's image near. "It's a historic event that's about to happen here," Marlis acknowledged.[53]

John Afraid of Hawk, a strong, quiet, hardworking, spiritual man, burned the sage and lit the *chanunpa*, passing the pipe to each person as we assembled in a circle around the gravesite. Richard Red Elk tapped a buffalo hide drum and sang. Daniel Jay Afraid of Hawk stood at the center of the circle and prayed first in Lakota, then spoke in English, emphasizing how happy he was to be here, telling of their long journey to reach Connecticut and how

Author consulting with Marlis and Daniel Jay Afraid of Hawk, Wooster Cemetery, Danbury, CT, August 2012. (Courtesy of Kenneth Beatrice.)

important it was for them to bring grandfather Albert home, completing his long journey. He prayed to the Creator, *Wakan Tanka*, and to all four directions, confidently announcing that Albert's remains would be found and returned to his homeland. John Afraid of Hawk blew an eagle bone whistle, its piercing sound calling out to Albert's spirit.

Through the beauty of the pipe ceremony, all of us realized that we were partaking in something very special. Tania Porta was awed by the occasion, inferring that "this is a once-in-a-lifetime thing"[54] that had made her feel she could better understand the faith the family possessed and their connection to the earth. Diane Hassan, who collaborated with Bob Young bringing to light Albert's story, said that the experience became very "personal."[55] Mary-Jo Young reflected on the Native American belief that things happen when they are supposed to happen, not necessarily when we want them to happen, recognizing that all the research, consultation, and waiting eventually brought us all together at this place in time, at the moment Albert was meant to go home.[56] We all felt a deep obligation to do our best for the family, and I personally felt the added anxiety of wanting the disinterment to come off perfectly with respect and professionalism.

As we prepared to proceed with the excavation, Marlis shared a thought that reminded me of Debbie Lee. She disclosed her feeling that the repatriation "should have happened a long time ago, but it didn't." Debbie expressed a similar sentiment about Henry ʻŌpūkahaʻia's return. I shared with the Afraid of Hawk family my experiences with the Lee family, and Marlis immediately understood the power of Debbie's calling, sensing an affinity with her own dream of Albert.

American Horse Count, Oglala Lakota, 1865-1866, "They killed one hundred white men at Fort Phil. Kearny."[57]

Though the *wasichus* continued to cross the plains in great numbers, the years after 1857 brought the Lakota an interlude of relative peace. Relocation to the Powder River Valley in Montana and Wyoming begat security, plentiful game, and distance from the southerly Oregon Trail. Time-honored Native enemies like the

Crow and Shoshone could be raided for horses and removed from unspoiled hunting grounds. Reputations of young warriors could be established within ritual combat traditions. Normalcy seemed to permeate these days. Hopefully, the confrontations with the *wasichus* were a thing of the past. The Lakota had always desired to be left alone in their own territory, free to roam, hunting buffalo. In spite of this, the Americans had been only temporarily distracted by a bloody Civil War, and once they had put their own house in order, they would re-emerge with a renewed passion for Manifest Destiny.

Gold had been discovered in southwestern Montana, stimulating renewed fervor for heading west and bringing with it the expectant horde of prospectors and settlers. The available route to the gold fields was the Oregon Trail to California, then backtracking eastward to Montana. A miner, John M. Bozeman, was convinced there was a faster and more direct course to Montana, so he began scouting a passage east from Virginia City, reducing nearly 400 miles off the Oregon-California route.[58] Unfortunately, the "Bozeman Trail" cut through the heart of the finest buffalo hunting ground available to the Lakota, who had already witnessed *Takanta*'s disappearance along the Platte and North Platte Rivers and would not tolerate similar desecration in the Powder River country. The Lakota confronted Bozeman in no uncertain terms; any attempt to travel through Lakota territory would be met by the wrath of warriors. Bozeman was apparently willing to call their bluff.

Gold-seekers inclined to test the fortitude of the Lakota on the Bozeman Trail found themselves under fierce attack and, like their earlier predecessors on the Oregon Trail, demanded U. S. Army protection. The government's response was a series of military forts safeguarding travellers to Virginia City. The Lakota response was Red Cloud's War, a series of battles staged in the Wyoming and Montana territories from 1866 to 1868, for which the Oglala were well prepared. When Red Cloud and Crazy Horse lured soldiers from Fort Kearny into an ambush on December 21, 1866, in the "Battle of the One Hundred Slain," it would not be the last time a U. S. military force would be totally decimated by Lakota warriors.

Swan Count, Minneconjou Lakota, 1867-1868, "Made peace with General Sherman and others at Fort Laramie."[59]

With anticipation of building the first transcontinental railroad linking Sacramento, California, to Omaha, Nebraska, and dealing with Reconstruction in the South, Congress was ready to end Red Cloud's War by establishing a Peace Commission headed by Civil War Gen. William Tecumseh Sherman. The governmental attitude was that the differing "races" could not live together so reservation systems had to be developed to separate them.[60] Ely Parker, a Seneca lawyer appointed by President Grant as commissioner of the Office of Indian Affairs and a proponent of Grant's Peace Policy, hoped that the large Indian reservations would eventually become states of the Union with Native populations assimilated into American life.[61]

In April 1868, the peace commission arrived at Fort Laramie to negotiate with Red Cloud and other Lakota leaders. However, the Oglala chief made it clear he would never participate in treaty discussions unless the Bozeman Trail was abandoned and the military forts removed.[62] When the peace council began, few Indians bothered to show up, gifts or no gifts. A month later the peace commission conceded to Red Cloud's terms: the forts were vacated and travel along the Bozeman Trail ceased. The Lakota had won. Red Cloud's War would remain the only time in history that the U. S. government sued for peace after having never won a major military engagement and agreeing to the terms of the enemy. On Nov. 6, 1868, the triumphant Red Cloud rode into Fort Laramie and signed the treaty.

The Fort Laramie Treaty of 1868 was divided into twelve Articles from which we highlight five main agreements: 1. Both sides promised to uphold the peace and allow for the Union Pacific Railroad to be built; 2. Land west of the Missouri River and east of the Bighorn River from the 46th parallel south to the Nebraska line (more than 60,000,000 acres), would be "given" for the "absolute and undisturbed use" as the "Great Sioux Reservation," including the hallowed Black Hills which the U. S. government formally recognized as sacrosanct to the Lakota; 3. In compensation for giving up their land for the railroad and in acknowledgement of the disappearing buffalo, provisions would be provided by the U. S. government, including schools, seeds, and clothing, as well as agencies for the distribution of services; 4. The Powder River area would be designated as "Unceded Indian Territory" where the *wasichus* would not be permitted to settle or build military posts, maintaining the land for the continual hunting of buffalo; 5. No part or portion of the Reservation shall be ceded unless at least three-fourths of all male Indian adults signed in agreement.[63] The treaty establishes Lakota sovereignty as a nation and compensates the tribe for U. S. appropriation of their lands and resources; it was considered the benchmark of Red Cloud's leadership.

One of the Miniconjous leaders signing the 1868 Fort Laramie Treaty was "Tah-tonk-ka-hon-ke-schne, his X mark, Slow Bull."[64] *Tatanka Hunkesin* was born (ca. 1819) in Minnesota and eventually traveled westward to reside with the Oglala sometime in the 1840s. He became one of Red Cloud's trusted warriors. Slow Bull's son, Afraid of Hawk (*Cetan Kokipapi*), born in April 1850[65] in what is now Wyoming, would continue in his father's fighting spirit at the Battle of Little Bighorn in 1876. In his elder years, Slow Bull shared a tipi with his grandson, Albert Afraid of Hawk, before the latter left the reservation to join Buffalo Bill's Wild West.[66]

With the treaty signed and peace restored to the plains, the Union Pacific tracks crossing the Nebraska Territory were laid out and connected with the Central Pacific Railroad coming out of Sacramento, California, in May 1869, rendering both the Oregon and Bozeman Trails obsolete. To feed the considerable crews laying thousands of miles of track, railroad bosses hired buffalo hunters, including a young Billy Cody, who together slaughtered millions of the Lakota "banquet of life." The U. S. government encouraged the killing of buffalo, recognizing that their elimination would speed up Indian dependency on the reservation system for food and supplies.[67]

Two years after the treaty signing, Red Cloud accepted an invitation to go to Washington, D. C., to speak with President Grant on behalf of his people. While the Lakota delegation to Washington did little to change conditions on the Plains, Red Cloud impressed the general public with his appearance, elegance, and oration, becoming quite the celebrity. However, Red Cloud was also overwhelmed by what he saw in the strength and numbers of the *wasichus*, realizing the fruitlessness of further resistance; he would fight no more and commit himself to a role of accommodation with the Americans as the only means of long-term survival for his people. Many Lakota would say of his trip to Washington, "Red Cloud saw too much."[68]

Once the opening ceremonies were concluded, excavation proceeded by delineating on the ground the location of Lot 19, Section 22, identified by Bob Young from the cemetery's archives as Albert Afraid of Hawk's burial plot. Norma Vinchkoski arranged for a small backhoe whose skilled operator, Tom Keane, worked carefully under our supervision, attaching a flat blade across the teeth of his bucket, carefully stripping the topsoil away. Bruce Greene and I graded the excavation by hand, hoping to highlight changes in the soil coloration indicating the location of the grave shaft. None appeared, so we directed the operator to remove another six inches for further inspection.

Layer after layer we continued in a similar manner until we reached the depth of twenty inches where the outline of the grave shaft formed. The rectangular feature, oriented with its long axis east to west, exhibited the same Christian mortuary pattern encountered with 'Ōpūkahaʻia's grave. With a fifteen-inch separation of natural, undisturbed soils to the right of the burial feature, another grave shaft consisting of mixed, mottled soils also appeared. Bob Young's archival research found a burial card for another unmarked grave residing to the right of Albert, identified as George LeLapp, thirty-nine-year-old Euro-American who had died in a railroad accident six days after Albert's death. Conversely, to the left of Albert lay the remains of eight-day-old infant Ira McLaughlan, having died of lockjaw on June 8, 1900. Adjoining burials in close proximity necessitated a narrow excavation unit so as not to disturb their remains during Albert's disinterment, resulting in a very tight unit in which to conduct our work, reminiscent of the same concerns and constricted excavation space for 'Ōpūkahaʻia.

Anticipating hardware associated with the coffin, we used metal detecting equipment to penetrate a foot beneath the soil, allowing us to predict the level of the coffin depth before actually encountering it. The detectors started ringing at a depth of three and one-half feet, so we dispensed with mechanical stripping and transferred to hand tools for the remainder of the delicate excavation. Hardware mesh screens were mounted, soils were sieved, and protective tents erected. Satisfied that we had located the grave shaft and were in range of metal, Bruce Greene and I decided to finish up the day's work in anticipation of encountering the coffin, and possibly Albert, the following day. Tom Keane covered the open burial unit with three vault lids, and further security was provided by Tania Porta and the mayor's office, who arranged for youth volunteers from the local Civil Air Patrol to remain in the cemetery throughout the night, guarding over Albert Afraid of Hawk's grave until relieved by our crew the following morning.

No Two Horns Winter Count, Hunkpapa Lakota, 1876-1877, "Long Hair (Pehanska) killed by the Sioux."[69]

Lt. Col. George Armstrong Custer, known as *Pehanska* (Long Hair) among the Lakota, led an expedition into the Black Hills in 1874 accompanied by civilians trained in geology to survey the region for its suitability toward establishing military forts and assessing its economic potential. While the 1868 Fort Laramie Treaty permitted the military to enter the Black Hills, it gave them no authorization to build forts, towns, or exploit natural resources. Since *Paha Sapa* had legally been given by treaty to the Lakota for their exclusive eternal use, Custer was trespassing.

George Custer was particularly lured on his Black Hills Expedition to explore possibilities of rumored gold deposits. The Lakota were well aware that yellow nuggets and dust which made the *wasichus* crazy existed in the hills. *Mazaskazi* (yellow white metal) had become a treasured exchange commodity when dealing with French traders.[70] Gold had no worth among the Indians, but they saw how much the white man desired it, coming in droves to obtain it, and willing to kill and die over it—always taking land containing it. The Lakota were so anxious about the consequences of the *wasichus* finding *mazaskazi* in *Paha Sapa*, it was resolved that any Indian who showed the gold fields to the white man would be put to death.[71] Even without Native assistance, the expedition found traces of gold; with a newspaper reporter along to record the discovery for the American public, hordes of prospectors soon followed Custer's trail to the gold fields. The Lakota called it, "The Thieves Road."

Only superficial consideration was given to the fact that they were trespassing in violation of the treaty. The nation was plunged into a global economic depression, the Panic of 1873, when post-Civil War inflation and collapse of the overly-built railroads plummeted the nation into a severe fiscal downturn. Newly discovered gold reserves were viewed as a valuable asset to the economically reeling country. Concocting a feeble attempt to uphold the treaty by impeding the flow of miners into the Black Hills using the U. S. Army to confront prospectors, President Grant prepared to confiscate the gold fields.[72] The Lakota went on the warpath against the interlopers, realizing that if they did not intercede, they would lose their beloved *Paha Sapa*.

Suppressed under the weight of internal corruption, Grant's administration attempted to purchase, or lease, the hills from the Lakota to ensure the safety of the miners. When the Teton would not consider selling their sacred *Paha Sapa*, the president decided that they necessitated permanent placement on confined reservations "for their own safety," though the real motive was to keep them out of the way of American economic advancement at such a critical time. Euro-Americans viewed the events as a "race war," pitting "civilization" against "savagery,"[73] and justified taking the Black Hills by rationalizing that the Lakota did not use the land and only occasionally visited the area to hunt and hold ceremonies, never occupying and developing the region.[74] Custer went so far as to imply that the Black Hills only served the Lakota as a place to hide after committing atrocities against white people.[75]

The president authorized the Office of Indian Affairs to send a decree to the Lakota ordering them to return to their respective agencies by Jan. 31, 1876, or be considered "hostiles" and forced into submission by the U. S. Army.[76] If the free-roaming Lakota bands failed to comply, then the American government would consider the 1868 Treaty dissolved, opening *wasichus* settlement and mining of the Black Hills. No doubt federal authorities were at a legal disadvantage having gold deposits discovered on Indian land, but this issue was viewed as one that was easily overcome by shifting the fault to the Lakota.[77] Gen. Phil Sheridan was given authorization to bring in noncompliant Lakota, an order he was most confident of fulfilling and enjoy doing, having been infamous for the phrase, "The only good Indians I ever saw were dead."[78]

The Lakota were outraged. As American messengers brought word of Grant's directive to the tribes scattered throughout the vast High Plains hunting buffalo, it became apparent to both sides that the wintertime deadline was impossible to meet because of the many miles and below-freezing weather that entire bands had to overcome to reach the far off agencies on time. Even for compliant bands, it meant potential conflict with the U. S. Army because of the impossibility in meeting the strict demands of the president's deadline, a fact not lost on Grant who was looking for an excuse to break the treaty.[79] For non-compliant "hostile" bands, it was of little concern since they had no intention of obeying orders imposed upon them by another nation.

Emissaries from Sitting Bull, a Hunkpapa *wicasa wakan* (holy man), invited Red Cloud and other Lakota to join him to discuss the *wasichus* invasion of their land and develop a collective military response to the coming peril. However, now past fifty years of age, Red Cloud, once the most-feared Indian warrior of the Great Plains, decided to honor his commitment to nonviolence and remained at his agency. Although his son, Jack Red Cloud headed north to join the "hostiles," the old warrior could foresee nothing but total annihilation by resistance.[80] Crazy Horse, Sitting Bull, and their followers were not deterred. They swore to avenge the desecraters of *Paha Sapa* and those Washington bureaucrats who would demand their obedience by enslaving them on reservations as if they were children.

The anticipated collision came on the High Plains during the summer of 1876. Early in June, "When Berries Are Good" (*Wipazuke Waste Wi*), 3,000 Lakota congregated on Rosebud Creek to conduct a Sun Dance. During the ceremony, Sitting Bull beseeched *Wakan Tanka*[81] to provide buffalo and protect them from the *wasichus*. The *wicasa wakan* danced and fasted for days seeking a powerful vision possessing a prophetic message for his people. Sitting Bull had his chest pierced by eagle claws tied to ropes looped over high poles set around the *waga chun,* the sacred (cottonwood) tree that stood in the center of the dancing circle. He cut 100 strips of flesh from his arms in a sacrifice of self-mutilation. He danced to the pounding and repetitive drumming until finally losing consciousness.

While comatose, Sitting Bull had had his vision: he had seen American soldiers and their horses falling from the sky head first into the Indian's camp; their hats flew off as they descended; their arms flayed as they crashed to the ground. *Wakan Tanka* was freely giving these soldiers as a gift to the People of the Buffalo Nation because the Americans had no ears, implying that the white men never listened to the Lakota's request to be left alone on their own land. There was only one interpretation of this foretelling vision: a great victory was ordained and many "bluecoats" would die.[82]

Dawn on the morning of June 25th promised to be a sweltering day on the High Plains. A combined village of Lakota and Northern Cheyenne were camped by the Little Bighorn River, tipis extending for more than a mile. Black Elk, a thirteen-year-old Oglala, set off on his morning chores tending to the horses along the Greasy Grass, the Indian name for the river possessing an oily grass along its banks. The encampment was large and most people went about their daily activities without worries of approaching trouble. Yet Black Elk sensed a discomforting emotion sweep over him. He felt ill and was overcome with a premonition that something bad would happen today.[83]

Sitting Bull had begun his day overlooking the needs of his family and tribal members. Crazy Horse's Oglala pitched their tipis to the north of the Hunkpapa and were also going about their daily activities.[84] So, too, were Slow Bull, Afraid of Hawk, his wife White Mountain, their two-year-old son, and two female children residing within the Oglala camp.[85] Nothing appeared out of the ordinary until just after 3 p.m. when from the hills to the south gunshots were heard and bluecoats were sighted astride their horses, charging down into the valley. Lt. Col. George Armstrong Custer's Seventh Cavalry was attacking the village.

The alarm sounded throughout the southern Hunkpapa encampment. Warriors, led by Gall, whose two wives and daughter were early casualties of the attack, ran to gather their horses and strap on their bows, arrows, and firearms, hurriedly organizing to meet the assault. Custer, anticipating a panicky withdrawal of the village, had split his battalions into three units to intercept fleeing Indians. Instead Lakota warriors counter-charged directly into Maj. Marcus Reno's attacking troops. Crazy Horse mounted a war pony, and accompanied by Oglala and Cheyenne warriors, including twenty-six-year-old Afraid of Hawk, entered the flail, providing encouragement and support to the Hunk-papa efforts.[86]

The ferocity of the warriors was unanticipated by the American soldiers. Custer led five companies of cavalry toward the northeast hills hoping to flank the village, while leaving Reno behind to absorb the brunt of the counterattack. After forcing Reno into a retreat, Crazy Horse and his men were drawn to the sound of increased gunfire along the northeastern bluff and gave chase. Whether Afraid of Hawk followed Crazy Horse in pursuit of Custer, or remained behind to keep Reno contained, is unknown. Nonetheless, through a series of calculated maneuvers, Indians repositioned and improvised as battle conditions warranted. Custer also attempted to regroup, but the Lakota had him ensnared with warriors flanking his lines, others coming out of the village, and Crazy Horse from behind,[87] reminding some Lakota of chasing buffalo to a place to be easily slaughtered.[88]

The fighting was intense and up-close with no lack of bravery on both sides. Within two hours, the Seventh Cavalry was overwhelmed and had collapsed at the northern end of the ridge with no escape routes available. Custer was shot by at least two bullets: one to the left temple and a second to the chest. He also suffered a wound in the right forearm, though this may have been from the same bullet that exited his chest.[89] All 210 soldiers under his command on the high ridge were eliminated to the last man, just as had been foretold in Sitting Bull's vision.

The Battle of the Greasy Grass, the Lakota name for the fight against Custer, had resulted in unimaginable losses for the Seventh Cavalry and struck at the confidence of the entire country at the time of its chest-pounding first centennial celebrations. When news of Custer's demise reached the eastern cities on July 5, 1876, the country was stunned, shocked into disbelief. How could a Civil War hero, a West

Point graduate, be wiped out by a bunch of "scarecrow savages"?[90] The nation and surviving Seventh Cavalry would remember, and the reverberations of Little Bighorn would sting fourteen years later at Wounded Knee Creek.[91]

Slow Bull's son, Afraid of Hawk (*Cetan Kokipapi*), represents hundreds of relatively nameless Lakota and Cheyenne warriors who participated in the Battle of the Greasy Grass and never had their personal accounts recorded by historians. His small but growing family was with him at the village where White Mountain protected their children during the fighting. Three years after the confrontation with Custer, White Mountain would give birth to another strapping son named Eagle Weasel (*Itankusun wanbli*), later to be christened Albert.

White Cow Killer Count, Oglala Lakota, 1877-1878, "Crazy Horse-killed winter."[92]

The U. S. Congress used the defeat of Custer's Seventh Cavalry to force agency Indians into another contract, the Black Hills Agreement of 1876, formally seizing *Paha Sapa*.[93] Congress stipulated that the government would deny food and other commodities to the Lakota until the agreement was signed.[94] To save their people from starvation, Red Cloud and other "friendly" chiefs had no choice but to sign and relinquish their sacred hills, even though the required three-fourths of adult male signatures stipulated by treaty was never achieved.

After the Battle of the Greasy Grass, the Lakota/Northern Cheyenne bands divided into smaller groups, some seeking game and independence while others returned to the agencies.[95] Crazy Horse's faction would travel south up the Little Missouri River to Slim Buttes while Sitting Bull would head north to the Killdeer Mountains and eventually Canada. The Afraid of Hawk family decided not to go back to the agency and instead remained with Crazy Horse to live as free-roamers for as long as they could. They hunted unmolested until Colonel Nelson "Bear Coat" Miles located their encampment in January 1877, opening a running series of battles in the dead of winter. Although Crazy Horse and his followers escaped, Miles was able to destroy much of their winter supplies.[96] Through the course of the frigid mid-winter with buffalo and other game decimated, little food could be found, leaving the defiant Lakota succumbing to a slow death of attrition. Painfully, Crazy Horse realized he could no longer protect or provide for them, so he encouraged many of his followers to return to the agency and receive treaty-promised rations as he continued to hold out. Nonetheless, Afraid of Hawk and his family remained loyal, enduring the hardships with Crazy Horse until they were forced to surrender in May 1877 at Fort Robinson, Nebraska.[97]

When the Oglala leader, accompanied by the Afraid of Hawk family and 300 other followers, rode slowly into the bluecoat's camp, the gaunt, emaciated features of the men, women, and children were hard even for the soldiers who had fought against them to behold. They had endured the winter, but the price of survival was exposed in blackened facial scars caused from frostbite; their clothes were rags, barely covering their bodies. As the sorrowful procession entered the fort, they conceded by singing peace songs. In greeting their kin many Lakota already at the fort lined the path of Crazy Horse's surrender route and sang along with them. To one disgruntled army officer it seemed like a victory march rather than admission of defeat.[98]

Crazy Horse was not content at Fort Robinson, though he assured army authorities that he had no intention of going back on the warpath. He desired his own agency where he could continue to lead his people in their assimilation into the modern world. When he left the Red Cloud Agency because his wife was ill and needed treatment, Crazy Horse was persuaded to come to the fort to explain his departure to post commander Lt. Col. Luther P. Bradley. The parlay planned for the late afternoon of September 5, 1877, was a pretext to arrest Crazy Horse and imprison him far away from his followers. When soldiers and Indian police brought him to a guardhouse instead of Col. Bradley's office, Crazy Horse fathomed the deception, lunging for his hunting knife. Amid confusion and wrestling, the combatants fought their way out the door and onto the parade ground. A soldier drove a rifle-mounted bayonet twice into Crazy Horse's side. He fell to the ground grievously wounded. A commotion erupted among his followers, but Red Cloud and the other leaders demanded restraint. Crazy Horse lay dying, his blood staining the ground beneath him.

Four days before the killing of Crazy Horse, Afraid of Hawk, finding it necessary to support his growing family, enlisted in the U. S. Army as an Indian Scout at Fort Robinson. His enlistment papers registered his name as "Afraid of a Hawk."[99] The day Crazy Horse was executed, Afraid of Hawk was among the soldiers in uniform. However, the Oglala chief's death had an emotional and detrimental effect on the young Lakota father, who had fought alongside of Crazy Horse and followed him through the severe winter while chased by the U. S. Army in pursuit of a traditional life pathway that was no longer possible. Afraid of Hawk's military conscription ended after serving for only one month. Thereafter, Slow Bull, Afraid of Hawk, White Mountain, and their children would remain loyal to Red Cloud, struggling to adapt to these confined and unaccustomed conditions. Their children would learn and respect Lakota ways but were now compelled to follow the "White Man's Road."

6 | "His Spirit Has Been Lifted"

Marlis Afraid of Hawk was only a child of four or five years in her dream. Adorned in a small white dress, she had been searching for her parents and siblings throughout their little house on the prairie without finding them. Worried she might have been left home alone, she went outside to look, but they were nowhere to be seen. Scanning the horizon, she saw an unfamiliar young man approaching on horseback out of the north. His long flowing hair swirled as he rode. He was dressed in traditional Lakota, not Western, clothing. Apprehensive, she retreated into the house, sitting alone on her parents' bed, frightened. Dismounting in the front yard, the stranger genuflected down on one knee and began playing a flute, producing a sweet, soothing sound so soft and melodic that Marlis was disappointed when he finished his song. No longer afraid, she went outside and saw that the mysterious man had remounted and was riding away. He pulled up on the reins of his horse, spun and called back to her in a distinct voice, "*Yu' pah*" (Come here). With a wave of his hand, the clouds began to move in unison, merging together, discharging a herd of pintos and palominos and, behind them, Lakota grandmothers, grandfathers, children, even a dog pulling a *travois*, and lastly, warriors on horseback, all descending from the sky. She thought to herself, "I know these people," and once again felt safe.

Marlis woke awestruck, pondering the meaning of her dream and the identity of this entrancing young Lakota man. In Native American cultures, dreams offer guidance from the spiritual world, often providing prophetic messages that require response in the awakened world, a call to action in fulfillment of the vision. Comparable to Debbie Lil'ikapeka Lee, Marlis was concerned that she was being chosen to do something, but did not know what. She questioned family and tribal members at the Cheyenne River Sioux Reservation, but they remained just as puzzled. In search of an explanation, Marlis attended an elders' ceremony, retelling her dream to Lakota spiritualists who listened, prayed, and provided explanation. The message received from the spirit world, she was told, concerned her grandfather's brother who left the reservation a long time ago, never returning home. She felt immediate relief and comprehension: the people descending from the clouds were ancestors, and the young man was her *lala* (grandfather) Albert Afraid of Hawk. He was seeking her help through the intimate power of her dream, and she felt immediate responsibility. Marlis realized, *"He wants to come home."*

The second day at Wooster Cemetery proved most memorable. With an early morning start, we resumed excavation deeper into the grave shaft and encountered hardware within moments. Coffin nails and the caps of six white-metal handles surfaced, outlining the wooden casket. Soil acidity decomposed any traces of the sideboards though some wood did survive adhering to rusting iron nails. Unlike 'Ōpūkaha'ia, there were no brass tacks with Albert's initials, no nameplate; the casket shape was rectangular, not hexagonal.

With the coffin positioned, apprehension centered on the distinct possibility that no organic remains of Albert Afraid of Hawk persisted in the highly acidic soils. So we invited Deborah Surabian, soil scientist with the Department of Agriculture's Natural Resources Conservation Service, to test and examine the profiles. Debbie confirmed the University of Connecticut's soil results for low pH by conducting her own independent analysis.[1] She informed us that along with the high degree of soil acidity, organic preservation is also a product of soil moisture that can affect the metabolism of decomposer microorganisms.[2] Fluctuations in water activity in the soil influence microbial biomass,[3] playing havoc on bone and wood. The location of Albert's grave in Wooster Cemetery, near the bottom of a steep slope with the area beyond his head built up for the dirt road bed, produced soils that retained runoff water, percolating down to lower levels. Debbie's results were not encouraging.

Nonetheless, we continued to hope, descending deeper into the interior of the casket outline without encountering human remains. Bruce Greene and I made a command decision to concentrate at the head of the coffin to expedite finding any evidence of Albert rather than conduct a complete horizontal excavation of the entire body. The headboard was eighteen inches in breadth, so I extended eighteen inches down the coffin toward the shoulders, creating a square unit where we anticipated the skull.[4] We would either encounter Albert or confirm that his remains had totally decomposed.

Around noon while the Afraid of Hawk family was absent conducting a ceremony where Albert had died, I was greatly relieved to find the first evidence of skeletal tissue when the forehead was uncovered. The entire crew was elated. Wendell Deer With Horns handed me sage to wash my hands and scatter the dried leaves of the purifying plant around the exposed remains. By the time the family returned, upper parts of Albert's face were revealed, his eye orbits distinct. However, it was also apparent that the thin bones of the cranio-facial complex (i.e., nasal) were completely dissolved.

Work continued until Tania Porta approached, announcing the family had returned. I swept loose soils into a dustpan for screening and climbed the ladder out of the burial shaft to greet them. Marlis and Daniel, arm-in-arm, looked down into the burial, viewing the superior portion of the face and forehead of their ancestor. I explained the change in my field procedure and how I had gently shaved the ground, dislodging a patch of soil, and there was Albert. I told them we could now anticipate finding additional remains. My voice faltered with emotion when I put my hand on Daniel's shoulder and told him that Albert "will come home."

John Afraid of Hawk honored the occasion by burning fresh sage in the abalone shell. "I was sure he would be here," he said. "I am happy you found him. It brings closure to a lot of anxiety for the Afraid of Hawk family." Looking down into the burial and dabbing her eyes with tissue, Marlis Afraid of Hawk felt relief for the first time.[5] "He's there! He's there!" she kept repeating. As she relaxed into a lawn chair to take it all in, she lifted her head and said, "He'll be with his family and his spirit will be at peace."[6]

His heart pounded with so much excitement he feared the blood-pumping organ would explode through his chest. The smoking rifle he commanded in his perspiring hands was red hot from repeated firing. He aimed at a Shoshone warrior, traditional enemies of the Lakota, lurking behind a tree across the field. Fired. The "Snake" crumpled to the ground, writhing in pain. Sensing someone approaching at his back, he whirled and saw a Crow brave about to plunge onto him with a tomahawk. He fired pointblank, throwing his would-be killer back in agony.

Albert Afraid of Hawk stood strong, his courage and fortitude never wavering. He was Oglala Lakota; his grandfather rode with the undefeated Red Cloud, and his father fought with the greatest Lakota warrior of them all, Crazy Horse at Little Bighorn. He had inherited a mantle of gallantry that he desperately longed to sustain.

Then, just as suddenly, when he cherished more engagement with his enemies, the firing ceased. Horses were pulled to a halt. Smoke covering the field began to rise and as it cleared, he studied the ground to see who were among the dead. Only then, as the adrenaline washed away, did Albert Afraid of Hawk hear the applause coming from

Sham Battle, American Indian Congress, Trans-Mississippian & International Exposition, Omaha, Nebraska, 1898, F.A. Rinehart, photographer. (Courtesy of Omaha Public Library, TMI-01005.)

Victorian men and women watching from wooden grandstands protected from the sun under parasols and bowler hats. The mock battle was over before he was willing to yield the field. It had seemed so real. But now the "dead" Indians rose, picking themselves off the ground, dusting off their leather clothing as they walked away in search of the food tables. He had not wanted the moment to end.

It was the summer of 1899, Omaha, Nebraska, where the Greater American Exposition was in full swing. The previous year, thousands of easterners journeyed west in droves to witness the marvels of the modern technological age, including for many the sight of their first automobile and flushing toilets, amid the promises of industrial farming in the Western Plains at the Trans-Mississippian and International Exposition. The follow-up Greater American Exposition utilized the buildings and fairgrounds of the International Exposition, as well as the concept of the American Indian Congress. Both Expositions strongly promoted an imperialistic vision of America to a broad audience in the same year that we went to war with Spain and Hawai'i was annexed to the U. S.[7] Many people came to Omaha especially to see the American Indian Congress. The International Exposition promoted the gathering of tribes as an ethnological and scientific event, but the highlight was the "mock battles" in which the Indians engaged. The Exposition's guidebook promised this would be "the last opportunity of seeing the American Indian as a savage, for the Government work now in progress will lift the savage Indian into American citizenship before this generation passes into history."[8] On the other hand, the Greater American Exposition made no claims of "ethnological" or "scientific" concerns and staged the mock battles as spectacles to entice crowds.

The Trans-Mississippian and International Exposition's board of directors invited in excess of twenty American Indian tribes and more than 400 indigenous peoples from across the U. S. under the direction of the Office of Indian Affairs (OIA) to participate in the Congress.[9] Even the fierce Apache warrior Geronimo attended, released from prison at Fort Sill, Oklahoma, specifically for the occasion. The OIA handpicked Indian representatives who possessed good morals, demonstrated temperance, were full-blooded, and of a "good type" to exemplify their tribes physically.[10] Forty-eight individuals represented the Lakota, including ten from the Pine Ridge Reservation.[11] For the following year's Greater American Exposition, Samuel McGowan, superintendent of the Phoenix Indian School, was hired to enlist Lakota from the Pine Ridge Reservation where he recruited seventy-five braves, including the teenaged Albert Afraid of Hawk.[12]

During that summer's Congress, Albert was approached by Herman Heyn, an Omaha photographer known for portraits of some of the leading citizens in the community. The Heyn family emigrated from Germany in 1856 and set up a photographic gallery where Herman and his brother George were able to take advantage of the two Indian Congresses and framed more than 500 portrait images of Native Americans. Their five extant prints of Albert Afraid of Hawk are currently in the Library of Congress, copyrighted as the Heyn & Matzen Collection.

The photographic images portray a youthful Lakota male of good stature and round face. His cheekbones are high, his eyes and mouth droop a bit to the sides and his loose shoulder-length hair is parted

Albert Afraid of Hawk, Photo by Heyn, #255 taken in Omaha Sept. 18, 1899 by Heyn and Matzen, photographers. (Courtesy of Library of Congress, Lot 3401.)

slightly left of center. There is health and pride in his appearance. He does not smile but looks earnestly into the distance, focusing on a far-off place. He is adorned in a combination of traditional Lakota clothing and Western shirts and pants. He wears arm and wristbands along with three feathers on his head, a hair-pipe bone breastplate, neck scarf, the strap from a bandolier over his shoulder, and a quilted "uncle of the world" with a trailer of beads and eagle feathers secured to the top of his head, extending down over his back, sitting on a chair with animal fur covering.[13]

In one photograph, he is posed in an eagle-feathered headdress and plaid Western cotton shirt. In another he holds a stone-headed war club, its handle decorated with beadwork; in yet another his arms are crossed, his head poised high, his gaze far off to his right, dignified and respectable. Albert Afraid of Hawk looks directly into the lens of the camera in only one image, his eyes piercing, left hand pensively along the side of his head, fingers extended upward, as if in meditation. Late

Albert Afraid of Hawk, Ogallala Sioux, Photo by Heyn, taken in Omaha 1899, Heyn and Matzen, photographers. (Courtesy of Denver Public Library, Western History Collection, X-31509.)

nineteenth-century photographic portraits of Native Americans are reflections of publicity and artistic creativity. The meaning of the images among the Indians that modeled for them were vastly different from the commercial value sought by the photographers. Albert communicates recognition in his bearing that he is being photographed proudly as Oglala Lakota, leaving a legacy of his people for the future.

James Mooney, an anthropologist with the Smithsonian Institution's Bureau of American Ethnology and later chronicler of the Ghost Dance, had hoped to make the Indian Congress an enlightening experience for the public. Invited tribal members set up tipis, wigwams, wiki-ups, and other native dwellings, recreating village atmospheres. Indians acted out everyday residential activities such as preparing food, conducting ceremonies, dancing, and demonstrating their technologies, handcrafting weapons, tools, clothing, and household goods manufactured from bone, wood, hide, and stone. Strolling among the villages, the public witnessed aboriginal life-ways up close, a living ethnography of a "vanishing race." However, Mooney's hopes for an

Albert Afraid of Hawk, Ogallala Sioux taken in Omaha 1899, Heyn and Matzen, photographers. (Courtesy of Denver Public Library, X-31510.)

educational attraction were dashed by the spectacle of the mock battles, which he detested, but were the authentic attraction of the Indian Congress.[14]

Native American contestants, in particular, got caught up in the excitement of the mock battles which allowed them the opportunity to demonstrate their "fearlessness, agility, (and) horsemanship," "in the excitement of the fray."[15] The performances were so realistic the public was immediately caught up in the drama, as were the Indians who entered the pageants with zest and determination, sometimes competing against traditional enemies in the ways of their ancestors. Indian delegates, 100 to 150 on each side, reenacted shooting, scalping, and torturing scenes using blank cartridges, animal furs, and good stagecraft to entertain the *wasichus* crowds.[16] Native men were so carried away with the action that they continued firing their guns until the last blank cartridge was dispatched and they were forced to cease.[17]

Native Americans performed at the Expositions for many reasons, mostly financial. However, for many first-generation Reservation Indians these shows represented an opportunity to be warriors like their grandfathers and fathers before them. Though role-playing, it provided the chance to experience the excitement of the field of battle, to demonstrate their athleticism and horse-riding abilities, and to remain "Indian" in the wake of assimilation. Albert Afraid of Hawk, at an age now when he would have been proving his courage as a Lakota warrior and buffalo hunter, found himself so overcome by exhilaration during the excitement of battle he would fail, for the moment, to remember that this was only play-acting. When the action ceased, for the first time in his young life away from the stifling colonization of the reservation, he felt like a true Lakota instead of a ward of the American government.

After the surrender and death of Crazy Horse, the Oglala Lakota found themselves in a situation they had not anticipated when they were forced onto the reservation—they were starving again. They had gone without food on the Northern Plains when the buffalo and other game became scare, so they gave up their independence and came to the agency with the assurance of rations and shelter promised in treaty resolutions. Yet by the end of September 1877, the Lakota remained hungry as pledged food did not arrive.[18] By winter a few families left to join Sitting Bull's band in the Cypress Hills of Saskatchewan. If they were going to starve, at least they would starve as freemen.

Government corruption and apathy lead to additional broken promises, leading even Gen. Sherman, never considered an "Indian-lover," to define a reservation as "a parcel of land inhabited by Indians and surrounded by thieves."[19] The forced injustice was not lost on some government officials. Henry Benjamin Whipple, chairman of the Bureau of Indian Affairs, reported on the taking of the Black Hills in disregard of the 1868 treaty: "I know of no other instance in history where a great nation has so shamefully violated its oath. Our country must forever bear the disgrace and suffer the retribution of its wrongdoing. Our children's children will tell the sad story in hushed tones, and wonder how their fathers dared so to trample on justice and trifle with God."[20]

The Oglala Lakota were given a permanent place of residence north of a ridge of pines, amid South Dakota's rolling hills on the Nebraska border along White Clay Creek. Afraid of Hawk and his young family would reside under Red Cloud's leadership at Pine Ridge, eking out a living by farming and providing care for his father, Slow Bull, and his wife, Comes Out (*Tankal Iyaya*), into their senior years.[21] Earlier in 1872 when Afraid of Hawk was twenty-four years old, he married White Mountain (*Re Ska*), an Oyuhpke Oglala, daughter of Paints Himself Yellow.[22] She was a year younger, and together they would have at least eight and possibly eleven children, the oldest of which was Richard, born in November 1874, most likely in Wyoming;[23] the youngest was Fannie Afraid of Hawk born twenty years later in May 1895. They would eventually settle in the Wounded Knee District of the Pine Ridge Reservation.

The family converted to Episcopal Protestantism in 1893. Adopting Anglo-Christian custom, Afraid of Hawk took the first name of "Emil," while his children maintained "Afraid of Hawk" as their surnames. The family attended services at St. Mark's Mission Church, north of Manderson, and Emil attempted to farm the hardpan soil near Rockyford.[24] By 1879-80, the year according to Battiste Good's winter

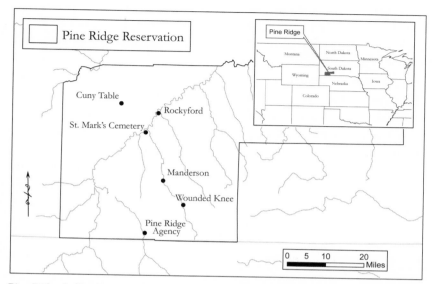

Pine Ridge Reservation

Pine Ridge

Montana | North Dakota | Minnesota

Wyoming | South Dakota

Nebraska | Iowa

Colorado

Cuny Table

Rockyford

St. Mark's Cemetery

Manderson

Wounded Knee

Pine Ridge
Agency

0   5   10   20
                    Miles

Pine Ridge Indian Reservation, South Dakota, highlighting places associated with the Afraid of Hawk family.

count, "Sent-the-boys-and-girls-to-school-winter,"[25] a third son was born to Afraid of Hawk and White Mountain, named *Itankusun wanbli* (Eagle Weasel), later, christened Albert.[26] The young Eagle Weasel/ Albert Afraid of Hawk, Lakota/Episcopalian grew up straddling two immensely dissimilar cultural worlds. As Eagle Weasel was taking his first formative steps as a "two-legged," the first reservation schools were founded to teach Lakota children English and the mores of Western society.[27] He was Lakota by birthright and self-identity, American by assimilation and acculturation.

Reservation life was extremely challenging in the late nineteenth century, even unbearable at times, but the Lakota used the same strength and determination they developed to survive by the hunt in the northern plains to adjust to the difficult changes thrust upon them.[28] Indian Agents ruled as lords and masters over confined Indigenous People. Elaine Goodale, who supervised education on Pine Ridge in 1890, said that agents ruled as "an absolute monarchy on a small scale—a little Russia in the midst of Republican America."[29]

Nonetheless the Lakota persisted, learning the new behaviors, adjusting to the demands of the dominant society. The Afraid of Hawk family strived hard to raise Albert and his siblings in a "sacred manner" with an emphasis on traditional ways[30] while being immersed into the most severe poverty and political domination they had ever experienced. Brought in at the bottom rung of the modern world system's economic ladder, the Lakota worked hard to cope with their new lives, both psychologically as well as physically. Farming and cattle ranching were the current economic production modes and the Lakota adapted, acquiring skills commensurate of settled life. Yet no matter how much toil they brought to their fields, farming the arid land yielded little in sustainable produce. Droughts and insects destroyed crops; cattle grew thin in the harsh winters and were prematurely slaughtered to feed starving families when government rations were not forthcoming. Epidemics, particularly tuberculosis and whooping cough, ravished the agencies, taking payment in human lives. The Lakota fought hard to ward off depression and maintain their sense of cultural identity. Alcohol took a heavy toll.

Assimilation focused primarily on Lakota children like Eagle Weasel, forcing them to attend day and boarding schools that were sometimes located within, or at great distances from, the reservations, separating students from their parents and friends for long, homesick periods of time; many never returned due to suicide and disease.[31] Along with the English language, boys were taught vocational skills such as carpentry, blacksmithing, and agriculture while girls learned domestic proficiencies primarily set around maintaining an orderly American household. When suspicious Lakota parents were reluctant to send their children to far-away boarding schools, American officials kidnapped and held children as hostages.[32] It was all for their betterment, Indian reformers rationalized. Richard Henry Pratt, who had experience as an army officer commanding a prisoner-of-war camp for the Seminoles in Florida and headed the infamous Carlisle Indian Industrial School in Pennsylvania, affirmed the government's goal at the boarding schools was to "kill the Indian in him and save the man,"[33] often justifying physical, mental, and sexual abuse to accomplish their goals.

Native religious beliefs were banned and dances restricted on the reservations and replaced with Christian theology. Roman Catholics (Black Robes), whose seven holy sacraments were viewed as analogous to the seven sacred rituals given by White Buffalo Calf Woman,[34] and Episcopalians (White Robes) set up missions at Pine Ridge and competed for Lakota souls. Traditional ceremonies were no longer permitted in public. The Sun Dance was especially prohibited. In a resistance movement, the sacred pipe, *chanunpa*, went underground, hidden by the Keeper for its preservation and protection. Lakota spiritualists responded by maintaining traditional rituals clandestinely in the privacy of tipis and plank houses and by modifying Christian concepts into patterns of their cultural worldview. The "Spirit of the World," *Wakan Tanka*,[35] became internalized in the Christian God. They amalgamated time-honored, cyclical forms of prayer into the linear form of catechism, merged healing ceremonies with stories of Jesus' miracles, and modified traditional beliefs within the adopted theology.

When Eagle Weasel was a mere seven-year-old student learning to read and write in English, Congress passed the General Allotment (Dawes) Act, which mandated the survey of Indian reservations for subdivision among individual tribal members. The act was designed to break up tribal unity by promoting individualism and capitalism. Each family head was allotted 160 acres of land as private property for farming and ranching. In Sen. Dawes view, assimilation of the Indian into western society was impeded because "there is no selfishness (among them) which is at the bottom of civilization."[36] Indian Nations remained powerless when Congress amended the act to allow the Secretary of the Interior to sell or lease "unallotted" lands to white settlers resulting in a massive land grab and a combined loss of more than ninety million acres of reservation territory across the country, depriving Native Americans of vital economic resources needed to survive.[37]

Based on the 1898 U. S. Indian Census for the Wounded Knee District of the Pine Ridge Reservation near Manderson, the teenaged Albert Afraid of Hawk was living in the household of his paternal grandfather, Slow Bull, where his education in the ethics and values of Lakota life would have been accentuated. Elders carry great responsibilities for the moral training of the young; it is meaningful that among all his sibs, it was Albert who moved into his grandfather's tipi. As a teenager Albert Afraid of Hawk's tutelage in conventional Lakota Ways would be enhanced under the guidance of Slow Bull, his mentor, his college professor in the mores of life and the traditional ways of the ancestors.

Albert's older brother, Richard, would also have been tutor to the developing youngster. Taking Albert under his wing, Richard taught his younger brother how to manufacture bow and arrows, how to shoot at prairie dogs and other small creatures, how to mount and ride horses without saddles, and even how to chase cattle, netting the animal in simulation of the buffalo hunt they were born too late to partake in. The boys strongly bonded with their common socialization into reservation life; their biological and cultural survival was predicated on their abilities to maintain Lakota heritage in their heart while travelling the White Man's Road. The brothers were inseparable.

Excavation proceeded slowly throughout the third morning due to the rate of skeletal decomposition. Where we were able to exhume Henry ʻŌpūkahaʻia in two full working days, Albert Afraid of Hawk would take seven. Gently working the edges of the compact bone with a bamboo pick, we attempted to avoid scraping away skeletal tissue which felt soft as the texture of butter, demanding a slow and tedious process but essential for the fullest recovery of Albert's remains. With the skeleton preserved, we called in our colleague, Dr. Gary Aronsen from Yale University's Anthropology Department, to conduct the forensic identification of Albert's remains. Gary and I had previously collaborated during the archaeological rescue of four historic burials inadvertently discovered during emergency room expansion at Yale-New Haven Hospital, which unwittingly had been built over a mid-nineteenth century Roman Catholic cemetery. Gary and I worked side-by-side during the final days of the exhumation.

Lightly brushing away soils on the left side of Albert's cranium in the area of the auditory canal, I encountered bristles emerging from the ground. My first impression was hair, but how could hair fibers survive in such acidic soils? We were fortunate to find the hard tissue of bone, I reasoned, let alone hair. Unsure, I removed a few more particles of soil, which yielded a green stain. Choosing a finer brush, I delicately swept the area, revealing the arrangement of three drilled copper beads and a short straight pin. Albert was wearing a copper/copper alloy earring. The metal had dissolved after decades in the ground, leaching cuprous minerals into the soil, neutralizing the pH in the immediate vicinity of the earring, and amazingly preserving strands of hair. In the field, Gary and I hypothesized that these strands could be horse, buffalo, or human hair, though such analysis would have to await laboratory results. Meanwhile, I cleared the right side of Albert's cranium and found evidence of a second copper earring.[38]

Absorbed in the discoveries and concentrating on the delicate work in the cranio-facial area, I hadn't realized that someone was calling down to me. "Nick, we need you up here. The family wants to do a ceremony."

"Of course," I said, slowly lifting myself up, needing a minute or two to respond after kneeling over the burial for hours. I covered Albert's face with a wet cloth to prevent drying and unwanted photographs. Soiled, wearing a sweaty tee shirt and dungarees ripped at the knees, I slowly climbed the ladder out of the burial unit and was told the family wished to conduct a Lakota Giveaway and Naming Ceremony.

Emerging to ground level, I noticed a large crowd of people, some invited, some not. Tania Porta had made a public statement in the city newspaper, asking people to respect the privacy of the family during the disinterment and not to come out to the cemetery,[39] but the curiosity of some could not be resisted. Reporters from various newspapers were on the scene, asking questions and taking photographs. The press was told in no uncertain terms that photographs of the skeletal remains would not be tolerated. Unaccustomed to this kind of media attention, Richard Red Elk laughed, "They are like magpies."

With members of the crew staying behind to watch over Albert's grave, we followed the family downhill to a grassy terrace above the small pond. With water and woodland as a backdrop, five lawn chairs were set up in a semi-circle and I was instructed to have a seat. Beside me were Bob and Mary-Jo Young, Christine Rose, and Tania Porta, none of us quite sure what to expect.

A family procession led by Richard Red Elk rhythmically beating a buffalo-hide drum and John Afraid of Hawk blowing the eagle whistle entered the grassy knoll and halted in front of us. Daniel spoke for the family, "This is a special day for Albert Afraid of Hawk. He has been here for 112 years. Now he can go home." Referring to St. Mark's Cemetery on the Pine Ridge Indian Reservation, Daniel continued, "My father, my mother, my aunts have been there for a long time. That is where we will take Albert."[40] Daniel prayed a Lakota prayer, turning in time to face the north, east, south, and west. Everyone in attendance, even newspaper reporters, paused from flashing cameras and note taking to follow Daniel's lead honoring the four directions.[41] With the scent of burning sage filtering through the air, Red Elk sang, drummed, and acknowledged that *Wakan Tanka*, the Creator, was at work in the cemetery. The family then gave special thanks to five of us instrumental in Albert's return, bestowing distinction in Giveaway and Naming Ceremonies.

Generosity is one of the venerated traits of the Lakota, the *otuhan* or "give-away," emphasizing its significance. Traditionally and in modern life all major events are occasions for a Giveaway Ceremony—birth, death, graduation, marriage, in times of sorrow, joy, or to give honor.[42] Initiated when the Lakota were buffalo hunters on the High Plains, the ceremony afforded a redistribution of wealth, providing poorer families with food and goods. As times improved for the receiving families, they would reciprocate, balancing the needs of tribal members so no one went without. Today among the Lakota, the Giveaway, *Wopila* (literally "thank you") remains a significant social event. The Afraid of Hawk family had their prayers answered with the discovery of Albert's remains, and they wanted to give thanks for the benevolence.

One of the seven sacred rituals given to the Lakota by White Buffalo Calf Woman is the *"Hunka"* or the making of relatives. The modern equivalent is the "Naming Ceremony" and is used to adopt non-relatives ritually into the *tiospaye*.[43] By receiving a Lakota name, the bearer enters into a special relationship with the sponsor, in this case the Afraid of Hawk family, establishing closely-linked social bonds. During the ceremony the sponsor explains the significance of the name bestowed on the adoptee, prays, and sings an honoring song.[44]

In his expression of gratitude, Daniel individually called out our new names while Richard sang and Marlis and John stepped forward with gifts—John presenting to the men, Marlis to the women. Bob Young was appropriately given the name "He Who Found Lakota Boy" while John draped a star quilt blanket around his shoulders and handed him a braided string of sweet grass. With a star quilt draped around her shoulders, Mary-Jo Young was christened "Her House is Always Happy." The name chosen by the family for Tania Porta, "She Is Always There to Help People," was presented together with a star quilt blanket and the Cheyenne River Sioux Reservation banner. Giving away the tribal flag was Marlis's way of thanking the people on the reservation for their support, allowing the Afraid of Hawk family to travel to Connecticut. Tania unsuccessfully fought back tears as the two women tightly embraced. Christine Rose was also bestowed with gifts and given the Lakota name "She Who Brings Good News." Lastly,

John Afraid of Hawk congratulates author during Lakota Naming Ceremony, Wooster Cemetery, Danbury, CT, August 2012. (Courtesy of David Smith.)

John Afraid of Hawk placed a star quilt blanket over my shoulders and removed a glass-beaded chain from around his neck and placed it over mine. The colorful medallion of the necklace was emblazoned with the image of a buffalo skull surrounded by a medicine wheel from which hung glass beads and five loops of buffalo hair. I was honored with the Lakota name *Tāku wan Waste' Okīlē*, "He Who Finds Good," a sweet sentiment impossible to live up to.

As the ceremony abated amid hugs and handshakes, Bruce Greene caught everyone's attention by pointing up at the clear sky. A large red-tailed hawk had flown out of the wooded area across the pond and begun circling overhead, screeching and looping above us. We were all silenced, marveling as we watched. This had been the second hawk attracting attention that week. The day prior to the Afraid of Hawk family's arrival in Danbury, Bob and Mary-Jo had observed a rarely seen hawk perched on a tree branch in their backyard. It announced itself by releasing a high-pitched cry until it was noticed, and having been, flying off to the west, the direction that the family was coming from as if to herald their arrival and escort them to Danbury. Marlis alone understood the true meaning. "(Albert's) spirit has been lifted," she said. "He has gone up into that hawk."[45]

Short Man Count, Oglala Lakota, 1889, "Three Stars made a treaty."[46]

As the brothers developed through childhood, they became increasingly aware of the continued threats to their cultural lives. They overheard the voices of their parents, Afraid of Hawk and White Mountain, speaking within the privacy of their tipi about increased *wasichus* demands for more Lakota land. With North and South Dakota statehood, railroad interests and land speculators were no longer satisfied with the reduction of the Great Sioux Reservation in 1876. Swelling numbers of white settlers beleaguered government officials in Washington to turn over more Indian land for their own farming and expansion.

The original Sioux Reservation stipulated in the 1868 Fort Laramie Treaty consisted of nearly 60,000,000 acres; with the Agreement of 1876 it was reduced to fewer than 22,000,000 acres. Even so, by

1888 white settlers clamored for more land. To pacify them, the federal government herded the Lakota into six smaller reservations carved from the existing agencies (Pine Ridge, Rosebud, Cheyenne River, Standing Rock, Crow Creek, and Lower Brule), opening further territory for white settlement. It would get worse. No Lakota residents were allowed to leave the boundaries of the smaller reservations without a pass from their respective Indian Agents, meaning that unless the government approved, they could not go out to hunt when food was limited or to visit relatives off their reservation. They were literally being held in concentration camps, confined by the authority of the U. S. government, creating "fear and resignation" as well as "resentment and resistance" among the Lakota, who were being treated as "colonial subjects."[47]

Eagle Weasel was ten years old when the drought of 1889 struck, forcing thousands of white farmers, who clamored for more Indian land, to abandon their fields as they dried up and fled South Dakota.[48] For the Lakota, whose cultivated fields also lay barren, there were no such options because of their containment. Wild game could not be found and even the normally productive creek bottoms yielded no wild plants to harvest. When these economic hardships were combined with government annuity reductions, malnutrition and starvation ensued. Compounding their dilemma, Lakota cattle contracted blackleg disease, reducing their herds dramatically.[49] With few economic alternatives available, the Lakota were once again famished and by now totally reliant on the federal government which continued to fail them.

To children like Eagle Weasel and his siblings, malnourishment made them particularly susceptible to epidemics. Communicable diseases such as measles, influenza, and whooping cough severely assailed Pine Ridge, resulting on average in the deaths of forty-five Lakota men, women, and children every month from 1888 to 1890. Their whole world seemed to be in upheaval. Man and nature were dying. The buffalo had disappeared. The Sacred Hoop was broken. Black Elk, having returned to Pine Ridge after a European tour with Buffalo Bill's Wild West, had seen hunger and death among his people before but never like this—"our people were pitiful and in despair."[50]

Short Man Count, Oglala Lakota, 1888, *Anpa wi wan te*, "Eclipse of the Sun."[51]

The sound was distant and indiscernible, coming from the mountain peaks, calling out to him in an inaudible voice. Jack Wilson put down his axe and ceased his woodcutting labor to concentrate, listening intently. The intonation remained indistinct, though seeming like a voice calling out to him.

Wilson was the surname of the white family he lived with and worked for in Mason Valley, Nevada, but his Northern Paiute name was *Quoitze Ow*. More often, though, he was called *Wovoka* (Wood-Cutter)[52] after his primary occupation felling cedar and pinion trees for use as mining shafts and charcoal smelting operations. He also cut cordwood for winter fireplaces and fences for his *tibo'o* (white) employers, which he was performing when he first heard the voice.[53]

Setting aside his labors, Wovoka ascended the steep slopes hoping to get closer to the sound and distinguish its command, but soon exertion yielded to dizziness. Grabbing hold of a tree branch for support, he pushed himself forward, compelled to hear the message calling out to him. His legs became heavy, his head spun, his body burned with fever; he became disoriented with the ground seeming above his feet and the mountaintop below. He fell exhausted, rolling onto his back. Lying amid the rocky slope and pinion, along the earthen trail, in search of the beckoning voice, he died. And when he died, the sun disappeared.

In death, Wovoka travelled to a resplendent spirit world: green and lush with vegetation, game abounded, people were young and healthy, dancing and singing. He recognized ancestors who had died years ago in their advanced ages looking in the vigor of their youth, and white men and Indians living peacefully together, enjoying the magnificence of their eternal domain.

In this exhilarating, heavenly world, Jesus Christ took Wovoka aside, disclosing the wonders of paradise and imparting a message for him to bring back to the Indian people who "must be good and love one another, have no quarrelling and live in peace with the whites; that they must work and not lie or steal; that they must put away all the old practices that savored war; that if they faithfully obeyed His instructions they would be reunited with their friends in this beautiful creation where there would be no more death, hunger, sickness, or old age."[54] God revealed to Wovoka a dance the Indians should do in intervals consisting of five consecutive days. If they were loyal to this ritual, He would hasten the date for their reunion with the dead and secure their personal happiness. Wovoka, the prophet of this revelation, was granted powers to control weather and perform miracles before being sent back to earth. And when Wovoka awoke on the bed of his lodge, the sun reappeared, and he was perceived as having saved the world.[55]

By the fall of 1889, amid the hardships of land reduction, drought, disease, and unyielding death, rumors of a Messiah had come to the Lakota. The Messiah, they were told, was grieved by the suffering of the Indian people. He had come to earth once before and was killed by white men. His Second Coming would favor the downtrodden Indian by destroying the world, not by water as in Noah's time, but by a new layer of earth, burying the world except for the believers, creating a new social order in which faithful Indians would be reunited with their ancestors in joy and everlasting happiness. But could all this be true?

Red Cloud and other Lakota leaders decided to investigate and sent a delegation west to meet this Messiah to confirm or refute the swelling rumors. Lakota representatives, including Good Thunder, Short Bull, and Kicking Bear, travelled to Nevada, heard and spoke with the prophet privately. Wovoka had them look into his hat and witness the beauty of heaven and the new world.[56] Convinced, they returned home disciples of the new religion, conveying a renewed zeal for the future, giving the Lakota reason for hope, for survival, for a future for their children, and a reunion with their ancestors.[57] They interpreted Wovoka's message to mean that the *wasichus* would disappear, and the Buffalo Nation would return to its former glory. *Tatanka* had disappeared, returning to its home within Wind Cave, not because it was slaughtered to near extinction but because of the disrespect given to its spirit.[58] Dance the "Ghost Dance" the Messiah taught, and the buffalo would reappear in the newly created world. Not all Lakota believed the message; many remained skeptical. But for those who had faith, Wovoka's message took on a sacred meaning, combining redemptive, messianic Christianity with its belief in the resurrection of the dead and Indigenous metaphysics and ritual dancing, spread joyously throughout the western reservations.[59]

Lakota believers danced, beginning with the participants fasting and undergoing purification rites in a sweat lodge. Cleansed, both men and women devotees arranged themselves in a large circle, clasping hands. In the center of the loop, a sacred cottonwood tree was mounted, adorned with offerings, taking on the familiar aspect of the prohibited Sun Dance. Celebrants wore specially decorated "ghost shirts" and dresses[60] made of white cotton cloth cut from flour sacks, embodied with images of eagles, moons, and stars drawn on their fronts and backs. Wovoka gave Good Thunder sacred red paint and told him that the people must apply it to their faces when they danced.[61] Sidestepping and singing continuously, around and around the circle, for hours on end, day after day, they danced until exhaustion overtook their fatigued bodies. Many fainted, lapsing into trance states that brought visions of their resurrected dead relatives; visions of large buffalo herds giving themselves freely for their Teton relatives; visions of a world with independence and freedom bereft of *wasichus* imprisonment; visions of their resurrected children who had died in their arms;[62] visions of a restored sacred hoop; visions so powerful and realistic that they cried when they awoke from their trance state and found themselves back among the living on the wretched reservation.

Black Elk remained a nonbeliever until he attended a Ghost Dance ceremony at Wounded Knee Creek, astounded by how personal it was to him. As a child, Black Elk had had a sacred vision, which in part included a "tree painted red with most of its branches cut off and some dead leaves on it."[63] He witnessed that very same tree at the center of the Ghost Dance ceremony. His youthful vision seemed recreated in life. Men and women, young and old, assimilationists and traditionalists,[64] holding hands in the circle mirrored the sacred hoop that would give the tree the power to bloom again. Overcome with happiness, he was henceforth a believer, dressing himself "in a sacred manner,"[65] fashioning Ghost Dance shirts with designs from his youthful apparition. Black Elk made his first ghost shirt for Afraid of Hawk.[66]

While conducting archival research, Bob Young was having difficulty finding primary sources for "Afraid of Hawk" in assorted Indian
documents. He was not a noted chief, not a signer of treaties, nor ever
interviewed by historians concerning accounts of his life. Nonetheless, Afraid of Hawk does represent thousands of Lakota men who
fought anonymously in battles to protect their Indigenous way of life;
who looked for means to accommodate the U. S. government in order
to feed and shelter their families; who taught traditional values within
a changing world; and who placed themselves in harm's way in hopes
of finding a better life for their children and grandchildren. With pro-
spective aspirations for his family, Afraid of Hawk embraced what the
wasichus called the "Messiah Craze."[67]

"Afraid of Hawk" is listed in a key government record suggesting
the family's participation in the Ghost Dance Movement. In 1891, the
U. S. government commissioned Special Agent James A. Cooper of the
Office of Indian Affairs to accept compensation applications from Pine
Ridge families who had suffered damage to their property from the per-
secution of Indian Wars culminating at Wounded Knee Creek. Agent
Cooper processed 755 compensation claims, including one from Red
Cloud, and distributed a total of $100,000 to tribal members. Cooper
denied only six applications, one of which was submitted by Afraid of
Hawk (Claim No. 191), seeking $600 for damages done to his prop-
erty by soldiers. When interviewed concerning his whereabouts during
Wounded Knee, Afraid of Hawk testified that he was in the Badlands
with Short Bull, one of the Lakota delegates who met with Wovoka
and a known Ghost Dance leader at the Stronghold where the last
ceremony was held prior to the Wounded Knee Massacre.[68] Afraid of
Hawk's application was denied due to his suspected participation and
possible leadership role in the Ghost Dance.[69] Written in hand at the
top of Afraid of Hawk's application was the word "Hostile."

The reservation police (*ceska maza*) burst through his front door
before the sun had crested above the horizon on the freezing, drizzly
morning of Dec. 15, 1890.[70] Sitting Bull was asleep on the floor of his
log house in the south central section of the Standing Rock Reservation along Grand River. The police, brother Hunkpapa, aroused him

and told him that he was under arrest and must come with them. He was half-awake but agreed to do so, sending a wife for his clothes at another house and having his favorite horse saddled.

By the time the Hunkpapa medicine man was escorted outside, a large crowd of camp dwellers, many there to participate in a Ghost Dance, had been awakened by the commotion of barking dogs and gathered outside Sitting Bull's cabin. When he was lead out into the front yard, his followers encircled, closing in on the police, pressing forward and demanding the chief's release. The *ceska maza* attempted to open a path to their horses whilst chastised by Sitting Bull's people for doing a white man's job. As he was led away, Sitting Bull, seeing the agitation among his followers and family, called out that he would not go and started to resist the arrest. The police wrestled him forward toward his horse.

Catch-the-Bear, a camp follower, demanded the chief be let go and pulled a rifle out from under his blanket. He fired directly at Police Lieut. Henry Bull Head, hitting him in the side of his body.[71] Before he fell, Bull Head instantly spun and discharged his rifle, not into Catch-The-Bear, but into the unarmed Sitting Bull, unleashing a bullet into his chest. Second Police Sergeant Red Tomahawk simultaneously put a second bullet into the back of Sitting Bull's head.[72] The Hunkpapa holy man, arguably the most famous and feared Native American in history, dropped limply to the ground. Chaos and panic ensued. Hand-to-hand combat erupted. Catch-the-Bear was shot and killed while the near forty Indian police[73] drove Sitting Bull's followers back into a timber area.[74] The fight lasted only a few minutes but resulted in the eventual deaths of six policemen and eight followers, including Sitting Bull's fourteen-year-old son, Crow Foot.[75] To the Lakota, Sitting Bull's death was a plotted assassination.

Short Man, Iron Crow and No Ears Counts, Oglala Lakota, 1890, *Si tanka ktepi*, "Big Foot is Killed."[76]

Word quickly spread through the "moccasin telegraph" that Sitting Bull had been killed resisting arrest as had Crazy Horse before him, and that the U. S. Army was preparing to hunt down and assassinate all Lakota chiefs involved in the Ghost Dance Movement. In fear of reprisals Sitting Bull's people fled south to Hump's camp on the Cheyenne River Sioux Reservation. Chief Spotted Elk, also known as Big Foot, was en route to the Standing Rock Agency at Fort Bennett to receive annuities when Sitting Bull's refugees arrived. Anticipating trouble because of his strong involvement with the Ghost Dance, Big Foot reversed his trek, heading home and taking with him more than seventy of Sitting Bull and Hump's people.[77]

Approximately 400 Lakota under the leadership of Big Foot, two-thirds women and children, were intercepted Dec. 21 by Lt. Col. V. C. Sumner's Eighth Cavalry, under orders to capture the refugees from Sitting Bull's camp and to arrest Big Foot for imprisonment at Fort Meade until the Ghost Dance "hysteria" died down. Counseling with Sumner, Big Foot gave the clear impression he and his Lakota were peaceful and would go with the colonel to Fort Bennett as commanded.[78]

Events changed rapidly, however, when Big Foot's people approached their homes and refused to go to the fort as ordered. The Miniconjou chief could do little to control their fears and anxieties. When the Lakota did not mobilize immediately for Fort Bennett, Sumner sent John Dunn, a local rancher friendly with Big Foot, to urge the chief to set off at once. However, the rancher created further angst when he told the Indians that he had overheard soldiers saying all Lakota men would be captured and removed from their families for transport to an "island in the ocean to the east."[79]

Worried warriors wanted to flee to Pine Ridge where Red Cloud had recently extended an invitation for Big Foot to join him to discuss the Ghost Dance with army officials and help convince the Stronghold participants, Afraid of Hawk apparently among them, to surrender. With an impending arrest, the Miniconjou chief agreed that Red Cloud offered the best means of protection for his followers. By the next morning Big Foot's camp had vanished, tipis were dismantled and wagons loaded during the night. They quietly eluded the soldiers heading south without detection. They were escaping.

The U. S. Army now had more than 3,000 soldiers in operation in the Lakota territory, its largest military buildup since the Civil War.[80] Believing Big Foot's party hostile and well-armed, orders were issued to arrest, subdue, and destroy them if resisted.[81] The Seventh Cavalry, revived since the Battle of Little Bighorn, arrived at Pine Ridge, Dec. 23, 1890[82] amid formation of a crisis situation.[83]

Big Foot's group moved rapidly until the chief came down with pneumonia on Christmas Day, slowing their rate of travel dramatically. The U. S. Cavalry searched for them along the main road leading to Pine Ridge, but Big Foot eluded detection by taking a little known trail through the Badlands that descended vertically for more than 200 feet. The path was just wide enough for a single horse to be coaxed down its steep slopes. To maneuver, the men used axes and spades cutting a wider path and made use of ropes to precipitously lower wagons one at a time. With care and perseverance the Lakota successfully navigated the drop descending onto the Pine Ridge Reservation.[84]

Big Foot's Lakota suffered greatly during the march with shadowing federal troops to their backs and winter blizzards in their faces. No fires were permitted, little noise made, insufficient sleep gotten as they camped late and rose early constantly in motion.[85] Hunger consumed them. The wintry winds shivered through their bones but they persevered, impelled on by hopes of reaching the safety offered by Red Cloud and food and shelter provided by their Lakota kin at Pine Ridge.

Eventually, Maj. Samuel M. Whitside's column of Seventh Cavalry intercepted them on December 28th at Porcupine Butte. Although the Lakota hoisted a white flag, distrust compelled both sides to form into immediate combat positions. Big Foot requested a parlay with Whitside while warriors and cavalry looked on in nervous anticipation. Whitside refused to talk and demanded unconditional surrender. Big Foot complied.[86] Whitside ordered the Indians to make camp along Wounded Knee Creek (*Cankpe Opi Wakpala*), and an army ambulance moved forward to receive the Miniconjou chief who was hemorrhaging blood through his nose. Big Foot relocated his people into a small vale, setting up temporary tipis made of brush and branches covered with blankets and robes.[87] Among them was 13-year-old Richard Afraid of Hawk, Albert's older brother.[88]

That night while encamped at Wounded Knee Creek, four additional cavalry troops under the command of Col. James W. Forsyth arrived, transporting two light artillery Hotchkiss cannons augmenting the two mounted from Whitside's command. Forsyth was now the ranking officer on the field, and his presence brought the total army force to 470 soldiers, far outnumbering the refugees, which consisted mostly of women and children. The Lakota erected a white flag outside Big Foot's tent as a visible sign of their pacifist intentions and hopeful safety as both sides settled into an uneasy evening, especially the Lakota, many of whom did not sleep or have stomach to eat as they watched troopers set up the four Hotchkiss cannons on a small knoll northwest of the camp, pointing ominously at their tipis.[89]

As the Seventh Cavalry attended to their sunrise details and Big Foot's Lakota awoke from their restless night, the morning of Dec. 29, 1890 in the "Moon of the Popping Trees" dawned cold, though clear and sunny. At approximately 8 a.m., Col. Forsyth positioned two lines of soldiers, infantrymen in front of mounted cavalry, around the perimeter surrounding the Indian camp. The Hotchkiss guns were primed and their ammunition stacked close by. Big Foot's followers were essentially corralled.

Forsyth summoned all the adult Lakota men out of the their tipis to convene at a designated council circle in front of Big Foot's tent. He explained through an interpreter that they were considered prisoners of war and ordered the surrender of all firearms and knives which none of the Lakota men were anxious to give up since they needed their guns for hunting and protection. They dreaded the moment of disarmament.[90] When only a few old guns were presented, Forsyth was convinced the Lakota were holding out, hiding their armaments for possible employment against him and his troops.

Although ordered by his superior, Gen. Nelson Miles, to keep his soldiers and Indians separated, Forsyth was irritated and as a show of force instructed his soldiers to advance as close as ten yards from the warriors and form a line, while ordering others in his command to search the Indian camp. Soldiers entered tipis, conducting their business in a brash and determined manner, driving women and children out, upending bedding, rummaging through personal belongings, spuming garments over the ground.[91] Some Lakota women were physically inspected and became overwrought at the disruption. Striving to assist their women, Lakota men were forcibly shoved back to the council area by the line of troopers.[92]

Big Foot, sick and incapacitated, was carried out of his hospital tent on a stretcher and set down in the council circle. His head was covered with a scarf, and he wore an overcoat for warmth. He was too weak to maintain an upright position so he spoke lying down, telling his warriors to be patient, do as Forsyth commanded, and take courage that there were too many women, children, and old men among them for anything bad to happen.[93]

Amid the council circle, a medicine man, Good Thunder[94] of the Rosebud Reservation, his face painted green and wearing his "ghost shirt," stood singing and dancing around the circle, stopping occasionally to scoop up dirt, casting the soil into the air in the direction of the soldiers behind the circle, symboling that the earth would soon swallow up the bluecoats as decreed in Wovoka's prophetic vision. Forsyth was able to get Good Thunder to sit down while the search continued for concealed weapons.

When only thirty-eight guns, some new but most old and worthless, were recovered, Forsyth further ordered the search of Indian men in the council circle for the possibility of weapons concealed under their clothing. Two soldiers approached Black Coyote,[95] who was deaf and carrying a rifle, surprising him from behind. Taking hold of Black Coyote's arms, they grappled with him to remove his firearm, which he held above his head, shouting in his Native language that he had paid plenty for the gun and was not going to give it up without compensation, none of which the soldiers understood. Amid the commotion, Good Thunder once again rose, tossing more dirt into the air and blowing on an eagle-bone whistle. As suspicion and uncertainty escalated, a gunshot rang out. In the struggle for Black Coyote's firearm, the gun accidently discharged skyward; it was the spark that set their world ablaze.

Impulsively, Forsyth ordered his line of soldiers to "Fire," setting off a volley in such unison that it sounded like a single shot[96] directly into the crowded council circle, killing more than forty Lakota men instantly at close range, their bodies toppled onto each other. While the wounded rolled on the ground in painful agony, Lakota survivors responded by attacking the soldiers with hidden knives, war clubs, concealed firearms, and whatever they could retrieve from the pile of confiscated weapons. With few Indian guns available, desperate hand-to-hand combat ensued. Panic and chaos took hold as each side thrashed against the other.

Hell broke loose when the four Hotchkiss cannons opened fire, pouring two-pound explosives from the northwest knoll, striking with the effect of bombs directly into the Lakota tipis, exploding them to shreds, entrapping women and children. Youngsters playing within the camp moments before, some dressed in reservation school uniforms,[97] were senseless victims of the carnage. The percussion shells of the Hotchkiss guns were unmerciful, wiping out every living thing in their range.[98] The killing was unrestrained, indiscriminate. Survivors of the immediate bloodshed ran in all directions, some for only short distances before soldiers' marksmanship felled them. When the bluecoats' line broke to race after Big Foot's fleeing people, Forsyth lost control of his army.

Thirteen-year-old Richard Afraid of Hawk was trapped in the melee.[99] Running amid the terror of the cannon explosions, he tripped, falling to the parched ground. Before he could right himself, an army trooper appeared, straddled over him, rifle pointed directly at Richard's head. The boy instinctively raised his arm to cover his face shielding him from impending death. The trooper squeezed the trigger but without report. The gun had jammed, overheated due to repeated heavy firing. The trooper scrambled to repair his firearm, but before he could engage the teenaged Lakota in a hand-to-hand struggle, Richard bounded from the ground, his young legs propelling him through an alignment of soldiers toward a ravine leading into Wounded Knee Creek, south of the encampment.[100]

Bullets swirled around Richard when he came to the steep embankment of the ravine, but rather than providing protection, he saw a company of soldiers shooting other Lakota attempting to flee down the slopes. The dry, fifty-foot deep ravine was filled with smoke from the guns and dust kicked up high by the soldiers' bullets. One of the Hotchkiss guns was rolled down to the ravine to be more effective in killing the refugees who amassed there, seeking shelter among dense plum bushes. Women with their children ran for the ravine while others spilled up the road, heading west toward an abandoned Lakota settlement. The majority would not get away. Enraged soldiers on horseback pursued women and children, chasing and killing their victims for a distance of three miles. One Lakota woman, whose baby's head was shot off her back while she ran to the ravine, grabbed the gun of a dead solider and fired at an Army officer who rode by her, killing him instantly with a bullet through the skull.[101] Women dug holes into the ravine to hide their babies from deadly gunfire.[102]

Unarmed amidst the chaos, Richard retreated back toward the encampment, finding an empty wagon in which to hide. When bullets penetrated the wagon's wooden sides, Richard jumped out. Running up a hill where he didn't see any soldiers, he was fast enough to escape over the distant hills.[103] Afraid of Hawk's son narrowly escaped death that morning, but for the remainder of his life he could not escape the anguished memory of the slaughter.

Big Foot, debilitated and lying on the ground in the council circle, had been mortally wounded, shot through the back. His agonizing movements caught the attention of soldiers who thought he was feigning death and shot him multiple times. Big Foot's daughter ran to her father's aid, but she, too, was shot in the back, collapsing beside him.[104]

Bodies of Lakota men were mostly concentrated around the council circle where the first burst of intensive gunfire occurred, but the dead corpses of women and children were scattered throughout the countryside, lying in pools of their own blood. The killing was not simply a terrible cross-cultural misunderstanding or a reflexive response to a supposed military threat; rather, it was a deliberate, systematic attempt to annihilate Big Foot's Lakota.[105] The Seventh Cavalry, some of whom shouted "Remember Custer!" during the bloodbath, finally had had their revenge.[106]

The last of the Ghost Dance participants at the Stronghold, including Short Bull, Kicking Bear, and possibly Afraid of Hawk, were travelling to Pine Ridge to surrender when they heard the gunfire. They learned of the slaughter of Big Foot's Lakota when they arrived. Some would flee and join follow Ghost Dance advocates at White Clay Creek to continue the fighting.[107]

When the guns ceased firing around noon, the U. S. Army picked up its dead and wounded and left for Pine Ridge Agency. Lakota bodies would remain on the killing fields, lying distorted in their death postures. That evening, snow fell and winter winds howled. The blizzard obscured the landscape; drifting snow cloaked the corpses. The ravine had become "one long grave of butchered women and children and babies."[108]

The Holy Cross Episcopal Church at the Pine Ridge Agency was still decked out with Christmas buntings when the first wagons arrived filled with Wounded Knee survivors. Pews had been removed and straw was scattered over the floor to tend to the mostly women and children who had been injured during the conflagration.[109] Big Foot's wife arrived among the refugees. She would join her husband and daughter in death within two weeks.[110] While the Christmas tree had been removed from the church, a sign proclaiming "Peace On Earth, Goodwill To Men," still hung behind the altar.[111]

Four days after the massacre, a burial party made up of an army escort and civilian workers descended on the killing fields. Tipi poles stood like skeletons, their blanket and hide coverings incinerated by the Hotchkiss cannons. Army officers counted forty-seven dead warrior bodies in the council area, while those of women and children lay throughout the distant hills. Fresh wagon tracks deposited on the snow revealed that the Pine Ridge community had already removed some of the deceased, keeping the body count lower than the actual number of deaths recorded.[112]

Relic hunters scavenged, removing moccasins, ghost shirts, and other personal items as souvenirs off the dead.[113] Good Thunder's corpse lay frozen, his face blackened by death and frost. A photographer placed a rifle by the side of the medicine man to enhance the visual effect of a battlefield confrontation.[114] Big Foot was photographed in his death pose, propped up so his face would be visible to the camera.[115] Four infants were found lying beside their dead mother, who had wrapped the babies in shawls to protect them from the bitter cold in a final effort to save her children. Only one survived.[116]

A trench, sixty feet long by six feet wide and six feet deep,[117] was dug to serve as a mass grave, caustically situated upon the knoll where the Hotchkiss guns poured down their lethal explosive shells. One hundred and forty-six bodies, some stripped of clothing and jewelry, were interred into the trench, "piled one upon the other like so much cordwood until the pit was full (and) the earth was heaped over them."[118] The Lakota would resent that the government did not provide individual graves for the victims[119] and interpreted the heartless burial process as evidence of revenge by the Seventh Cavalry.[120] Mourners painted posts erected at the burial site with red pigment given to them by Wovoka for the Ghost Dance.[121] Although accounts differ on the number of Lakota casualties— to this day it is impossible to know— accepted estimates suggest that somewhere between 250 and 350 tribal members were killed at Wounded Knee Creek, including more than 200 women and children.[122]

Wounded Knee was the horrific, concluding act of the government to colonize American Indians through genocide, ethnocide, and ecocide. The "Ghost Dance" was a religious revitalization movement that preached tolerance and benevolence toward the *wasichu*s, adopting fundamental precepts of Christianity as its foundation.[123] It has been argued that for adherents to go on the warpath against the U. S. government would be the equivalent of the followers of a Christian evangelist threatening our armed forces.[124] It denied the Lakota and other tribes, who had been dehumanized, starved, and confined to concentration camps, the religious freedom granted all white settlers on which the country was founded.[125] Red Cloud presented the case for his people's acceptance of the new religion, "We felt that we were mocked in our misery....You who eat three meals a day, and see your children well and happy around you, can't understand what starving Indians feel. We were faint with hunger and maddened by despair. We held our dying children and felt their little bodies tremble as their souls went out and left only a dead weight in our hands.... There was no hope on earth and God seemed to have forgotten us....They screamed like crazy men to Him for mercy. They caught at the promises they heard He made."[126]

In the immediate aftermath, the Seventh Cavalry was celebrated but soon found itself in desperate need to persuade the American public that Wounded Knee was a military battle and not a massacre initiated for Custer's revenge. As a result, U. S. Army officials cited thirty-two soldiers for bravery, and Congress awarded twenty soldiers the Medal of Honor.[127] Considering that only three Medal of Honor awards were given out to South Dakota soldiers during World War II, the inflated honors given for Wounded Knee suspiciously exaggerated the battle, condoning the army's actions in killing women and children.[128] General Nelson Miles officially reprimanded Col. Forsyth for his conduct at Wounded Knee, charging him with disobedience and incompetence. Miles was convinced that the majority of the army's thirty-five casualties had resulted from "friendly fire" because of Forsyth's troop arrangement encircling the Indians.[129] A military court of inquiry had to exonerate Forsyth; failure to do so would officially admit to the slaughter of innocents. Miles considered the whole affair a great embarrassment, labeling the Army's actions an "abominable criminal military blunder."[130]

In the year following Wounded Knee, William "Buffalo Bill" Cody received permission from the federal government to have the Lakota Ghost Dance leaders, including Short Bull and Kicking Bear, who were being held prisoners at Fort Sheridan, Illinois, released into his custody for his 1891 European Wild West tour.[131] When the Wild West was originally formulated, Cody employed Pawnees as his primary "Show Indians," though he also included Cheyenne, Arapaho, Crow, and Lakota. Placing long-time enemies in close proximity to each other created too many problems, so after he persuaded Sitting Bull to spend one year (1885) with his exhibition, he preferred to rely exclusively on Lakota performers.

"Indian Reformers" and the federal Office of Indian Affairs expressed their annoyance at the War Department for releasing the Ghost Dance prisoners and directed their criticism at Cody, who they accused of using "coercive powers to control the Indians."[132] Thomas Morgan, OIA commissioner, began an investigation into the effect the Wild West had on Indian performers, noting that six Lakota had died in Europe while with Buffalo Bill in 1889. Morgan cited their ill health to improper care by the show's management, also arguing the production held Indians back from making assimilative progress by permitting them to "relive" their fading past, recreating rituals, dances, and acts of violence.[133] Morgan was so distraught about the decision that he warned tribal members at Pine Ridge to be strongly advised that anyone cooperating with Buffalo Bill should not look for any further assistance, in any way, from the OIA.[134]

Cody refuted these attacks testifying that Indians performing with his show were self-supporting, reducing government spending and lessening the potential for further Indian troubles. He also countered that he provided them with regular food, medical care, and income, as well as the right to employment at a job of their choice like other American workers. Addressing the question of Indian fatalities while overseas, Cody was quick to point out the death rate among his Indians in Europe (10%) was comparable to the percentages of death on the Pine Ridge Reservation (5-10%) in 1889.[135] If anything, Cody argued, he was educating the Lakota by introducing them to the ways of Western civilization, and the opportunity to travel throughout America and Europe was a positive factor in furthering the process of assimilation.[136] The Department of Interior agreed and overruled Commissioner Morgan, removing the recruitment ban and releasing the Ghost Dance prisoners to travel to Europe with Cody for one year.[137] Morgan and the Indian Reformers were incensed.

To their further dismay, Native Americans in general did not share the Reformers' concerns. Although being stereotyped in their "savage state," Indians often welcomed the opportunity to travel and leave the hardship of the reservations where they were banned from wearing traditional clothing and performing rituals and dances, all of which Cody allowed his show Indians to do on the road.[138] Travelling with the Wild West was a means of escape from the fixity of reservation life, providing opportunities to take part in the modern world.[139] A Lakota delegation that travelled to Washington after Wounded Knee signed a document saying they had no objection to their young men travelling with Buffalo Bill's show.[140] Nonetheless, the OIA discouraged the Lakota from joining the Wild West, threatening to arrest any managers from the show attempting to recruit Indians at Pine Ridge.

Regardless of these controversies, Albert Afraid of Hawk was more than willing to join up with Buffalo Bill ten years later and continue the excitement of participating in the regeneration of Plains Indian battles he performed in Omaha. Albert longed to accomplish what his father and grandfather before him had when they were his age: taking part in buffalo hunts, wearing Lakota dress, maintaining rituals, fighting for honor, and preserving traditional Lakota culture.[141] Though role playing, it would be seem real for the brief moments he was on horseback in the arena, riding hard and shooting, appreciating what it must have felt like to have lived unrestricted on the High Plains in search of honor and glory. Riding with Buffalo Bill could also enhance his reputation back home, giving his family respect, a meaning vital to young Native performers.[142]

Albert may also have seized an opportunity to present to the American public a sense of traditional Lakota lifestyles, have them appreciate the skills and talent identified with Native heritage. But, most of all, going with Buffalo Bill allowed Albert to leave behind the stifling colonization of the reservation, to exhibit his bravery by going to faraway lands with the "enemy,"[143] and to alleviate the circumstances of his family's harsh poverty by sending money home. Decent pay, travel, and the opportunity to interact with non-Indian people would have been attractive reasons to join the Wild West, although Albert Afraid of Hawk may well have set out on his long journey into the *wasichus* world much like 'Ōpūkahaʻia—to express what was hidden and repressed inside him and escape the containment of his early life. As he stepped onto the "iron wagon" to join Buffalo Bill and start his journey into lands unknown, Albert for once seemed free.

William Frederick Cody embodied the exaggerated personification of Western dime store novel heroes of the American West. Born on the plains of Iowa in 1846, Cody would scout for wagon trains, pan for gold, ride for the Pony Express, enlist in the 7th Kansas Volunteer Cavalry during the Civil War, serve as a U. S. detective, fight in Plains Indian battles, labor for the Kansas Pacific Railroad, win the Congressional Medal of Honor, perform on stage in melodramas as a Western hero, write his autobiography by the age of thirty-three, and kill more than 4,000 buffalo single-handedly, earning the brand "Buffalo Bill." Yet for all these histrionics, Cody will forever be remembered as one of the grandest showmen, second only to Phineas T. Barnum, in American

William F. "Buffalo Bill" Cody, unknown photographer, said to have been taken during performance of the Wild West at the Gentleman's Driving Park, Hartford, CT, 1900 (Courtesy of Library of Congress, LC-USZ62-2051.)

history. He *was* the Wild Western frontier to millions of people in the U. S. and Europe who had never been beyond the Mississippi River.

Although Cody always considered himself a friend of the Indian, he killed his first Native American at eleven years of age, and he seemed to do everything he could personally to wipe out their basic subsistence resource. In July 1876, soon after the Battle of the Little Bighorn, Cody slayed Yellow Hair, a Cheyenne Indian, while scouting for the Fifth Cavalry, and in so doing, according to sensational writers of the day, took the "First Scalp for Custer."[144] To recreate the drama and myth of the American West, Cody required an enemy to overcome and his Show Indians filled this role.[145]

Even so, Cody was often an advocate for Native Americans, once telling a newspaperman that when there was "trouble between the white man and Indians, it will be found that the white man is responsible. Indians expect a man to keep his word. They can't understand how a man can lie. Most of them would as soon cut off a leg as tell a lie."[146] He paid Indians the same wages as white performers, treated them equally, and often highlighted their cause in the show's programs. Cody opened the Indian encampment to the public, who were permitted to freely stroll through the tipi village after the performances and meet the Native players, interacting with them as peaceful, educated, and unexpectedly modern human beings.[147] In turn, the show Indians learned to trust him; on the road Cody often preferred to sleep in a tipi at the Lakota camp rather than lodge in a comfortable hotel.[148]

Conversely, Cody stereotypically portrayed Indians in his Wild West as violent savages who massacred Custer and attacked innocent settlers and stagecoaches, unleashing the potential fear of violence among his white audiences. The reenactments purposely contained an element of dangerous outbreak among the Indians, upholding the white narrative of winning the West.[149] Only the safety of the grandstand seats and Buffalo Bill's bravery seemed to save the audience from these "rapacious killers."[150] And, most tellingly, he disappointed the Lakota when his 1913 silent feature, *The Indian Wars*, did not tell the truth about Wounded Knee, but supported the military's version of a heroic battle against "savages" rather than depicting the carnage it really was.[151] Contradictions in Cody's relationship with his "Show Indians" mirrored the general public's muddied perceptions of Native Americans, ambiguities that persist to this day.[152]

William Cody purchased land and established the Scout's Rest Ranch in North Platte, Nebraska, in 1878 with aspirations of settling down. However, the wanderlust remained within him. When asked by the town's fathers to produce a Fourth of July celebration in 1882, Cody brought together cowboy and Indian acquaintances to perform in the "Old Glory Blow-Out," which many historians consider the first rodeo in the Western states.[153] Years earlier, Cody starred in the theater in Ned Buntline-staged Western melodramas. Though a poor actor, he felt confined by the proscenium and craved the openness to perform outdoors with an extravaganza of horses, buffaloes, stagecoaches, and a cast of hundreds. Encouraged by the success of the "Blow-Out," he sought backers and in 1883 launched his "Wild West," which toured America and Europe up to the First World War, thrilling audiences with Cody's brand of the real and mythical American West.[154]

The first officially scheduled performance was May 17, 1883, in the "Gateway to the West," Omaha, Nebraska.[155] While the show's program would change through the years keeping up with modern political developments, the basic themes—re-creating historic battles, sharp-shooter exhibitions, horse races, buffalo hunts, and stagecoach attacks—were crowd favorites from the beginning, remaining staples in all the performances in one form or another. Although nowhere near the Battle of the Greasy Grass, for years the Wild West would stage "Custer's Last Stand," climaxing with Buffalo Bill riding up to the scene of the Seventh Cavalry defeat with the words "Too Late" flashed upon a screen.[156] By 1900, when Albert Afraid of Hawk performed with the Wild West, the show would be updated to include a reenactment of Col. Theodore Roosevelt's charge up San Juan Hill and have an entourage consisting of Mexicans, Cossacks, Arabs, gauchos, Russians, Cubans, cowboys, and, of course, Lakota Indians.[157]

Life was hard on the road—long tours and one-night stands. The grueling daily schedule of sleeping onboard moving trains, up at dawn, arriving in a new town, setting up the show tents and tipis, unloading all the animals, stagecoaches, wagons, and equipment, morning parades through Main Streets, afternoon and evening performances; then dismantle the whole operation, jump onboard the train, start all over again the next day in a new town from March to October in a continuous state of weariness.[158]

For the Lakota, the 1900 season started in early March when the performers left their families at Pine Ridge, travelling east by rail to Bridgeport, Connecticut, where Cody shared his winter quarters with the Barnum and Bailey Circus to rehearse the show. Unknowingly for the Afraid of Hawk family, seeing Albert off on his journey to join Cody in the east would be the last time they would ever see him alive.

The 1900 Wild West tour began on April 23rd at New York City's Madison Square Garden before a packed house of enthusiastic fans. Though the program was the same as the previous year, every seat at the Garden was sold out with many celebrities in attendance, including among others, Gen. (Bear Coat) Nelson Miles and Chief Joseph of the Nez Perce.[159] After a circuit through Pennsylvania and New Jersey, Cody's troupe set out on a month-long tour of New England where they performed almost daily throughout Massachusetts, Rhode Island, New Hampshire, and Maine before coming to Hartford, Connecticut, the last week of June.[160]

Arriving in the state's capital on June 25, 1900, the Wild West erected their grandstands and tents at the Gentleman's Driving Park, a harness racing track on Albany Avenue. Later that morning Hartford welcomed Buffalo Bill and his entourage as thousands of people lined the anticipated parade route. A warm sun was shining brightly as the grand procession left the Driving Park promptly at 9:30 a.m., heading south toward the City Hall on Main Street. Buffalo Bill led the hour-long convoy in a carriage, followed by Lakota Indians on horseback. The demand for transportation to see the Wild West was so high that the Hartford Street Railway Company was forced to put into service every available trolley car, motorman, and conductor. Afternoon and evening performances were jam-packed, living up to expectations with even the aging Buffalo Bill demonstrating he was never a truer shot with his firearm, hitting all but one of the glass balls tossed into the air by a Lakota Indian as the two galloped side-by-side on horseback around the arena.[161]

Hartford's Wild West "Programme" opened with the Star Spangled Banner conducted by the Cowboy Band, followed by the "Grand Review," which got the spectacle off to a rousing start with Lakota Indians in full regalia at the lead of the "Rough Riders of the World" parading before the grandstands. Albert may have been adorned in an eagle-feathered war bonnet, bone breastplate, and armbands astride a swift Lakota pony. The kickoff act was "Miss Annie Oakley," who amazed the audience with her firearm proficiency, setting the pace for the remaining performances. Oakley was followed by the "Race of Races" which pitched a competitive match between "a cowboy, a Cossack, a Mexican, an Arab, a gaucho, and an Indian," all desperately yearning to win that day in honor of their compatriots and the quality of their swift horses.

Non-Native performances included Capt. Thorpe's U. S. Artillery Drill, booming cannon throughout the arena; the Pony Express, demonstrating how mail was delivered before the building of the railroad and telegraph and emphasizing how seventeen-year old Billy Cody rode through the plains as an Express rider; the Battle of San Juan Hill, reenacting Roosevelt's charge of the Rough Riders during the Spanish-American War; the horsemanship of Arab equestrians; Johnny Baker, sharpshooter; Cossacks; cowboy "fun;" military musical drills and exercises; and Col. W. F. Cody providing an additional sharpshooting demonstration.

Albert Afraid of Hawk and the Lakota participated in the majority of the performances, including a strike on an immigrant wagon train crossing the plains, demonstrations of Indian fighting, war dances and games, an attack on the Deadwood mail-coach, racing bareback horses, a reenactment of the last buffalo hunt, and an assault on a settler's cabin.[162] Moreover, some Lakota may have been enlisted in the scenes defending San Juan Hill. Clearly the Lakota were star attractions of the show based on the number of performances they participated in, and without whom the Wild West would never have developed into the definitive entertainment variety.[163] Subsequently, generations of Americans, unfamiliar with the diversity of Indian cultures, would think of the Lakota as representative of *all* Native American tribes, even stamping their likenesses into U. S. coin and paper currencies.

Between performances, the troupers filed into the galley tent for supper. The company was served three hot meals a day cooked over twenty-foot-long ranges.[164] The Lakota sat together at their usual Table No. 7 and were provided the same fare as other performers though they favored meat and preferred not to eat desserts.[165] Luther Standing Bear divulged that at times the Indians were served inferior food because of the prejudices of the cooks, but when it was reported, Cody put an immediate stop to the practice.[166] Included in the Hartford meal consumed that evening was a side dish of canned corn; by the time the show reached New Haven the next day, many performers started feeling ill, so ill that nearly fifty of them were incapacitated with stomach complaints, unable to execute their duties. As a result, Cody's extravaganza was crippled and only partially performed. Consulting physicians agreed that the common ailments stemmed from something they had all eaten. The accepted culprit was the canned corn ingested the previous day in Hartford. The Lakota were the last group to succumb to the food poisoning. However, two among them, Albert Afraid of Hawk and Eagle Bear, were in the most severe distress.[167]

Buffalo Bill's Lakota "Show Indians," unknown photographer, 1900. Albert Afraid of Hawk is on top the Deadwood Stagecoach, upper left. (Courtesy of the Buffalo Bill Center of the West, Cody, Wyoming, U.S.A., P.6.234.)

After a stop in South Norwalk, the Wild West pulled into the Danbury train station amid 4 a.m. darkness on June 28th. The company disembarked from the platform and hauled their equipment and animals to the arena grounds about a mile away on White Street. The weather was cloudy most of the day, and around 6 p.m. a violent windstorm came through, gusting down the sideshow tents and dressing room backings. Fortunately, the winds subsided and the crew repaired the damage in time for the evening performance.[168]

Afraid of Hawk was unable to participate, convulsed by abdominal pain and constant vomiting. He lay prostrate, paralyzed in his tipi. After the evening's performance, Johnny Baker checked on Albert and was concerned enough to summon Dr. MacDonald, who recommended transferring the patient to Danbury Hospital for further medical care. While Albert appeared grateful for the doctor's efforts, his fellow Lakota looked upon him with grave and anxious faces while two women started to sing his death song. Johnny Baker urged the physician, "Spare no expense! Save his life if you can, no matter what the cost may be."[169]

Carefully handling Albert's pain-ridden body, show performers maneuvered him gently onto the back of a horse-drawn wagon for transport to the *wasichus* hospital. Accompanying Albert were David Bull Bear, a childhood friend who lived near the Afraid of Hawk family in the Wounded Knee District at Pine Ridge, and Eagle Bear, who would recover from his ravages with food poisoning. Bull Bear, interpreter for the Lakota, would stay by Albert's side during his ordeal. Black Hawk, one of the Lakota chiefs, spoke quiet words of encouragement as the wagon prepared to leave, and Albert weakly responded that he knew he was going to die and would do so honorably. Tribal members followed the wagon for a short distance and looked on until it disappeared from sight.

Albert Afraid of Hawk was carried on a stretcher into the men's ward, a wooden story-and-a-half wing off the left side of the large Victorian house that served as Danbury Hospital. The men's ward was a long rectangular dormitory room with abutting beds spaced underneath fourteen tall windows that provided extensive light during the day. Assigned a bed for his relief, Albert was made as comfortable as possible while other patients and hospital personnel ogled at the exoticness of a full-blooded Indian placed tenderly beside them. Given full attention by the hospital staff, Albert continued to suffer without complaint. David Bull Bear was provided a chair and quietly sat next to Albert's bed, conversing with doctors and nurses, watching over his friend.[170]

Sometime after midnight, Albert Afraid of Hawk, Oglala Lakota, son of warriors and buffalo hunters, far from home on a journey to find meaning and fulfillment in the modern world, convulsed into a stupor, dying of a body racked by the infection of botulism. In an era before antibiotics, death from infection was common. The irony of his fatality at the hands of contaminated, processed food of the "civilized" *wasichus* diet, an ailment that "primitive" buffalo-hunting Lakota could never have imagined, would have been apparent to David Bull Bear as he sorrowfully observed his friend's death in unstated agony. As 'Ōpūkaha'ia had died a truly Christian death, Albert Afraid of Hawk died a courageous Lakota death.

David Bull Bear left the hospital, returned to the fair grounds, and reported Albert's death to the Lakota. Black Hawk requested to see Afraid of Hawk before the Wild West left for Pittsfield, so while the show's crew continued loading the train cars, Black Hawk and Bull Bear paid their final respects at the hospital. Black Hawk stood silently by the bed, his eyes moistened, then announced that he was ready to leave.[171] The 1900 Route Book impassively recorded the event:

**"Thurs. June 28, 1900. Danbury, CT. An Indian,
Albert Afraid of Hawk,
died in the hospital there."[172]**

The following morning, David Bull Bear and L. C. Decker, secretary for Buffalo Bill's Wild West, remained behind as the rest of the company rode the train to Pittsfield. Preparing final arrangements for Afraid of Hawk's burial, Decker purchased a coffin and cemetery plot while gravediggers at Wooster Cemetery excavated a six-foot-deep rectangular shaft near a small pond downslope behind the hospital. His clothing was removed from his body by funeral directors at

Reynolds and Fuller Co., and he was wrapped in a black shroud held together by straight and safety pins, his face uncovered, and placed in a hardwood casket held by six decorative, silver-plated handles.

Dressed in his formal regalia, David Bull Bear was the lone Lakota listening as Rev. J. D. Skene performed a funeral rite of Episcopal tradition.[173] He looked down on the face of his boyhood friend for the last time as the lid closed on the casket and was lowered by ropes into the ground. As the cemetery grounds crew shoveled dirt on top of the coffin, David Bull Bear climbed into a coach and left to catch the next train to Pittsfield in time for the evening performance of the Wild West.[174] The sexton registered the event on a burial card placed into the cemetery's files. The grave, unmarked, would soon be forgotten, Albert's journey unfinished.

7 | After Afraid Of Hawk

Researching historical archives can be analogous to archaeological excavation. In lieu of digging through the earth's soil to uncover material culture of the human past, historians leaf through dusty papers to uncover written evidence of the human past. Library shelves are like stratified sites. We scrap soil layer after layer, centimeter after centimeter, deeper into the earth; historians turn page after page, review paragraph after paragraph, delving deeper into documents. Both methods of research, along with oral traditions, represent the universe of what we will ever know about the historical past. Both are probably the most exciting when something unanticipated is discovered.

Undertaking a research project to remap historic Wooster Cemetery in Danbury, Connecticut, historian and genealogist Robert (Bob) Young was scanning through card files in 2008, documenting a number of unmarked graves lying within an older section of the cemetery. Running his fingertips across the top edges of vintage index cards, pulling them forward in the same manner as searching through an old-fashioned library card catalog system, he noticed the name "Afraid of Hawke" (sic) in large script at the top of one entry.

As a student of Danbury history, Bob had heard anecdotes of a Sioux Indian dying in the city while performing with Buffalo Bill's Wild West long ago. However, no one had ever proved the story was true, and Bob was reluctant to give credence to unsubstantiated assertions. Yet here in front of him was a cemetery burial card documenting the event: Issued Permit No. 3013. The card was dated June 29, 1900, and noted Afraid of Hawk's age as 20, his burial in Section 22, Single Grave No. 19, and handled by Reynolds & Fuller Company, Undertakers.[1]

Young's interest was piqued. He searched an old map of Wooster Cemetery, located Section 22, Lot 19, and went out to the gravesite to confirm it was unmarked, speculating it might be that of "Afraid of Hawke." Intrigued further, Diane Hassan, researcher at the Danbury Museum and Historical Society, visited City Hall and located a death certificate in the clerk's office listing "Alfred" (sic) Afraid of

Hawk's occupation as "Rough Rider."[2] Diane Hassan and Bob Young extended their pursuit by exploring old newspaper accounts of Buffalo Bill's appearances in their city. Before long, Bob found himself totally consumed by the story, absorbing all he could find on Albert Afraid of Hawk as if the mystery of this young, handsome Lakota from the city's past possessed some kind of spell on him.

His sleuthing included an Internet search, locating a painting of Afraid of Hawk auctioning for $120,000 online and the 1898 Indian Census with names of Afraid of Hawk family members listed as tribal members in South Dakota. Aware of the federal government's Native American Graves Protection and Repatriation Act of 1990, Bob made phone calls and sent letters to the Pine Ridge tribal government whose burial assistance office was willing to contact the family on his behalf. He was told that the Afraid of Hawk family left Pine Ridge decades ago and were now residing at Cherry Creek on the Cheyenne River Sioux Reservation in north central South Dakota. Pleasantly surprised, Bob Young soon received a phone call from the family inquiring about his discovery and making arrangements to meet.

Unable to contain himself, Young immediately booked a flight to Rapid City in early October 2009, flying into the first South Dakota snow and ice storm of the season. He drove across long, isolated roads covered with snow and drifts to the Pine Ridge Indian Reservation while the Afraid of Hawk family was subsequently motoring the four-hour trip south from Cheyenne River. They converged at Big Bat's, a gas station, restaurant, and convenience store at the crossroads of the old Pine Ridge Agency. There amid tribal members drinking coffee and eating buffalo burgers, Bob met eighty-year old Daniel Jay Afraid of Hawk, family patriarch, youngest and only surviving offspring of Richard, nephew of Albert and legendary rodeo cowboy in his own right. Bob recounted his rediscovery of the grave and the current research he was doing into Albert's life.

Daniel was staggered. He was aware of his father's brother and that one of his older brothers was named after Albert, but the family had no knowledge of what had happened to his *lala* (grandfather), only that he had left the reservation before any of them were born and had never returned. Daniel was beside himself with emotion. He vowed that his uncle must come home and be laid to rest with his family at Pine Ridge. Hurriedly, Daniel escorted Bob across the icy street to the Oglala Sioux Tribe's brick administrative offices, seeking a letter permitting the family to have Albert's remains reinterred at Saint Mark's Cemetery north of Manderson where those of his father, mother, and grandparents were buried. Daniel felt deeply that this was important to his family, important to the Lakota people, and important for the spirit of Albert to be home again. It would have been hard to speculate who was more enthusiastic and uplifted by the meeting, Bob Young or Daniel Jay Afraid of Hawk.

Returning home to Danbury, Young awaited word from the Afraid of Hawk family to activate the repatriation. However, no communication from South Dakota was forthcoming, so all he could do was anxiously continue to wait. The delay frustrated and haunted him. But try as he might, he could not get the thought of Albert out of his mind. He busied himself with other research projects but wondered why he was not hearing from the family. Doubts surfaced. Had they given up on the repatriation or lost interest? More than two years passed before the phone finally rang. On the line was Marlis Afraid of Hawk.

She had had a dream.

Word of Albert Afraid of Hawk's death never made its way back to his family at the Pine Ridge Reservation. His parents, Emil Afraid of Hawk and White Mountain, wondered if Eagle Weasel would suddenly reappear at their home in the Wounded Knee District. Slow Bull offered prayers to *Wakan Tanka* for his grandson's safety. Richard thought often of his missing brother, eventually naming one of his sons after Albert.

For a brief time at Wooster Cemetery, children would visit Albert's gravesite, bringing flowers to honor Buffalo Bill's fallen "Rough Rider," and there was talk of erecting a tombstone. But, soon the kids stopped coming[3] and no tombstone was ever raised. Before long the citizens of Danbury no longer remembered the Lakota Indian who spent less than one day in their city, died in their hospital, and was buried in their cemetery.

Albert Afraid of Hawk died the same week the 1900 United States Indian Census for the Pine Ridge Reservation was published.

Obviously, he was not included. Only Richard, Annie, Mary, Julia, and Fannie are listed as siblings living with their parents, Afraid of Hawk and White Mountain. As a young adult, Richard would soon be living in his own household, marrying Mabel Lone Elk in 1902. With his grandson gone, Slow Bull is listed in the 1904 census as living alone at the age of eighty-four.[4]

The last citation for the sixty-four-year-old Afraid of Hawk is the 1913 U. S. Indian Census.[5] White Mountain, who outlived him by more than twenty years, can be found in the 1930 Population Census for Pine Ridge,[6] residing at age seventy-eight with her son Richard and his family, which included that year the infant, Daniel. Three years later she petitioned the U. S. Army for a military headstone for her husband's grave at St. Mark's Mission,[7] eligible after serving as an Indian Scout in Sept. 1877. The War Department application form furnishes Afraid of Hawk's date of death as April 14, 1914.

The youngest child, Fannie, would live with her parents until her father died. She met the future Lakota spiritualist and nephew of Black Elk, Frank Fools Crow, at a Fourth of July celebration in 1918, marrying him soon after. Afraid of Hawk and White Mountain had previously discussed a possible marriage arrangement with Fools Crow's parents, Eagle Bear and stepmother, Emily Big Road,[8] and both families appeared delighted with the match. Fannie set up a residence with Frank in Pine Ridge's Porcupine District, named after Fools Crow's maternal grandfather, Porcupine Tail, a prominent Lakota leader.

Pursuant to federal legislation, further land allotments were granted to individuals at Pine Ridge from 1904 to 1911, providing each family member with parcels held contiguously. In 1910 Richard Afraid of Hawk was endowed 640 acres in the northwest area of the reservation in Shannon County at Cuny Table, the rugged land adjacent to where the Ghost Dance disciples isolated themselves in the fall of 1890. The Lakota called this land *Mako Sica* (bad lands) because of its lack of water, steep terrain, and desolation. As part of the allotment system procurements, Richard received another 320 acres in 1913,[9] along with a wagon, plow, horses, harnesses, and an axe. Compared to conditions a decade earlier, reservation life in the early 20th century had improved with a degree of economic consumption and self-sufficiency.[10]

The 1900 Federal Population Census lists Richard's profession as farmer while a decade later he is listed as a rancher, correlating with new allotment lands providing enough grazing area to feed his developing herds of cattle. The government encouraged the switch from farming to ranching, and the Afraid of Hawk family embraced the role of cowboys, providing a livelihood more in tune with a traditional Lakota life of riding, herding, and capturing large animals.[11] However, the duration of the reservation cattleman was short-lived.

World War I brought high prices for beef, and many Lakota ranchers started selling off large quantities of their herds for top dollar. After the war, the economic downturn brought hardship when the cattle market crashed, and Lakota ranchers had few animals left to support themselves.[12] Additionally, by selling off their cattle, the Lakota opened up their grazing lands to *wasichus* neighbors who were lying in wait for the opportunity to obtain increased acreage. Before the turn of the decade, more than two million acres of Pine Ridge grassland were being leased to white ranchers with meager or non-existent compensation to Lakota land owners.[13] The government reversed itself and encouraged ranchers like Richard to revert to tilling the soil. Hence, by 1930 Richard's occupation is once again listed in the Census as "Farmer" with remaining members of this family recorded as "Ration Indians."

Regardless of the emotion conveyed during the naming and give-away ceremonies, a lot of delicate excavating still lay before us in uncovering the remains of Albert Afraid of Hawk. So Bruce Greene and I descended the ladder and resumed our effort. With the cranium uncovered, we concentrated on the post-cranial elements and leveling the entire burial. By the end of the day we had revealed the pubis bone of the pelvis, which is the highest post-cranial element in a supine position.

With another early start on the fourth day of excavation, we were told that the Afraid of Hawk family would be leaving for the long drive back to the Cheyenne River Sioux Reservation. I apologized for my inability to finish the removal of Albert's remains before their departure. The bones were simply too fragile and we had to labor slowly.

Marlis understood, saying, "We've been patient all this time. We can be patient a few more days."[14]

The family did have one request, though. Could we remove Albert's cranium to honor him during the closing pipe ceremony? I had anticipated its recovery since we first discovered Albert, knowing the extent of decomposition would make removal a very delicate procedure. Gary Aronsen and I discussed the best methods and eventually developed a strategy for lifting the skull out of the burial unit. Since the facial bones had disintegrated, the cranial vault, upper, and lower jaws were in three sections held together by moist compact soil. The brain case was packed entirely with earth, covered by an outer layer of thin, decomposing skeletal tissue. Removing them in one unit without the skull exploding into fragments due to the weight of the interior soil would be precarious. Albert's cranium was far too fragile to lift; we would have to slide it carefully onto a supporting container with strong bottom and sides. When all the necessary equipment and receptacles were in place, Gary and I worked side-by-side in the cramped burial unit.

Wearing a glass-beaded, leather bracelet given by the family, I cleared soil around the cranium so it sat on a pedestal higher than the surrounding matrix. With the scent of burning sage wafting overhead, I extended my right leg over the far side of the coffin straddling the burial. Bending at the waist, I pedestaled soil that contained the copper earrings from both sides of the head. Employing bamboo picks and trowels of various sizes, I lifted them *in situ* onto the receptacle to the left and right of where we anticipated placing Albert's cranium, maintaining their anatomical positions. Gary, lying alongside the grave, steadied a battery-operated light illuminating the work area. Once tiered, I carefully probed under the mandible feeling for resistance, loosening any materials such as small stones. Our most serious impediment was deep root systems intertwined under and into the cranial cavity. If the roots were not disconnected, their pull would crush the cranium with any attempt to move it. Clipping every root I could distinguish, we slowly freed the bones. All the while, Gary had his hands firmly supporting the cranial vault so it would not shift during our efforts to release it.

My heart was in my throat, understanding that the slightest movement could bring the whole cranium crashing down into a hundred fragments. We worked painstakingly slow to present Albert intact to his family. Every move was anticipated ahead of time and only undertaken once Gary and I agreed to proceed. Slowly, the cranium was pedestalled, raised enough for us to begin sliding it forward. Gary laid a sturdy cardboard tray at the level of the cranial base. One side was cut open and laid flat to receive Albert without lifting. We brought the box as close as we could without threatening our transfer ability. Gary cuddled the cranial vault and face firmly in his hands while I slid a large mason trowel under the cranium to provide an extensive, solid base. We probed gingerly leaving a soft bed of soil for the cranium to lie on. Sensing another root underlying the skull, prohibiting its further transfer, we ceased. Releasing the trowel, I probed gently with my fingers, found it and clipped it free, a movement we had to replicate twice before the cranium was liberated. With Gary cradling the vault, I began to slide it toward me gingerly. The initial movement was less than an inch, and encouragingly the cranium held together. We painstakingly moved another inch, all the time praying that the remains would not explode into countless pieces.

We only needed to slide Albert's cranium seven inches and it probably took fifteen minutes, but it seemed like a mile and eternity before he was secured in the container. The open side was lifted back into place and taped tightly, enclosing all four sides. The crew handed down finely screened soil to pad the area around the cranium and the container's sides creating further support. So far so good, but we still had to lift Albert over our heads to reach ground surface level without shattering.

A piece of plywood had been placed on the grass to the left side of the burial above the excavation platform. Taking our time, Gary and I embraced the container in our four arms, supporting underneath the box. One at a time, we unhurriedly rose from our knees to a standing position. Once secured, we lifted the receptacle in unison slowly above our heads and slid it onto the plywood, intact. I felt like I could take my first breath in over an hour.

Albert Afraid of Hawk's face soaked in sunlight for the first time in 112 years. Gary and I scaled the ladder and, assisted by Jeremy Pilver, picked up the plywood, carrying it around the tent to the medicine wheel and carefully placing it on the ground, presenting Albert to his *tiospaye*.

Marlis Afraid of Hawk was the first to advance. Bending deeply at the waist, she looked closely into the features of her ancestor whom she had first seen in a photograph, later in a dream, and now face-to-face. She said a silent prayer and walked towards me. We embraced. Crying softly, she could hardly speak, but wanted to say thank you. Daniel Afraid of Hawk followed his daughter, and as we hugged, I told him how happy I was for him and his family. As Richard Red Elk and John Afraid of Hawk prepared to perform the closing pipe ceremony, I stood quietly, and my thoughts returned to Debbie Lee and Henry 'Ōpūkaha'ia. I sensed we were all together again.

An altar was prepared at the foot of the medicine wheel pole whose base was adorned with two framed photographs of Albert Afraid of Hawk, the buffalo skull, and abalone shell. John knelt and stripped off fresh sage leaves from their stems, washing his hands with the sacred plant before removing the stone pipe from a leather bag and leaning it on the buffalo skull. Richard Red Elk heated a natural stone taken from the grave shaft, carried it on the blade of a shovel and poured cold water over it, issuing purified steam. He asked us all to pray silently to ourselves while he placed the stone by Albert's side and sang a Lakota song of gratitude.

John, remaining on his knees in front of Albert, continued to fill the pipe bowl with sacred tobacco. He enveloped Albert with the smoke emitting from the freshly lit pipe and the burning sage from the abalone shell while Richard stood by him singing. John spoke in English, "Today we are going to smoke the pipe with you guys for the last time. I want to thank you all for being here for him. Also, we are thankful for a safe journey home and for him, also. On behalf of my family, I want to say thank you to all of you."

As we aligned in a circle around the gravesite, John rose and presented the pipe to his father, Daniel, who held it with both hands above his head, intoning a prayer. In English Daniel announced, "It is a great, big day for us. Albert, grandpa Albert, he has been over here for 112 years, and today my family and my daughter—she is the one who is working on it—will bring him home. Also to Mr. Bob Young and his wife and to everyone down at home—Pine Ridge Reservation. I am really proud of the people back home. He will go back, and we are going to give him a new name." Daniel again meditated in Lakota, invoking the supremacy of both *Wakan Tanka* and Jesus Christ, concluding with a loud "Amen!" John followed with four powerful blasts on the eagle whistle. Then in his Native language, he harmonized in song with Marlis, Daniel, Richard, and Wendell Deer With Horns.

Daniel pulled on the pipe while his son held a flame over the bowl. Once relit, John passed it around the circle, starting with Gary Aronsen. Everyone of us in turn drew the sacred smoke into their mouths, releasing its aromatic power into the summer air. Overwhelmed by the goodwill expressed by all, Marlis wiped tears from her eyes as John kept the tobacco burning until all had a chance to share the smoke of peace. Daniel said in their celebration that his family wished to thank us all personally for what we had done by going around the circle and shaking our hands individually, expressing a final gratitude to every person present.

When the Afraid of Hawk family finished their Lakota rites, Ed Sarabia bestowed a blessing from the Connecticut tribal community. Stepping into the circle, Ed prayed aloud in his native Tlingit tongue, translating into English,

> "Thank you, Creator, for my relatives,
> Thank you, Creator, for my friends,
> Thank you, Creator, for bringing us together,
> Thank you, Creator, for the food that is here,
> Thank you, Creator, for sharing time with us . . .
>
> We are all related, all one, in the end we are all one people.
> A family member dies, and we hear their voice in the wind,
> In a bird's song, and we're with that person again."

Upon conclusion of the pipe ceremony, Richard Red Elk quietly presented Ed with the buffalo drum as a gift of friendship from the Lakota Nation. We were all immensely moved. Wendell Deer With Horns handed out stones from Albert's grave, saying, "You can feel Albert's spirit right here. This is his eternal energy." Once again, it was Marlis who placed the repatriation of Albert Afraid of Hawk into perspective when she eloquently envisioned, "I can just picture him at home, riding a horse across the field of green, with other family members. Home is where he belongs."[15]

The Great Depression brought uncertainty and suffering to tens of millions of Americans, but few struggled more than reservation Indians in the Great Plains. With the adverse effects of the Dust Bowl drought blowing away topsoil and desiccating grasslands, accompanied by grasshopper infestations that devoured whatever crops could grow, making a living at either farming or ranching on the Pine Ridge Reservation in the 1930s became near impossible. The Lakota did not have the option available to their white neighbors of packing up and heading for California or other parts of the country to avoid the environmental devastation. Many impoverished Indian families resorted to gathering what wild vegetables they could find and eating horsemeat to survive.[16] The Lakota were no strangers to starvation, and the hardships of the 1930s were comparable to the suffering of the late 1880s during the days of the incipient reservation system.

Lakota families creatively found ways to obtain money to support their paltry incomes, some selling farm machinery, even dishes and other household items to generate needed cash, pooling resources to avoid starvation.[17] The average family's annual income at Pine Ridge was $150.80 during the Depression.[18] In 1931 the elderly White Mountain applied for a widow's pension based on her husband's military service as an Indian Scout. There is no record she received any appropriations. Two couples, Emil Afraid of Hawk Jr., half-brother to Albert and Richard, and his wife Agie Hollow Horn, and Fannie Afraid of Hawk and Frank Fools Crow, left the reservation for a year to join Col. Miller's famous 101 Ranch,[19] performing around the country, making money as best they could.

President Franklin D. Roosevelt's New Deal initiative brought some relief. The Civilian Conservation Corps' Indian Division placed a few Lakota men in salaried positions to build telephone poles, string lines, construct dams, wells, and fences; the Works Progress Administration employed Indian men building roads; and the Farm Security Administration subsidized grants for Indian farmers and assisted ranchers in rebuilding their herds. These government programs alleviated some of the poverty experienced by the Lakota during the Great Depression, but basically little changed to overcome the famine once again facing the people.

Probably the most controversial piece of federal legislation pertaining to Native Americans during the Roosevelt Administration was the Indian Reorganization Act (IRA) of 1934, an initiative of John Collier, Commissioner of the Bureau of Indian Affairs, whose purpose for the "reorganization" was to reverse the attempt to assimilate the Indian into American society. The IRA ended land allotment and aimed at transferring the management of Indian reservations and their natural resources back to the tribes by creating a $2 million fund for the purchase of property lost to white homesteaders. Each tribe was required to develop a constitution with a tribal council to govern the reservations.[20]

Although Pine Ridge narrowly passed acceptance of the IRA, Frank Fools Crow and many traditional Lakota initially opposed the legislation primarily because they believed that mixed-bloods, who had a better command of the English language and had already acquired the best and largest land holdings, would control the tribal council to the detriment of full bloods.[21] Collier, in his zeal for democracy on the reservations, had created a model constitution he expected all the tribes to abide by, assuring Fools Crow that the new tribal council would have full bloods involved giving them decision-making capability.[22] However, the prevailing view among many tribal members saw the Bureau of Indian Affairs as paternalistic and scheming.[23]

Another sore point among the full-blooded Lakota was the IRA's undermining of traditional chiefs. Tribal elders and district leaders gave way in favor of elected council members. Often the mixed-blood majority controlled governance and steered tribes away from the time-honored Lakota political organization. Nonetheless, the passage of the Pine Ridge constitution created a new form of government on the reservation. To assist his tribesmen in an effort to make the new law work for the people and hopefully provide a voice for the full bloods, Richard Afraid of Hawk was elected and served on the first Pine Ridge Reservation Tribal Council in 1934 and then again in 1936, representing the Manderson District.[24]

As one of the *takini* (to die and come back, survivor), Richard Afraid of Hawk had privately shared his horrific experience at Wounded Knee with his children, who have subsequently maintained the oral tradition of his escape from the carnage to the present generation.[25] In the 1930s Richard was vigorously involved with the "Survivors of the Wounded Knee Massacre," an advocacy group working through Pine Ridge Reservation Superintendent James H. McGregor to petition Congress for reparations for themselves and their descendants. In the long-standing Lakota tradition of conflict restitution, survivors sought compensation as a symbolic means of healing between the Lakota Nation and the U.S. government.[26]

The *takini* would meet every summer at the Wounded Knee Memorial to promote awareness and gain Congressional support. "Richard A. O. Hawk" would be one of the signatories on a 1933 resolution sent to Commissioner John Collier presenting as evidence "the marks of the wounded men and women, together with their written statements" of the atrocious events on the morning of December 29, 1890, seeking compensation for their suffering.[27] For all that, their petitions were denied when the War Department refused to acknowledge Wounded Knee as a "massacre." Richard also drafted a sample bill in 1935 with Cheyenne River tribal members James Hi Hawk and Philip Blackmoon calling for the federal government to compensate families of all Lakota killed at Wounded Knee, including prenatal infants, $50,000 and a stipend of $75 a month for wounded survivors, retroactive to 1890.[28] Until his death Richard would never stop advocating for his fellow survivors and their families.

The U. S. government officially continued to uphold the notion that what happened that sorrowful morning at Wounded Knee Creek was a military "battle" and has yet to remove the Medal of Honor awards given out for the indiscriminate slaughter of Lakota women and children. Ultimately, concerns by Congress that liability claims would set a precedent for future compensation for other war victims and the harsh economic realities of the Great Depression rendered Lakota compensation efforts in vain. In his testimony, Richard narrated his grim story for public consumption to McGregor, who through interpreter Bill Bergen published the account in 1940.[29]

Richard Afraid of Hawk died February 15, 1941, at Pine Ridge where his mortal remains were buried at St. Mark's Mission Cemetery near the graves of his father and mother. His tombstone lists his date of birth as December 1876, two years later than most U. S. Indian Census records indicate.[30] The epitaph reads, "We Will Meet Again," evoking a belief in eternal life and maybe eluding to the disappearance of the brother he grew up with during the difficult times on the burgeoning reservation; the brother he taught to ride bareback, to hunt with a bow and arrow, to shoot a rifle while astride a horse, and in whom he instilled the self-esteem of being Lakota; the brother he never saw again but would hopefully reunite with in death.

Emil Afraid of Hawk, Jr., half-brother to Albert and Richard,[31] was another prominent member of the Pine Ridge Reservation in the early 20th century and played a pivotal role introducing John Neihardt, the poet-laureate of Nebraska, to the Lakota spiritualist Black Elk in 1930. Though a generation younger than the elder Lakota *wicasa wakan*, Emil shared Black Elk's conversion to Roman Catholicism. Together they served as catechists for the Holy Rosary Church and were known as community leaders of the Roman Catholic mission.[32] On acquainting them, Emil served as the initial interpreter between Neihardt and Black Elk.[33]

At the time, Neihardt was interviewing a number of Lakota elders for the final volume of an epic poem he was composing on the Ghost Dance and Wounded Knee. Emil had warned Neihardt that he was not likely to get much cooperation from the Lakota elders since Black Elk had refused to be interviewed by Eleanor Hinman in her study of Crazy Horse.[34] The Oglala holy man remained reluctant and suspicious of speaking about his experiences to white people, but Neihardt remained confident, indicating that he had known Indians for many years and they had always talked to him.[35] Remarkably, Black Elk saw something singular in Neihardt, and, for whatever reason, decided to trust him, inviting the *waschius* poet back to his home to converse at greater length. In subsequent interviews, Black Elk would divulge his life story, including his childhood vision, his participation in the Battle of the Greasy Grass, his experiences with Buffalo Bill, the Ghost Dance, and the horrors of Wounded Knee. The result is the literary classic, *Black Elk Speaks: Being the Life Story of a Holy Man of the Oglala Sioux as told to John G. Neihardt*,[36] which was originally published in 1932 but did not find a receptive audience until the turbulent late 1960s when it became a best-seller. Emil Afraid of Hawk can be considered the matchmaker of one of the most significant Native American literary partnerships of the 20th century.[37]

About the time Emil Afraid of Hawk Jr. was working with Neihardt, he was also deeply involved in a federal case before the U. S. Court of Claims for the return of the beloved *Paha Sapa*. Officially seized by the federal government in 1877 after the discovery of gold and in direct violation of the 1868 Fort Laramie Treaty, the sacred Black Hills, where the Teton emerged from their subterranean world, remains a point of contention between the U. S. and the Lakota people to the present day.

By the turn of the 20th century, the battle for *Paha Sapa* was being fought in American courtrooms as actions were organized by all the Lakota reservations: Standing Rock sent a delegation to Washington, D. C.; Cheyenne River organized the Black Hills Treaty Council; Red Cloud and his people at Pine Ridge requested of their agent to travel to Washington and meet with Congressional representatives to promote their case. Charles Eastman, a Santee Dakota, and Henry Standing Bear organized the Society of American Indians to lobby Congress for legislation that would allow the U. S. Court of Claims to have jurisdiction on Indian land disputes.[38]

They succeeded when Congress passed a bill in 1920 permitting the Lakota to obtain counsel and petition the Court of Claims for the Black Hills.[39] Represented by Lakota tribal attorney Ralph Case, the appraised value of the Black Hills was estimated for purposes of compensation, and a document was prepared for submission to the courts. The process was slow but proceeded steadily so that by 1934, in the midst of the Great Depression, Case filed a series of petitions under the Fifth Amendment seeking $750 million in compensation for the taking of the Black Hills which included the estimated value of the land and accrued interest since 1877.[40]

While the claim was still in preparation, Pine Ridge took a pro-active role by sending a delegation to Washington, D. C. in 1930 to meet with Indian Commissioner Collier over the pending land claim. Four delegates were selected to represent the Lakota Nation: Henry Standing Bear, Iron White Man, George Little Wound, and Emil Afraid of Hawk.[41] Though the trip probably gave them a better understanding of the deliberate judicial process and politics in Washington, it would be another decade before the claim would receive a ruling from the courts.

On June 1, 1942, shortly after the U. S. became engulfed in World War II, the Court of Claims rendered its decision on the Black Hills. The court rejected the land claim, citing that the Lakota had made no adequate legal case, only a moral assertion.[42] The court furthermore placed blame on the Lakota for the War of 1876, emphasizing that the U. S. government did everything in its power to rid gold miners from the Black Hills and supporting the 1876 agreement that relinquished the land even though the federal government failed to secure the consent of the necessary three-quarters of the adult male Lakota population as stipulated in the 1868 treaty before any land transactions could be sanctioned.[43] In other words the court decided the United States was within its legal right to take the Black Hills from the Lakota, regardless of moral issues. Ralph Case's appeal was denied, and *Paha Sapa* would endure in the hands of the *wasichus*.

The Lakota were recipients of yet another insult to the Black Hills. For years during the 1930s, high granite exposures were blasted with tons of dynamite, not to mine gold but to carve the facial images of four U. S. presidents on the peak of Mount Rushmore:[44] George Washington, who believed Indians were only temporary inhabitants of the continent to be subdued by white civilization, established the precedent of the federal government's treatment toward Native

Americans; Thomas Jefferson, who purchased Louisiana from the French and directed Lewis and Clark to survey land "owned" by the United States as a Christian nation, resulting in the Lakota standoff on the banks of the Missouri River; Abraham Lincoln, who demonstrated no effort to work with Indian tribes and who put to death by hanging thirty-eight Dakota, which remains to this day the largest mass execution by the federal government; and Theodore Roosevelt, who once wrote that it was of "incalculable importance that America... should pass out of the hands of (its) red....aboriginal owners and become the heritage of the dominant world races."[45] These monumental figures enshrined onto the mountains of Lakota origin were painful reminders of all that had been lost, the desecration of their sacred hills, and the insults they had received. Eight months prior to the court verdict on the Lakota land claim for the Black Hills, Mount Rushmore National Park officially opened as a major tourist destination. The Lakota agonized over the defilement occurring to *Paha Sapa*, and now the courts reaffirmed they would remain powerless to stop further destruction.

While the Afraid of Hawk family drove back to Cheyenne River, Gary Aronsen and I continued our excavation of the fragile post-cranial remains of Albert Afraid of Hawk. Soon his figure began to emerge. Albert was lying supine with the left arm relaxed parallel to the body, hand resting palm down on the left femur (thigh) while the right arm was flexed across the waist at the elbow with the hand residing over his left side. The legs appeared slightly bent at an oblique angle from the upper body, as opposed to being straight.

In working the complicated series of finger, hand, and wrist bones associated with the left arm, black fibers appeared. The fibers were not hair as the bristles identified with the earrings but were intertwined as part of a fabric. Considering the discovery of the earrings, I anticipated copper in the area, and two pins soon materialized, one straight, the other a safety pin; however, the metal was a steel alloy. The green coloration of copper finally surfaced around the decomposed fourth finger of the left hand (the ring finger) where we found a plain copper band, clarifying the textile's preservation.

What did the black textile and ring represent? Discussion ensued among the crew. Was Albert holding something in his left hand? Was it clothing? A shroud? When the possibility of a medicine bundle was proposed, the thought brought anxiety. Medicine bundles contained sacred objects that often had healing powers and were highly personal. Bundles are holy and often consisted of small, natural items held within a pouch; bundles are private, kept secretly from others, and to open a bundle without the proper ritual would risk calamity. Fortunately, to our relief, the textile turned out to be the remnants of a burial shroud. Like ʻŌpūkahaʻia, Afraid of Hawk had been buried naked with a shroud enclosing his body. The funeral director's records for Albert Afraid of Hawk mentioned the removal of his traditional Lakota clothing, their replacement being a simple shroud secured by safety and straight pins.

The ring remains more of a mystery. Bob Young's historical research has found no references to suggest that Albert had ever married. Was the ring ornamental or a wedding band? Of the five extant photographs of Albert taken in Omaha (in 1899), three provide images of his hands and no copper ring is visible in either. However, photos of young Lakota men performing with Buffalo Bill's Wild West display decorative rings on numerous fingers of both hands.[46] In Albert's case the ring may have been part of his adornment and have no marriage symbolism. U. S. Indian Census records prior to his leaving the reservation have Albert living with his grandfather and not the head of his own household. It is furthermore unlikely that Albert could have married while performing with Buffalo Bill without the occasion being recorded in the Route Book; there is no mention of a wife in any newspaper accounts during his sickness and death or in family records.

Once the entire skeleton was exposed and documented, we began the delicate removal process, a full day's work. The coffin handles were easily detached and secured for shipment to Pine Ridge. Each skeletal element was loosened and supported for transport to Cornell Memorial Funeral Home under Tania Porta's supervision. We excavated below the burial feature until we encountered sterile, glacial soils underneath the grave shaft, establishing that there were no other burials stacked under Albert.

Throughout the completion of the disinterment, I was at a loss to explain scientifically why Albert's skeleton had survived the acidic soils of Wooster Cemetery for 112 years. One soil scientist supposed that we got lucky. However, I prefer to believe that Albert was waiting for his family to take him home, persisting in the ground until they arrived; not a scientific explanation, but one I want to believe.

Richard and Mabel's youngest child, Danny Jay Afraid of Hawk, *Wambli Anukansan* (Bald Eagle), was born in 1930. Daniel grew up on horseback at Pine Ridge, and in 1954 he would help to develop a ranch at Cherry Creek on the Cheyenne River Sioux Reservation. With a loan from the Department of Agriculture's Farmland Repayment Program, Daniel began by purchasing land and cattle. He expanded the ranch, seeking assistance under USDA's Federal Service Agency, and by 1970 had paid back all his loans and established the "Afraid of Hawk Ranch" as a viable Native American enterprise. Daniel provided for his family while embracing the role of a Lakota cowboy.

As the late 19th century reservations developed, Lakota men could still recapture the glory of their tribal past by demonstrating skills of breaking horses, branding, roping, racing, and other abilities associated with the rodeo concept.[47] In those years, rationed cattle were distributed "on the hoof" so Lakota men could chase them in the manner of the buffalo hunt, sometimes deliberately riding a mile after steers rather then killing them immediately, simply to enjoy the chase.

This love of horseback riding was further demonstrated by the frequency of Lakota participating in various Wild West shows across the country, in particular with Buffalo Bill, who benefited from his relationship with the Lakota Show Indians as expert riders and shooters.[48] Enthusiasm for participating and staging horseback-riding displays led to the development of the Pine Ridge Sioux Rodeo, which reached its highest popularity in the 1920s and 1930s.[49] For example, more than 3,000 people from both on and off the reservation attended the Sioux Rodeo at Pine Ridge in 1931.[50] Undoubtedly, his father and older brothers brought the young Danny to many rodeo performances which offered important opportunities for community celebrations on the reservation[51] and instilled into the youthful Lakota a passion for horses and ranching, similar to many *wasichu* boys attending their first baseball game amid the lush green grass of multi-tiered stadiums, forever wanting to be major leaguers.

The love and enthusiasm for the cowboy life, as well as the demanding work ethic, were instilled in the Afraid of Hawk family as among many of the ranching Lakota. The skills acquired on the range could be displayed at the rodeo, as their ancestors did at free-roaming tribal gatherings in the High Plains. The concept of the Lakota cowboy found an educational outlet for Indian youth in the 1954 publication of *The Singing Sioux Cowboy Reader*, written by Ann Clark, with drawings provided by Andrew Standing Soldier. Emil Afraid of Hawk translated Clark's children's story about a Lakota boy whose family tends cattle and loves rodeo into the Lakota language.

My father and I are cowboys.
We ride horseback to Rodeo
We sing as we ride along.

Ate kic'I pte'ole hoksila kg he'unc'api
Sunk'akanyanka Oskate ekta unyanpi.
Unyanpi kin ec'unhan low an unyanhanpi.

Yip-e-ye. Yip-e-ye.
I'm going to Rodeo.

Yip-e-ye. Yip-e-ye.
Pteyuha Oskate ekta ble lo.

Yip-e-ye. Yipe-e-ye.
I am a singing Sioux cowboy.

Yip-e-ye. Yip-e-ye.
Lak'ota pte'ole lowans'a henac'a.[52]

Danny Afraid of Hawk matured into a legendary bronco-busting cowboy, taking first-place prizes at the Dupree Rodeo in the Bareback Event.[53]

Two young *wasichu* **brothers** named Hare picked up and assaulted Raymond Yellow Thunder, a middle-aged Oglala cowboy, during the winter of 1972. The Hares had been drinking, and their intoxication turned to violence when the brothers started to abuse Yellow Thunder just for the fun of it, beating him for hours and locking him in the trunk of their car while driving around bumpy dirt roads at high speeds. The beating and bouncing took its toll. The next morning, Yellow Thunder lay motionless in the vehicle, dead from a brain hemorrhage, his body found two weeks later. The Hare brothers were arrested, released without bail, and charged with only second-degree manslaughter in Custer, South Dakota.[54]

The following year, another Oglala Lakota, Wesley Bad Heart Bull, was stabbed in a fight outside a bar near the Pine Ridge Reservation. Bad Heart Bull was a known alcoholic who had been involved in many public disturbances through the years and when he got into an argument with Darold (Mad Dog) Schmidt, the quarrel extended into the parking lot. According to one witness, Schmidt had bragged earlier that "he was going to kill him an Indian"[55] and soon Bad Heart Bull lay dead with a knife plugged into his back, severing his aorta. Like the Yellow Thunder killing, Bad Heart Bull's assailant was tried for second-degree manslaughter and received a light jail sentence.

In the states where the West was still considered "Wild," murders of Indian men, especially those involved with public intoxication, were often disregarded by the judicial system. White perpetrators, judged by white juries, often received minor penalties when violence and hatred erupted in the deaths of Indians. In the Bad Heart Bull case, the courts would disregard the testimony of another Lakota male who had witnessed the stabbing and related a story of deliberate, premeditated murder. To the Indian community, miscarriages of justice were being repeatedly perpetrated. When Sarah Bad Heart Bull, the victim's mother, asked the American Indian Movement to intervene, the county court seat erupted into violence. The Lakota were back on the "warpath," precipitating a confrontation that would escalate to the federal government.

The American Indian Movement (AIM) originated in Minneapolis, Minnesota, established by a group of disenfranchised Native Americans who were relocated off their reservations. Originally focusing its efforts on police brutally in the Twin Cities, AIM advocated for needed public services for urban Indians who sought jobs and educational opportunities around the country as part of the government's relocation program. AIM soon became a national assistance organization on and off the reservations, though more militant than other similar support groups.[56]

Militancy was in the air as "Red Power" was taking a page from the African American Civil Rights Movement, staging "fish-ins," the occupation of Alcatraz Island, marches, and other demonstrations to highlight the plight of American Indians. By the early 1970s, frustration with the Bureau of Indian Affairs, the double standard of justice in the court systems, the corruption of tribal governments, and the lack of job opportunities with its resultant poverty pushed Native American communities toward an activist and sometimes confrontational approach to their quandary.

The Yellow Thunder and Bad Heart Bull murders and the subsequent slap on the wrist given their assailants by the *wasichus* courts led to a confrontation between AIM protestors and the civic authorities of Custer, South Dakota. When court officers refused to let the AIM activists into the courtroom during the trial of Bad Heart Bull's killers, a disturbance exploded when the police enforced their eviction. Forty Lakota were arrested as rioters, including Sarah Bad Heart Bull, who was beaten on the courthouse steps. Wesley's mother now faced a possible forty-year prison term while her son's murderer faced a maximum of ten years for the senseless killing.[57] The injustice was blatant and battle lines intensified. The Custer courthouse riot was the first violent engagement between Lakota and the U. S. government since Wounded Knee in 1890.[58]

Irate over AIM's influence which he blamed for the altercations in Custer, Pine Ridge tribal chairman Richard (Dick) Wilson obtained an order from the tribal courts to ban AIM representatives from attending public gatherings on the reservation. Regardless of Wilson's counter actions, traditional Lakota elders and spiritualists, who viewed his regime as corruptly mismanaging the reservation, supported AIM. The community formed the Oglala Sioux Civil Rights Organization and invited AIM delegates, including Russell Means, an Oglala raised at Pine Ridge, and Dennis Banks, a Chippewa, to speak at their meeting on Feb. 27, 1973.

At the parley, two Lakota women stood and addressed the gathering. Helen (Ellen) Moves Camp and Gladys Bissonette spoke first in Lakota and then in English for all in attendance to understand. They beseeched AIM to work with the Pine Ridge community. Gladys cried that the Oglala Lakota had been beaten so badly they had forgotten how to defend their rights. Helen was adamant they should fight and fight there.[59] The district chiefs, including Frank Fools Crow, widower of Fannie Afraid of Hawk, agreed and recommended, "Go head and do it. Go to Wounded Knee."[60]

Wounded Knee was on the minds of many Americans after the publication of Dee Brown's 1970 bestselling book, *Bury My Heart at Wounded Knee*,[61] and the rejuvenation of Neihardt's *Black Elk Speaks*, bringing the story of Big Foot's Lakota and the 1890 carnage by U. S. Army troopers to public consciousness. With the immense popularity of Brown's book and Black Elk's spiritual narrative, the massacre site at Wounded Knee received renewed national recognition, and tribal elders understood its solemn symbolism for their contemporary cause.

After the evening meeting, a caravan of fifty-four cars and trucks transporting 200 Oglala Lakota activists and AIM supporters advanced on the small village of Wounded Knee. Frank Fools Crow and other Lakota *wicasa wakan* who backed AIM because of the respect these young "warriors" showed to traditional Indian spiritualism rode in the front car and conducted a prayer at the mass grave of the 1890 victims, seeking sacred guidance for the protesters.[62] Armed with rifles, handguns, knives, and clubs, the militants took the town's residents as hostages.

With the reservation's community divided and with little advance planning, AIM made a public demand that the U. S. government recognize signed treaties, especially the 1868 Fort Laramie accord; that an investigation be conducted into BIA practices; and that Dick Wilson be removed from office as Pine Ridge tribal chairman, taking with him a "goon" squad he was accused of using to intimidate local tribesmen who disagreed with his polices. Within hours, police and federal agents had the town surrounded, blocking protesters from leaving or sympathizers from entering, resulting in a standoff that would last seventy-one days and lead to martial conflict.[63] The federal government brought in armored vehicles, machine guns, helicopters, and other military equipment to reinforce FBI, BIA police officers, and U. S. marshals, surrounding the militants with a massive show of force. The activists' small array of handheld firearms was a mismatch to the federal arsenal assembled.[64] Parallels to 1890 were becoming evident.

Throughout the coming days, while both sides exchanged sporadic gunfire, negotiators negotiated. The FBI did what it could to keep media away, but AIM found ways of getting their message out through blockade runners, who were often Lakota women bringing food in at night. When the National Council of Churches attempted to use its influence to settle the siege peacefully, the FBI escorted their representatives off the reservation. Lakota traditional chiefs and ceremonial leaders met in a tipi and emerged with a declaration that the Oglala were an independent, sovereign nation based on the Treaty of 1868 and that they intended to send a delegation to the United Nations for recognition. Wounded Knee was declared a corporate state under the Independent Oglala Nation.[65]

The siege continued day in and day out. The national evening news carried images of the shootings at Wounded Knee to an American public already tired of watching the violence and death from Vietnam traversing their television screens. Two activists died, victims of sniping: Buddy LaMonte (Lakota)[66] and Frank Clearwater (Cherokee). U. S. Marshal Lloyd Grimm was severely wounded, and FBI agent Curtis Fitzgerald was shot in the left hand and forearm.[67] A Lakota baby was born inside the compound.

Saddened by Buddy LaMonte's death, Frank Fools Crow met with a representative from President Richard M. Nixon's office at a fence along the perimeter of the compound. Fools Crow told the AIM activists it was time to end the holdout. AIM and the chiefs signed an agreement with the federal government that guaranteed fair treatment toward the activists and an investigation into the political tribal affairs of the reservation, formally ending the siege.

Were the skeletal remains those of Albert Afraid of Hawk? Gary Aronsen, Bruce Greene, and I reconvened at Cornell Memorial to conduct the forensic examination. The funeral home provided space, and we began by cleaning and laying out the fragile bones anatomically for analysis. Before us was a far more complete inventory of skeletal elements than I ever thought possible considering the acidic soil in which they had reposed. However, all the bones exhibited some damage/destruction associated with taphonomic changes due to high soil acidity and microbe action.[68]

With the skeleton spread out on a gurney, Gary conducted an examination for estimates of age and sex. Even with articular ends damaged, it was clear all the long bones had been fused and the third molars completely erupted, hence a fully adult individual. The pubic symphysis morphology most closely resembled Suchey and Brooks Scale 1, which correlated with males aged between 15 and 23 years of age.[69] Sexual dimorphism is relatively pronounced in the human species with males tending to be larger and exhibiting more bone density. We observed that the cranium exhibited prominent brow ridges, a very rugged nuchal area (where the neck muscles attach in the lower back of the skull) and a relatively large mastoid process. In addition, the pelvic morphology, having a deep sciatic notch, strongly indicated a male individual. We were very comfortable suggesting the remains were that of a young adult man, probably aged between twenty and twenty-three years.

So far so good, but is the individual of Native American ancestry? The family asked that DNA analysis be conducted only as a last resort for identification of Albert since genetic testing at the time required destruction of the skeletal sample. Though needing only a minute portion, testing would necessitate forfeiture of bone, and many Native Americans do not want destructive techniques applied on their ancestor's remains. Instead Gary relied on gross skeletal morphology, not as accurate as genetic testing but helpful in determining ancestry. The degree of skeletal decomposition made cranio-metric data impossible to use, so he had to rely on morphological characteristics with the dental incisors as the strongest indicator of Native American origin. Fortunately, the teeth were in excellent condition and the incisors exhibited a pronounced lingual (tongue-side) shoveling, a prevalent genetic characteristic among Asians and Native Americans that is all but absent among African and European populations.[70]

The skeleton showed virtually no indicators of pathology or traumas. Stature was estimated based on femur (thigh bone) maximum length and tibial physiological length. Using specific formulae calculated from Native American populations, including Plains Indians,[71] stature was estimated as between 192 and 196 centimeters or slightly taller than six feet.

The most interesting results of the forensic examination of Albert's skeleton were biomarkers exhibited. For instance, the labial crown surfaces of the incisors and canines showed evidence of enamel hypoplasia, which is observed as small horizontal bands across the crown and are indicators of nutritional stress during childhood growth and development. As the teeth grow, enamel is laid down like rings on a tree. If nutritional foods are unavailable, the growth pattern is disrupted. If nutrition is restored, growth resumes. This interchangeable pattern produces bands marking each episode of stress/recovery. Though the hypoplasia expression is minimal, it does suggest that nutritional food was periodically lacking in the diet of Albert's childhood. Gary and I hypothesized this may be a reaction to periods of starvation among Lakota children during the late 19th century when food rations often arrived late or were nonexistent. The evidence of enamel hypoplasia provides a powerful biological marker testifying to the harsh conditions Lakota children suffered under the early reservation system.

One unanticipated observation was the unusual rugosity on the distal tibiofibular joints (ankles), symptomatic of pronounced, uneven surfaces that made the ankle largely inflexible, either having been injured or subject to high stress. This condition would not have altered the mobility of the ankle joint, but may be indicative of lifestyle pathology associated with horseback riding[72] where controlling the horse, especially without a saddle, requires the inward rotation of the ankle. Albert's condition was not severe, but the remodeling of the ankle suggests he rode horses regularly and is consistent with expectations of a reservation rancher and Wild West performer.

The hair particles recovered around the left ear were submitted to microscopic inspection. The samples compared well with the diagnostic characteristics of human hair. Enhancement of organic preservation due to the copper earrings remarkably allowed Albert's hair to survive over 100 years in the grave.

There were no indicators on the skeleton of major infections or traumas that would be severe enough to cause death. Unlike 'Ōpūkaha'ia, the acute infection Albert suffered from food poisoning leaves no lesions or other indicators of death for the skeletal investigator. Albert's immediate death from botulism left behind no visible signatures on the skeleton.

Even without the genetic testing, we were extremely confident these were the remains of Albert Afraid of Hawk. Archival, archaeological, and biological data were remarkably concordant. This type of analysis is not proof of identity but the result of showing no falsification. That is, there were no negative outliers suggesting the skeleton was *not* that of Albert Afraid of Hawk. Every observable skeletal indicator Gary Aronsen could discern was positive in terms of the biology and lifestyle of Albert's known history.

When Fannie Afraid of Hawk died in April 1954, Frank Fools Crow remained adrift for quite a while without his beloved spouse. Nonetheless, he continued his spiritual journey and promotion of traditional Lakota ways. He would marry Katie Red Paint, and together they would develop a wonderful relationship as Frank aged into a respected spiritual tribal elder. He would serve for two years (1960-62) on the Pine Ridge Tribal Council representing the Medicine Root District. His staunchest support went to the AIM activists and their efforts on behalf of Indian people across the country. After Wounded Knee II, Frank Fools Crow travelled to Washington and met President Gerald Ford as part of an Oglala delegation to discuss tribal issues with White House aides. He was invited to give the opening prayer for a session of the U. S. Senate on Sept. 5, 1975, becoming the first Lakota spiritualist to receive such an honor.

Even as he aged, Fools Crow assisted the Oglala Tribe in filing another claim for the Black Hills, which was opposed by a number of corporate and governmental interests.[73] Regardless, in 1979 the U. S. Court of Claims overruled its earlier 1942 decision and agreed that the Black Hills was taken in violation of the Fifth Amendment. The federal Supreme Court upheld the ruling and awarded the Sioux Nations $106 million in compensation. However, the land claim for *Paha Sapa* remains unresolved, primarily due to Lakota insistence that they do not wish monetary compensation—they want their sacred hills back![74] Fools Crow presented a joint statement with Frank Kills Enemy before a Congressional Sub-Committee on Interior and Insular Affairs, opposing a House Bill to provide compensation to the Lakota for the illegal taking of the Black Hills. Fools Crow made clear to Congress that his people were against financial compensation because "the Black Hills are not for sale under any circumstances...The Black Hills are sacred to the Lakota people... (it) is our church, the place where we worship... our burial grounds. The Bones of our grandfathers lie buried in those hills. How can you expect us to sell our church and our cemeteries for a few token white man dollars? We will never sell."[75]

Frank Fools Crow's dream of Lakota self-determination for his people stands in union with the visions of Wovoka and Black Elk.[76] He died at ninety-nine years of age after devoting his remarkable life to the furthering of traditional Lakota culture in the modern world and at a time of the resurgence of their cultural ways.

8 | "Home Is Where He Belongs"

As the rhythmic sound of drums and incantation of Lakota singers cascaded across the open plains at the foot of the Badlands on the northern section of the Pine Ridge Indian Reservation, the skeletal remains of Albert Afraid of Hawk, wrapped in a buffalo robe, were hoisted upon a five-foot-high wooden scaffold. He will stay suspended until evening when he will be brought down and buried beneath the earth. Daniel Jay Afraid of Hawk sang traditional songs. Rick Two Dogs, a Lakota medicine man and relative of the Afraid of Hawk family, conducted smudging ceremonies to bless Albert on his final journey to the spirit world. In Lakota mortuary belief, the journey will take four days. Wilma Thin Elk recited the family's genealogy before and after Albert. White Plume noted that Albert would have been a ten-year-old boy when Wounded Knee occurred, declaring, "He is our lost elder."[1] Buffalo meat and cherry juice are buried with him to sustain his travel. Once arriving in the spirit world, whatever food is left over is shared with family members who have gone before.

The long journey of Albert Afraid of Hawk has brought him to St. Mark's Episcopal Mission Cemetery, north of Manderson, South Dakota, Sept. 9, 2012. The mission church that once resided on a hill adjacent to the cemetery is no longer standing, though remnants of the wooden structure can still be seen lying on the ground. It was here that the Afraid of Hawk family attended Christian services after their conversion in 1893 and where they have been buried into the 21st century: Albert's brother, Richard Afraid of Hawk, survivor of the Wounded Knee Massacre; Richard's wife, Mabel Lone Elk; his mother, White Mountain Woman; and his father, Afraid of Hawk. As the sun began its descent behind the rolling, western hills, Albert was laid to rest behind his father in this consecrated ground. The long road home that started 112 years ago was complete. Marlis defined the occasion, "(The repatriation of Albert) is sacred to my family and the (entire) family of Pine Ridge."[2]

When the autopsy of Albert was finalized at the Cornell Memorial Funeral Home in Danbury and his remains verified, the Afraid of Hawk family requested he not be placed in any artificial containers—no plastic, aluminum, or metal—but rather wrapped only in natural products. In compliance, cotton pouches were provided, and Albert's bones were delicately placed in them and secured for transportation by plane to Rapid City, South Dakota where they were brought to the regional hospital and placed in the custody of the Sioux Funeral Home, which handled the arrangements for the last leg of the trip to Pine Ridge.

On Sept. 8, 2012, less than three weeks after Albert Afraid of Hawk was exhumed in Danbury, Connecticut, a two-day service was held at the Wounded Knee District School auditorium in Manderson. The Eagle Mountain Singers served as traditional drummers and Rick Two Dogs presided over the spiritual services. The Sitanka Wikisuye Riders of 1986 assisted as pallbearers and more than seventy members of Albert's *tiospaye*, including delegates of the recently adopted Connecticut family represented by Bob and Mary-Jo Young, Christine Rose, and Wendell and Nancy Deer With Horns were in attendance. The five of them, with those of us who were unable to make the trip west, were given the privilege of being honorary pallbearers, reminding me of the distinction of carrying 'Ōpūkaha'ia's *koa*-wood casket in Cornwall during his farewell service. The Afraid of Hawk family adhered to traditional details providing Albert with the funeral he would have gotten had his body been returned in 1900. The following morning, the buffalo robe containing Albert's remains would be taken to St. Mark's Cemetery for final internment.

The auditorium where Afraid of Hawk's wake was conducted also functioned as the community gymnasium and had been decorated with a number of brightly colored star quilts, poster-sized photos of Albert, and the Oglala Lakota Sioux (Pine Ridge) flag with blue fringe inscribed,

Albert Afraid of Hawk
1879
6-29-1900
The Oglala Sioux Nation

Under the banner, a black, red, white, and yellow star quilt draped a table with multicolored freshly-cut flowers overlooking the simple wooden box that contained the buffalo-robed remains. To the right side on the gym floor were two tables covered with blue linen on which photos of Albert and his brother Richard were set, along with a number of specialty cakes welcoming Albert home to Pine Ridge.

Once the Afraid of Hawk family arrived, four pallbearers conveyed Albert, in an open wooden palette, into the auditorium, placing him on high sawhorses, which were draped with a light blue, white, and brown star quilt. Now settled, family and friends approached Albert, gently touching the buffalo robe, praying as they passed. As the Eagle Mountain Singers drummed and sang, all the attendees proceeded from Albert to his family, paying their respects and offering congratulations to Daniel, Marlis, and John for his return.[3] A Lakota prayer was tendered,

> **O *Tunkasila* (Grandfather),[4] whose voice I hear in the wind**
> **and whose breath gives life to all the world—hear me—**
> **I come before you,**
> **one of your many children. I am small and weak.**
> **I need your strength and wisdom.**
> **Let me walk in beauty.[5]**

Oglala spiritual leader Rick Two Dogs spoke, remarking that while this young Lakota's return to Pine Ridge brings closure to Albert and the Afraid of Hawk family, it is also a part of a larger issue of repatriation. "A lot of (our) people need to come home," Two Dogs lamented, noting their ancestors were still held in museums and cemeteries around the world.[6] The return of Albert Afraid of Hawk is more than one family bringing home a lost relative; the return represents the wishes of the community for closure and respect to their ancestors who, in the words of Floyd Westerman, have been "imprisoned" far from their homelands.

During a quiet moment during the afternoon wake, Darius Afraid of Hawk, cradling his seven-week-old daughter, approached Bob Young and asked to have his picture taken with Bob and the infant. Darius had come from Lincoln, Nebraska, to be present in welcoming his ancestor home to Pine Ridge. He came because he wanted to honor Albert as well as pay respect to Daniel for all he had done in his life and for the example he had set for the entire Afraid of Hawk family by honoring their history and traditions. Darius wanted the photograph taken so when his daughter grew older, she could appreciate the historic occasion of Albert's return and say she was there, hopefully inspiring her with an appreciation of her family's heritage.[7]

Most funerals are solemn occasions and while emotions were high at Albert's wake, many noted it contained an element of celebration in bringing family together—more like a reunion. Wendell Deer With Horns suggested, "It is more of a joyous and happy occasion to return (a family member home)."[8] The Afraid of Hawk kin had prepared food for all the attendees; once everyone had been fed, they withdrew to their homes in preparation for the next day's funeral and reburial. Daniel remained behind, spending the entire night in the auditorium so that Albert would not be alone.[9]

The following morning, Sunday, Sept. 9, 2012, the funeral and reburial of Albert Afraid of Hawk began in Manderson where his *tiospaye* assembled for their final farewells. After prayers and songs by Daniel Afraid of Hawk and Rick Two Dogs, Albert's remains were carried out of the building into a hearse for the fifteen-mile ride to St. Mark's Episcopal Cemetery outside of Rockyford. The jars of buffalo meat and cherry juice, prepared by three women in the family, were set at the head of the casket palette. With the drummers rhythmically beating a requiem, Marlis and Daniel walked closely behind the pallbearers, then boarded their car and drove behind the hearse as it slowly travelled to the small mission burial ground.

As the hearse proceeded north from Manderson, Mary-Jo Young was struck by the empathy displayed among Pine Ridge Reservation tribal members encountering the funeral procession in the course of their daily activities. Cars approaching in the opposite direction of BIA Route 33 pulled over to the side of the road and waited silently until the entire procession had passed. She noted to herself that back home in Connecticut, drivers on the other side of the road would continue on their way with little notice of the passing hearse and at intersections people would view the procession as an inconvenience, forcing them to wait until bypassed. But as Albert travelled the final leg of his epic journey, vehicles pulled over and came to a complete stop of their own volition. Cowboys took their hats off as a sign of respect, waiting reverently in their trucks or on their horses. While many tribal members were aware of Albert's return, most were simply showing deserved respect to any deceased member of the Pine Ridge community.[10]

Pulling off the paved road, the funeral procession moved slowly westward along a rutted, dirt lane, a half-mile leading to the cemetery. Each vehicle stirred up the dry soil, creating heightened invisibility as the vehicles that followed entered the dust storm. Brown soil particles permeated the air, decelerating the traffic until the prairie winds could disperse the dust and once again reveal the road ahead. Cattle, some so far away they appeared as black dots on the horizon, were grazing in abutting pastures. The multi-colored columns of the Badlands peaked in the distance.

Burial Scaffold of Albert Afraid of Hawk, St. Mark's Mission Cemetery, Pine Ridge Indian Reservation, South Dakota, September 2012. (Courtesy of Mary-Jo Young.)

Approaching an open gate secured by barbed wire, the caravan entered the cemetery. Young Lakota men shoveled four small round holes deep enough into the ground to secure the wooden legs of the scaffold. Four horizontal poles were lashed to the legs five feet off the ground, standing the scaffold erect. Albert Afraid of Hawk was carried from the hearse, smudged, and raised to the top of the scaffold where a blue star quilt had been draped over the horizontal poles as a soft bed. The jars of buffalo and cherry juice still rested in the wooden palette, and three vases of simple yet colorful flower arrangements were placed on the ground at the foot of the scaffold.

Tiospaye and friends filed past Albert in single formation one last time, reaching up to touch the buffalo robe before moving on to the immediate family. Drumming and traditional songs filtered through the countryside carried by the wind over the High Plains. Sage and sweet grass smoldered, releasing its sacred fragrance. Daniel stood solemnly at the head of the scaffold with his right arm raised on the box and head bowed.[11] He spoke softly to Albert in his Native language, words only his *lala* (grandfather) on the scaffold would hear.

Alex White Plume stayed behind once everyone returned to the auditorium in Manderson. He would linger in the cemetery until sunset, then remove Albert's bones from the scaffold and bury him in the row behind his mother and father, a short distance from his brother Richard. The Afraid of Hawk family had last seen Albert as he set off for the train station to travel east and join Buffalo Bill's Wild West. Now, one hundred and twelve years later, they were together again, reunited in death. If bones could cry, tears of joy would have been shed.

The attendees returned to the Manderson auditorium where food was once again shared. The family honored Albert by hosting a "Give-Away" Ceremony, expressing thanks to the *tiospaye* for assistance in his return to Pine Ridge. Once again, Bob and Mary-Jo Young and Christine Rose received star quilts and blankets in appreciation of their efforts in bringing Albert home. Joined by Wendell and Nancy Deer With Horns, who were also honored in the ceremony, the Connecticut *tiospaye* were once again acknowledged by the Afraid of Hawk family.

Bob and Mary-Jo were deservedly singled out by Daniel, advancing to the front of the room where they were instructed to dance to the beat of the drums playing an "Honor Song." Arm-in-arm, Daniel escorted Bob and Mary-Jo, circling the room three times, passing people who would shake their hands and offer appreciation.[12] Mary-Jo was so moved she struggled to contain her emotions, her face scrunching up to fight back tears welling in her eyes. Even Bob swallowed hard in an effort to maintain his composure. The Afraid of Hawk family had bestowed a fitting honor on them, and they were overwhelmed by the consideration. "We love you all dearly," Bob told the assembly. "I'd like to say, Albert, you have become like a grandfather to us."[13]

Wendell Deer With Horns joined the Eagle Mountain Singers, drumming and singing in celebration well into the afternoon. Marlis Afraid of Hawk danced with her grandchildren and felt relief, satisfied that Albert was finally "home where he belongs" and humbled by her meaningful dream that moved the repatriation forward. Daniel Jay Afraid of Hawk, the family patriarch, rodeo performer, last surviving offspring of Albert's brother Richard, and the genealogical link between Wounded Knee of 1890 and 1973, served in the manner of a traditional Keeper of the Winter Count, preserving his family's history and instilling them with pride in their cultural traditions, stood gratified, reflecting in the moment as the drums and prayers of the Lakota singers swirled within his head.

Six months after I paid my respects at Henry 'Ōpūkaha'ia's burial monument on the Big Island of Hawai'i, I travelled to the Pine Ridge Reservation, reuniting with the Afraid of Hawk family and paying my respects to Albert at St. Mark's Mission Cemetery. Bob Young and I had been invited by the Oglala Lakota College Library in Kyle to tell the story of our roles in Albert's homecoming to students and the Pine Ridge community, so I joined him and Mary-Jo in Rapid City and together we travelled to the reservation.

Even though Bob and Mary-Jo had attended the reburial ceremony the previous year, they couldn't quite recall which of the numerous dirt roads lead to St. Mark's Cemetery, so Marlis asked a cousin to meet and escort us along BIA Route 33. Driving over the bumpy dirt road, kicking up clouds of brown dust, gave me an appreciation of what had been experienced the year before with dozens of vehicles crossing over the rugged yet flat terrain. Studying the landscape outside the car window, I was mesmerized by the open plains, rolling as far as the eye could see, providing a stark contrast from the developed and dense eastern woodland of Connecticut. Up ahead, erect tombstones of the burial ground came into view. Albert Afraid of Hawk's scaffold, still erect, is the highest landmark; its red ribbons, placed at the tops of the four leg poles during the reburial ceremony, continued to flutter in the open wind. A small mound of ashen earth, which hadn't settled, defined Albert's burial plot. He lies directly behind the prominent marble military tombstone of his father, "Afraid of a Hawk."

The graves are laid out in the Christian east-west pattern in preparation for the Day of Resurrection. The remnants of flowers still secure within their vases have tipped, blown over by the wind, lying upon the burial mound. Dry prairie grass had grown knee high in areas, extending above low tombstones, some dating to the late 19th century when St. Mark's was established. A few older markers have tumbled or have cracked, lying on the ground; others have been repaired, but the majority are firmly erect and in place. We searched for the gravestone of Albert's brother, Richard Afraid of Hawk, paying our respects and giving thought to his survival at Wounded Knee. On an adjacent knoll to the east, ruins of a timber structure lie on the ground; they are all that remain of St. Mark's Church where the Afraid of Hawk family attended religious services and prayed for Albert's safe return. It had taken more than a century, but their prayers have been answered.

Albert Afraid of Hawk left the Pine Ridge Reservation in South Dakota in March 1900, journeyed by train throughout the eastern U. S., and died unexpectedly in Danbury, Connecticut, far from his homeland. In the 112 years he resided beneath the ground in Wooster Cemetery, his grave had become lost and forgotten. But his memory, preserved by his family, waited for the occasion of his return. He had become more than an image in old photographs. He had become an inspiration, the representative of a time of momentous culture change in Lakota history. Albert overcame repression and set out on a journey to find a way to remain "Lakota." He triumphed in death in a way he could never have imaged during his short life.

I allowed myself a satisfied moment, as I had at Henry ʻŌpūkahaʻiaʻs grave, taking pride in the minor role I was privileged to play in the return of Albert Afraid of Hawk to Pine Ridge. I also think about how much the two experiences have changed me, professionally and personally. I am grateful.

Wopila Tunkasila Albert. Thank you, Grandfather Albert.

Epilogue

Twenty-thirteen was a special year. In April, after a two-decade interval, my wife and I were finally able to travel to Hawai'i and reunite with Debbie Lee. In August, we trekked out to the Pine Ridge Indian Reservation with Bob and Mary-Jo Young, reconnecting with Marlis and the Afraid of Hawk family. During the two trips, I was able to pay my respects at the final resting places of both Henry 'Ōpūkaha'ia and Albert Afraid of Hawk, walk through the lands of their upbringing, stand silenced at Wounded Knee and Kealakekua Bay, marvel at the natural and cultural significance of the Black Hills and Mauna Loa, and ascend the Badlands and the Kilauea Caldera. The physical characteristics of their two worlds are dramatically different, but the themes of their cultural stories are comparable.

Bringing Henry and Albert home grew beyond immediate family interest, extending to the entire Hawaiian and Lakota communities a continuity with their past while emphasizing the significance of repatriation. Facilitating the completion of their long journeys developed into something beyond the bringing home of an individual ancestor; it brought families together and provided a sense of self-esteem, cultural identity, and kinship within their communities. Since both young men defined a time of enormous culture change transitioning into the modern world system, Henry and Albert became the personification of all that had been lost, and yet, all that was to be gained.

I, especially, learned that interpretation of the past is not abstract or esoteric. How heritage is construed has significant import to descendants and people searching for meaning in their contemporary lives. Our collective and individual pasts contribute immensely to the quality of our lives. I often remind my students that we weren't suddenly dropped here in the 21st century with Internet technology and smartphones, but that we emerge out of a deep history with traditions that give meaning by connecting us to those who have gone before—through their struggles, hopes, aspirations, and sheer survival. We honor them by studying their lives. They honor us by giving life.

These are some of the important lessons that Henry ʻŌpūkahaʻia and Albert Afraid of Hawk have taught me. They emphasized to me that my work is not about an ambiguous historical past, but that what I do as an archaeologist affects the personal lives of people today; that it is relevant to the modern social world, not obscure, but influences how people think of themselves and the cultural other. Working closely with the Lee and Afraid of Hawk families, having their trust in my ability to handle the remains of such cherished ancestors; having collaborated with my archaeological colleagues and forensic investigators; and, having experienced the deep sense of satisfaction of helping each family fulfill their aspirations to repatriate an ancestor has been the most profound and crowning achievement of my career. To have played a role in returning these two extraordinary young men home to their families was not simply a professional obligation as a state archaeologist, but a very personal, moving experience. I came to believe that my forty year calling in archaeology had prepared me for these specific moments—to have facilitated the archaeological recovery of Albert Afraid of Hawk and Henry ʻŌpūkahaʻia, assisting in their long journeys home.

Since the repatriation of Henry ʻŌpūkahaʻia, both of Debbie Lee's parents, Kwai Wah and Elizabeth Kapeka Hoʻomanawanui, have entered the Eternal Kingdom. Without their support and encouragement, it is unlikely that Debbie would have been able to bring cousin Henry home in such a timely manner. Their deaths have left a great void, but memory of their achievement will always remain prominent and visibly present in ʻŌpūkahaʻia's magnificent burial monument. Deborah Liʻikapeka Lee and her extended ʻohana are the bearers of Henry's legacy into the future and they all take that responsibility seriously.

A number of pivotal events in Henry's story are reaching their bicentennial. In May 2017, the Town of Cornwall marked the 200th anniversary of the founding of the Foreign Mission School with the dedication of the Steward's House as a National Historic Landmark by the Department of the Interior, a stage performance, church and cemetery ceremonies, and a colloquium of scholars discussing various aspects of the school's legacy. Families of Henry ʻŌpūkahaʻia and John Ridge were in attendance. February 17, 2018 commemorated the 200ᵗʰ year anniversary of the death of ʻŌpūkahaʻia with remembrance ceremonies timed simultaneously in Hawaiʻi and Cornwall. October 23, 2019 will mark the bicentennial of the departure of the *Thaddeus* from Boston harbor, followed by a celebration acknowledging the landing of the Protestant missions at Kailua-Kona on April 4, 2020. All ceremonies are open to the public and are being planned for Cornwall, Oahu, Kailua-Kona, New Haven, and Boston. We all hope that the bicentennial calendar and observances will give renewed recognition to the inspiration of Henry ʻŌpūkahaʻia.

Recreating the 1890 footsteps of Chief Big Foot's Lakota from Cheyenne River south through the Badlands to Pine Ridge, the Wounded Knee Bigfoot Memorial Riders were organized in December 1986 with nineteen horsemen participating in a Wiping of the Tears Ceremony. Four years later, commemorating the 100th anniversary of the massacre, the tour was renamed the Future Generation (*Oomaka Tokatakiya*) Ride to create awareness of what happened that tragic winter morning for Lakota children in order for them to heal, honor, and remember always the slaying of their ancestors.

One of the earliest and most prominent riders was Daniel Jay Afraid of Hawk, Oglala Lakota rodeo performer and rancher, whose father was one of the small number of survivors at Wounded Knee. Only months after the repatriation of his father's brother Albert, Daniel suffered a stroke that restrained his physical movements. Though partially blind and deaf, his spirit and Lakota pride remained unaffected by his bodily limitations—so much so that when the 125ᵗʰ anniversary of Wounded Knee arrived in 2015, the eighty-five-year-old Lakota cowboy insisted to his family that he once again, despite his disabilities, desired to be one of the Bigfoot Memorial Riders.

Unable to traverse the entire 150 miles on horseback in the dead of winter, Daniel joined the riders five miles north of Wounded Knee, where he accompanied the Sitting Bull and Bigfoot Riders for the final leg of their journey. Although his son, John Afraid of Hawk, rode alongside holding onto the reins leading Daniel's horse, the old patriarch sat erect upon his steed with his gloved hands grasping the saddle horn firmly, riding as he had done so often since childhood with dignity and happiness.

The riders had travelled through snow and bitter cold temperatures, withstanding wind chills below zero for two weeks, but were reminded that their suffering was trifling compared to the conditions Big Foot's people were made to endure. On December 28, 2015, they arrived at Wounded Knee Creek. Upon reaching the site of the killing fields, the riders culminated the march at the foot of the hill below the cemetery and memorial, circumnavigating their horses to the right until all the riders joined the sacred circle where they prayed to the spirits of *Wanka Tanka* and Jesus Christ in commemoration of their slain ancestors and for the healing of future generations of Lakota children.

Daniel's perseverance was a proud moment for the entire Afraid of Hawk family. As the last living member of first generation Wounded Knee descendants, Daniel was revered that evening as he was escorted around the sacred circle three times, surrounded by the sound of an "Honor Song" while the riders and their families paid respect to him and his courage, acknowledging all that he represents in Lakota history. Sadly, Daniel, the family's "Old Timer Cowboy," died in April 2018. He was the personal and cultural link to 1890.

While in Hawai'i and Pine Ridge, we had the opportunity to meet with family and friends of Albert Afraid of Hawk and Henry 'Ōpūkaha'ia who shared their experiences and emotions about the repatriations. Hearing their stories made me appreciate even more the power and influence that ancestry and our common humanity have on our contemporary lives. Though as humans we possess differing traditions, languages, and even ways to pray, down deep we are all related (*Mitakuye Oyasin*). Our collective and individual pasts are meaningful, contributing to the quality of our lives and giving rise to our social identities and self-worth; together, they provide all peoples across the globe with hopes for their children and the future. In this, there is a little bit of Henry and Albert in each of us—the ability to overcome hardship, persevere through tragedy, continue the search for true meaning in our lives, and give optimism to our descendants. My hope is that these two young Native men, unconquerable in death, are forever content to be embraced by the love of their families. Through their passion and influence on future generations, their journeys will continue.

Notes

PROLOGUE

1. Dwight, Edwin W., *The Memoirs of Henry Obookiah, A Native of Owhyhee, And A Member of the Foreign Mission School; Who died At Cornwall, Connecticut February 17, 1818, Aged 26 Years*, Honolulu: Woman's Board of Missions For the Pacific Islands, reprint, 2012.

2. Campbell, Joseph, *The Hero With A Thousand Faces*, Novato, CA: New World Library, 3rd edition, 2008.

3. Floyd "'Red Crow" Westerman, Dakota, was invited by the Connecticut River Powwow Society in 1988 at the Farmington Polo Grounds to be the main speaker. Red Crow appeared in a number of television and movies, including the drama, Dances With Wolves" in 1990. He was a strong advocate for Indian Rights throughout his life, a singer and songwriter, environmentalist and artist.

4. In 1969, Floyd Red Crow Westerman composed a song based on Vine DeLoria, Jr.'s book *Custer Died For Your Sins* (London: MacMillan and Company, 1969) entitled "Her Comes The Anthros," https://www.youtube.com /watch?v=vWaI9UZ-LYw.

5. DeLoria, Vine, Jr., *Custer Died For Your Sins*, London: MacMillan Company, 1969, pp. 78-100. Also see, Vine DeLoria, Jr., *Red Earth, White Lies: Native Americans and the Myth of Scientific Fact*, Golden, Colorado: Fulcrum Publishing, 1997.

6. For a full discussion of the relationship between archaeologists and Native Americans, we recommend, Swidler, Nina, Kurt E. Dongoske, Roger Anyon and Alan S. Downer, eds, *Native Americans and Archaeologists: Stepping Stones to Common Ground*, Walnut Creek, CA: Altamira Press, 1997, and Dongoske, Kurt E., Mark Aldenderfer, and Karen Doebner, *Working Together: Native Americans & Archaeologists*, Washington, D.C.: Society for American Archaeology, 2000.

7. Atalay, Sonya, *Community-based Archaeology*, Berkeley: University of California Press, 2012.

8. Colwell, Chip, *Plundered Skulls and Stolen Spirits: Inside the Fight to Reclaim Native America's Culture*, Chicago: University of Chicago Press, 2017.

9. West, Richard W., Repatriation, IN *Encyclopedia of North American Indians: Native American History, Culture, and Life From the Paleo-Indians to the Present*, ed. By Frederick E. Hoxie, Boston: Houghton Mifflin Company, 1996, pp. 543-546.

10. Colwell, Chip, *Plundered Skulls and Stolen Spirits: Inside the Fight to Reclaim Native America's Culture*, Chicago: University of Chicago Press, 2017.

11. For other detailed case studies and discussion on repatriation issues, see Michael F. Brown, *Who Owns Native Culture*, Boston: Harvard University Press, 2004;

and David Hurst Thomas, *Skull Wars: Kennewick Man, Archaeology and the Battle for Native American Identity*, New York: Basic Books, 2001.

12. See Dongoske, Kurt E., Mark Aldenderfer, and Karen Doebner, *Working Together: Native Americans & Archaeologists*, Washington, D.C.: Society for American Archaeology, 2000.

13. At times in this book I refer to both Native men by their first names which suggests famililarity with them. My useage is not out of disrespect, but due to my personal feelings of involvement in their journey's completion.

PART I. THE REPATRIATION OF HENRY ʻŌPŪKAHAʻIA

1. "OH, HOW I WANT TO SEE OWHYHEE"

1. Dwight, Edwin W., *Memoirs of Henry Obookiah, a Native of Owhyee, and a Member of the Foreign Mission School: Who Died at Cornwall, Conn. Feb. 17, 1818, Aged 26 Years*, Honolulu: Women's Board of Missions For The Pacific, Revised Edition, 2012, p. 66.

2. Ibid.

3. Ibid., p. 64. Henry's uncle, Pahua, *Kahuna Pule* at the Napoʻopoʻo temple, had been training his nephew to follow in his priestly footsteps prior to ʻŌpūkahaʻia's island departure.

4. Ibid., p. 64.

5. Ibid., p. 66.

6. Riegert, Ray, *Hidden Hawaii The Adventurer's Guide*, Berkeley: Ulysses Press, 1979, p. 1.

7. Silva, Noenoe, *Aloha Betrayed: Native Hawaiian Resistance to American Colonialism*, Durham: Duke University Press, 2004.

8. Ibid. p. 102.

9. Riegert, Ray, *Hidden Hawaii The Adventurer's Guide*, Berkeley: Ulysses Press, 1979, p. 11.

10. While we will probably never know exactly when and where the first Polynesians set foot on the Hawaiian Islands, some of my colleagues see this "discovery" as early as 300 Common Era (C.E.), while the latest archaeological evidence suggests a shorter chronology, dating to 1000-1200 CE.

11. Buck, Sir Peter H. (Te Rangi Hiroa), *Vikings of the Sunrise*, Wellington, New Zealand: Whitcombe and Tombs Limited, 1964, p. 39.

12. Ibid., p. 35.

13. Okihiro, Gary Y., *Island World: A History of Hawaiʻi and the United States*, Berkeley: University of California Press, 2008, p. 45.

14. Michael W. Graves and David J. Addison, The Polynesian Settlement of the Hawaiian Archipelago: Integrating Models and Methods in Archaeological Inter-

pretation, *World Archaeology*, Vol. 26, No. 3, Colonization of Islands, pp. 380-399 (Feb., 1995).

15. Okihiro, Gary, *Island World: A History of Hawai'i and the United States*, Berkeley: University of California Press, 2008, p. 215.

16. Kame'eleihiwa, Liliklalā, *Native Lands and Foreign Desires: Ko Hawai'i 'Āina a me, Nā Koi Pu'umake a ka, Po'e Haole*, Honolulu: Bishop Museum Press, 1992.

17. Hale, James L., *Captive Paradise: A History of Hawaii*, New York: St. Martin's Press, 2014, p. 12.

18. Van James, *Ancient Sites of Hawai'i: Archaeological Places of Interest on the Big Island*, Honolulu: Mutual Publishing, 2008.

19. Service, Elman, *Origins of the State and Civilization: The Process of Cultural Evolution*, New York: W.W. Norton & Company, 1975.

20. Kame'eleihiwa, *Native Land*, and Noenoe Silva, *Aloha Betrayed*, Durham: Duke University Press, 2004, pp. 98-102.

21. Malo, David, *Hawaiian Antiquities* (Honolulu: Hawaiian Gazette, 1898).

22. Ibid.

23. Hough, Richard, *Captain James Cook: A Biography*, New York: W.W. Norton, 1994, states that there is good reason to believe that Cook was preceded in his discovery of the islands by the Japanese and Chinese. Similar to Columbus, Cook may have not been the first but was one to bring the knowledge of Hawaii back to the Western world. Also see Braden, Wythe E., "On the Probability of pre-1778 Japanese drifts to Hawaii", *Hawaiian Journal of History*, vol. 10, 1976. Also, see Noenoe Silva, *Aloha Betrayed: Native Hawaiian Resistance to American Colonialism*, Durham: Duke University Press, 2004, Chapter 1, for detailed discussion of contact accounts.

24. Hale, James L., *Captive Paradise: A History of Hawaii*, New York: St. Martin's Press, 2014, p. 4.

25. Ibid., p. 12.

26. Pryor, Alton, *Little Known Tales in Hawaiian History*, Roseville, CA: Stagecoach Publishing, 2004, p. 21.

27. Letter to William A. Dinneen, President, Cornwall Cemetery Associated, from Henry L. Fuqua, dated 10 August 1993, Hartford, CT.

28. CT General Statutes, Section 10-388 *et seq.*

29. Poirier, David A. and Nicholas F. Bellantoni, *In Remembrance: Archaeology and Death*, Westport: Garvin, 1996.

30. Cook, Christopher, *The Providential Life & Heritage of Henry Obookiah*, Waimea, HI: Pa'a Studios, 2015, pp. 2-4.

31. www.mythichawaii.com/weapons.htm

32. Alexander, William, D., *A Brief History of the Hawaiian People*, New York: American Book Company, 1891

33. Barrere, Dorothy B., ed., Mary Kawena Pukui, translator, Fragments of Hawaiian History as Recorded by John Papaʻi, *Bernice P. Bishop Museum Special Publication* 70, Honolulu: Bishop Museum Press, 1983.

34. Dwight, Edwin W., *Memoirs of Henry Obookiah, A Native of Owhyee, and a Member of the Foreign Missions School, Who died at Cornwall, Connecticut February 17, 1818, Aged 26 Years*, Honolulu: Woman's Board of Missions for the Pacific Islands, 2012, p. 2.

35. Brumaghim, Wayne H., *The Life and Legacy of Heneri ʻŌpūkahaʻia: Hawaiʻi's Prodigal Son*, MA Thesis, University of Hawaiʻi, 2011.

36. Dr. Waterhouse, www.pleaseantfields.com/heritage/2011/04/23/obookiah/

37. Cook, Christopher, *The Providential Life & Heritage of Henry Obookiah*, Waimea, HI: Paʻa Studios, 2015, p. 175. Wayne H. Brumaghim, *The Life and Legacy of Heneri ʻŌpūkahaʻia Hawaiʻi's Prodigal Son*, MA Thesis, University of Hawaiʻi, 2011, p. 33-34.

38. Wayne H. Brumaghim, *The Life and Legacy of Heneri ʻŌpūkahaʻia Hawaiʻi's Prodigal Son*, MA Thesis, University of Hawaiʻi, 2011, p 19-36.

39. Ibid.

40. Gold, Theodore, *Historical Records of the town of Cornwall, Litchfield County, Connecticut*, Cornwall, CT: Case, Lockwood & Brainard Company, 2nd edition, 1904, p. 30.

41. David Malo, Hawaiian Antiquities, Honolulu: Hawaiian Gazette, 1898, p. 97.

42. Cook, Christopher, *The Providential Life & Heritage of Henry Obookiah*, Waimea, HI: Paʻa Studios, 2015, p. 5.

43. Dwight, Edwin W., *Memoirs of Henry Obookiah, a Native of Owhyee, and a Member of the Foreign Mission School: Who Died at Cornwall, Conn. Feb. 17, 1818, Aged 26 Years*, Honolulu: Women's Board of Missions For The Pacific, Revised Edition, 2012, p. 22.

44. Ibid., p. 3.

45. Cook, Christopher, *The Providential Life & Heritage of Henry Obookiah*, Waimea, HI: Paʻa Studios, 2015, p. 6.

46. Beckwith, Martha, *Hawaiian Mythology*, Honolulu: University of Hawaii Press, 1970, p. 36.

47. Though no historic documents exist to verify, Pahua may very likely have been present during Cook's initial contact with the Hawaiians, witnessed Cook's burial service of William Whatman in February of 1779 at the Heiau, and was a possible participant in the rituals that gave Cook a chief's funeral upon his death.

48. Dwight, Edwin W., *Memoirs of Henry Obookiah, A Native of Owhyee, and a Member of the Foreign Missions School, Who died at Cornwall, Connecticut February 17, 1818, Aged 26 Years*, Honolulu: Woman's Board of Missions for the Pacific Islands, 2012, p. 3.

49. Ibid.

50. Cook, Christopher, *The Providential Life & Heritage of Henry Obookiah*, Waimea, HI: Paʻa Studios, 2015, p. 6.

51. Dwight, Edwin W., *Memoirs of Henry Obookiah, A Native of Owhyee, and a Member of the Foreign Missions School, Who died at Cornwall, Connecticut February 17, 1818, Aged 26 Years*, Honolulu: Woman's Board of Missions for the Pacific Islands, 2012, p. 3.

52. James, Van, *Ancient Sites of Hawaiʻi: Archaeological Places of Interest on the Big Island*, Honolulu: Mutual Publishing, 1995, pp.24-25.

53. Cook, Christopher, *The Providential Life & Heritage of Henry Obookiah*, Waimea, HI: Paʻa Studios, 2015, p. 5, 7-8.

54. The Enfield Shaker farming community continued into the early 20th-century before it was disbanded due to declining enrollment. The State of Connecticut purchased the property and currently it is home to the state's maximum-security prison. Many extant Shaker buildings are used by the corrections facility and the property is listed on the National Register.

55. Interviews with laborers who had dug graves by hand for a living insinuated that historic burials in New England were usually placed at a depth of five feet, unless a layer of heavy gravel or clay deposits necessitated shallower placement. The proverbial six-foot grave was considered a "heart attack" and avoided. Personal communication, David Smith, superintendent, Wooster Cemetery, Danbury.

56. Dwight, Edwin W., *Memoirs of Henry Obookiah, A Native of Owhyee, and a Member of the Foreign Missions School, Who died at Cornwall, Connecticut February 17, 1818, Aged 26 Years*, Honolulu: Woman's Board of Missions for the Pacific Islands, 2012, p. 3.

57. Ibid., p. 4.

58. Ibid., p. 6.

59. Cook, Christopher, *The Providential Life & Heritage of Henry Obookiah*, Waimea, HI: Paʻa Studios, 2015, p. 12.

60. Ibid., p. 11. Prior to Christopher Cook's research, historians thought that the *Triumph* was obtaining seal furs in the Aleutians. The ship's log clarified the location as Baja.

61. *Narrative of Five Youths From The Sandwich Islands, Now Receiving An Education In This Country*, New York: J. Seymour, 1816.

62. Dwight, Edwin W., *Memoirs of Henry Obookiah, A Native of Owhyee, and a Member of the Foreign Missions School, Who died at Cornwall, Connecticut February 17, 1818, Aged 26 Years*, Honolulu: Woman's Board of Missions for the Pacific Islands, 2012, p. 5.

63. Ibid., p. 8.

2. "I HAVE EITHER A FATHER OR A MOTHER. . . BUT, HE"

1. Personal Communication, Deborah Lee, July 1993.
2. Cook, Christopher, *The Providential Life & Heritage of Henry Obookiah*, Waimea, HI: Pa'a Studios, 2015, p. 28.
3. Ibid., p. 25
4. Benson, John L., History of New York City: Embracing an Outline Sketching of Events from 1609 to 1830, and a Full Account of its Development from 1830 to 1884", Vol. I, New York: Perine Engraving & Publishing Company, 1884. Pp. 55, 56.
5. Dwight, Edwin W., *The Memoirs of Henry Obookiah, A Native of Owhyhee, And A Member of the Foreign Mission School; Who died At Cornwall, Connecticut February 17, 1818, Aged 26 Years*, Honolulu: Woman's Board of Missions For the Pacific Islands, reprint, 2012, p. 9.
6. Hopoo, Thomas, *Memoirs of Thomas Hopoo*, Manuscript, Andover Newton Theological School Library, n.d., p. 45.
7. Dwight, Edwin W., *The Memoirs of Henry Obookiah, A Native of Owhyhee, And A Member of the Foreign Mission School; Who died At Cornwall, Connecticut February 17, 1818, Aged 26 Years*, Honolulu: Woman's Board of Missions For the Pacific Islands, reprint, 2012, p. 9.
8. Hopoo, Thomas, *Memoirs of Thomas Hopoo*, Manuscript, Andover Newton Theological School Library, n.d., p. 9.
9. Dwight, Edwin W., *The Memoirs of Henry Obookiah, A Native of Owhyhee, And A Member of the Foreign Mission School; Who died At Cornwall, Connecticut February 17, 1818, Aged 26 Years*, Honolulu: Woman's Board of Missions For the Pacific Islands, reprint, 2012, p. 10.
10. Ibid., pp. 10-11. According to Noenoe Silva, the sound is similar to the Japanese where l and r sound the same. Kamehameha II often signed his name "Rihoriho." This has been lost in "Hawaiian today simply because of the choice of l over r in the orthography—it could have gone the other way." Personal Communication, 2016.
11. Dwight, Edwin W., *The Memoirs of Henry Obookiah, A Native of Owhyhee, And A Member of the Foreign Mission School; Who died At Cornwall, Connecticut February 17, 1818, Aged 26 Years*, Honolulu: Woman's Board of Missions For the Pacific Islands, reprint, 2012., pp. 11-12.
12. Ibid., p. 12.
13. Silverman, Kenneth, *Timothy Dwight*, New York: Twayne Publishers, 1969.
14. Dwight, Edwin W., *The Memoirs of Henry Obookiah, A Native of Owhyhee, And A Member of the Foreign Mission School; Who died At Cornwall, Connecticut February 17, 1818, Aged 26 Years*, Honolulu: Woman's Board of Missions For the Pacific Islands, reprint, 2012, p. 12.
15. Shelton, Elizabeth W., *Faith, Freedom, and Flag: The Influence of American Missionaries in Turkey on Foreign Affairs, 1830-1880*, Dissertation, Georgetown University, Washington, D.C., 2011, p. 153.

16. Richards, Thomas C., *Samuel J. Mills, Missionary, Pathfinder, Pioneer and Promoter,* Boston: The Pilgrim Press, 1906, pp. 29-31.
17. Dwight, Edwin W., *The Memoirs of Henry Obookiah, A Native of Owhyhee, And A Member of the Foreign Mission School; Who died At Cornwall, Connecticut February 17, 1818, Aged 26 Years,* Honolulu: Woman's Board of Missions For the Pacific Islands, reprint, 2012, p. 12-13.
18. Cook, Christopher, *The Providential Life & Heritage of Henry Obookiah,* Waimea, HI: Pa'a Studios, 2015, p. 53.
19. Dwight, Edwin W., *The Memoirs of Henry Obookiah, A Native of Owhyhee, And A Member of the Foreign Mission School; Who died At Cornwall, Connecticut February 17, 1818, Aged 26 Years,* Honolulu: Woman's Board of Missions For the Pacific Islands, reprint, 2012, p.13.
20. Ibid.
21. Ibid., p. 14.
22. Cooke, David, *David Cooke's Report,* hand-written unpublished manuscript, on file at the Office of State Archaeology, Connecticut Archaeology Center, University of Connecticut, Storrs, 1993
23. Dwight, Edwin W., *The Memoirs of Henry Obookiah, A Native of Owhyhee, And A Member of the Foreign Mission School; Who died At Cornwall, Connecticut February 17, 1818, Aged 26 Years,* Honolulu: Woman's Board of Missions For the Pacific Islands, reprint, 2012, p.13.
24. Cooke, David, *David Cooke's Report,* hand-written unpublished manuscript, on file at the Office of State Archaeology, Connecticut Archaeology Center, University of Connecticut, Storrs, 1993, p. 20.
25. Dwight, Edwin W., *The Memoirs of Henry Obookiah, A Native of Owhyhee, And A Member of the Foreign Mission School; Who died At Cornwall, Connecticut February 17, 1818, Aged 26 Years,* Honolulu: Woman's Board of Missions For the Pacific Islands, reprint, 2012, p. 17.
26. Ibid.
27. Ibid.
28. Ibid.
29. Ibid.
30. Ibid., p. 18.
31. Ibid.
32. Ibid.
33. Ibid.
34. Ibid., p.21.
35. Ibid., p. 22.
36. Ibid., p. 19.
37. Ibid., p. 21.
38. Ibid., p. 22.

39. Ibid.
40. Ibid.
41. Ibid., p. 23.
42. Ibid., p. 26.
43. Ibid., p. 55.
44. Ibid.
45. Ibid., pp. 55-56.
46. Ibid., p. 25.
47. Ibid., p. 22.
48. Ibid., p. 25.
49. Orcutt, Samuel, *The History of Torrington, Connecticut from Its First Settlement in 1737, with Biographies and Genealogies*. Albany: J Munsell, Printer, 1878, reprint 1990 edition, p 60.
50. Ibid., p. 218.
51. Ibid., p.538.
52. Demos, John, *The Heathen School: A Story of Hope and Betrayal in the Age of the Early Republic*, New York: Alfred A. Knoff, 2014.
53. Dwight, Edwin W., *The Memoirs of Henry Obookiah, A Native of Owhyhee, And A Member of the Foreign Mission School; Who died At Cornwall, Connecticut February 17, 1818, Aged 26 Years*, Honolulu: Woman's Board of Missions For the Pacific Islands, reprint, 2012, p. 49.
54. Ibid.
55. Richards, Thomas C., *Samuel J. Mills, Missionary, Pathfinder, Pioneer and Promoter*, Boston: The Pilgrim Press, 1906, pp. 94-95.
56. Unpublished field notes on file with the Office of State Archaeology, Connecticut Archaeology Center, University of Connecticut, Storrs.
57. Reuman, Otto G., *The Influence of One Man–Henry Obookiah*, published by the First Church of Christ in Cornwall, CT, 1968.
58. Bellantoni, Nicholas, Roger Thompson, David Cooke, Michael Park and Cynthia Trayling, The Life, Death, Archaeological Exhumation and Re-interment of ʻŌpūkahaʻia (Henry Obookiah), 1792-1818, *Connecticut History*, 2007, Vol. 46, No. 2, p. 219.
59. Two-piece shroud pins with copper heads were manufactured in New England prior to the 1840s, when they are replaced single-piece metal pins without copper heads. This provided another measure that the burial dated prior to the 1840s.
60. Cook, Christopher L., *The Providential Life & Heritage of Henry Obookiah: Why did Missionaries Come to Hawaiʻi From New England and Tahiti?*, Waimea, HI: Paʻa Studios, 2015, p. 104.
61. Park, Michael Alan, *Biological Anthropology*, New York: McGraw-Hill, fifth edition, 2008, pp. 8-11.

62. Barber, John Warner, *Connecticut's Historical Collections, Containing a General Collection of Interesting Facts, Traditions, Biographical Sketches, Anecdotes, etc., Relating to the History and Antiquities of Every Town in Connecticut with Geographical Descriptions*, New Haven: B. L. Hamlen, 1836, pp. 465-467.

63. Andrews, John, "Educating the Heathen: The Foreign Mission School, Controversy and American Ideals", *Journal of American Studies*, Vo. 12, No. 3, p. 332-333.

64. Spoeher, Anne Harding, "George Prince Tamoree: Heir Apparent of Kaua'iand Niihau", *Hawaiian Journal of History*, Vol. 15, 1981, p. 38.

65. Herman Daggett was appointed principal in 1817.

66. Andrews, John, "Educating the Heathen: The Foreign Mission School, Controversy and American Ideals", *Journal of American Studies*, Vo. 12, No. 3, p. 333.

67. Forbes, Robert, UConn historian, personal communication.

68. Cook, Christopher L., *The Providential Life & Heritage of Henry Obookiah: Why did Missionaries Come to Hawai'i From New England and Tahiti?*, Waimea, HI: Pa'a Studios, 2015, pp. 166-167.

69. Forbes, Robert, University of Connecticut, personal communication, 2014.

70. Letter from Henry Obookiah to Samuel Welles Jr., June 301817, Cornwall Historical Society, CT.

71. The Steward's House was designated as a National Historic Landmark by the Department of the Interior in 2017.

72. Dwight, Edwin W., *The Memoirs of Henry Obookiah, A Native of Owhyhee, And A Member of the Foreign Mission School; Who died At Cornwall, Connecticut February 17, 1818, Aged 26 Years*, Honolulu: Woman's Board of Missions For the Pacific Islands, reprint, 2012, p. 56.

73. Spoeher, Anne Harding, "George Prince Tamoree: Heir Apparent of Kaua'iand Niihau", *Hawaiian Journal of History*, Vol. 15, 1981, pp. 36.

74. Dwight, Edwin W., *The Memoirs of Henry Obookiah, A Native of Owhyhee, And A Member of the Foreign Mission School; Who died At Cornwall, Connecticut February 17, 1818, Aged 26 Years*, Honolulu: Woman's Board of Missions For the Pacific Islands, reprint, 2012, p. 56.

75. Okihiro, Gary Y., *Island World: A History of Hawai'i and the United States*, Berkeley: University of California Press, 2008, p. 93.

76. Conlon, Joseph, *The Historical Impact of Epidemic Typhus*, entomology.montana. edu/historybug/Typhus

77. Cook, Christopher L., *The Providential Life & Heritage of Henry Obookiah: Why did Missionaries Come to Hawai'i From New England and Tahiti?*, Waimea, HI: Pa'a Studios, 2015, pp. 99-100.

78. Wayne H. Brumaghim, *The Life and Legacy of Heneri 'Ōpūkaha'ia Hawai'i's Prodigal Son*, MA Thesis, University of Hawai'i, Manoa, 2011, pp. 87-88

79. Dwight, Edwin W., *The Memoirs of Henry Obookiah, A Native of Owhyhee, And A Member of the Foreign Mission School; Who died At Cornwall, Connecticut*

February 17, 1818, Aged 26 Years, Honolulu: Woman's Board of Missions For the Pacific Islands, reprint, 2012, p. 62.

80. Ibid.
81. Ibid., p. 63.
82. Ibid., p. 64.
83. Ibid., p. 65.
84. Ibid. p. 67.
85. Beecher, Lyman, *A Sermon Delivered at the Funeral of Henry Obookiah, A Native of OWHYHEE, and A Member of the Foreign Mission School in Cornwall, Connecticut*, Elizabethtown, NJ: Edison Hart, 1819, p. 30.
86. Reuman, Otto G., *The Influence of One Man–Henry Obookiah*, published by the First Church of Christ in Cornwall, CT, 1968.
87. Orcutt, Samuel, *The History of Torrington, Connecticut from Its First Settlement in 1737, with Biographies and Genealogies*. Albany: J Munsell, Printer, 1878, reprint 1990 edition, p 742.
88. The latest edition of the *"Memoirs"* was published by the Women's Board of Missions for the Pacific Islands in 2012. ISBN: 061565033.

3. AFTER ʻŌPŪKAHAʻIA

1. Dwight, Edwin W., *The Memoirs of Henry Obookiah*, Hilo: The Larry Czerwonka Company, 2012, p. 55.
2. The following description is based on the unpublished 1993 report by Dr. Michael Park, on file with the Office of State Archaeology, University of Connecticut, Storrs.
3. Ibid.
4. Todd, T. W., Changes in the pubic bone: The male white pubic, *American Journal of Physical Anthropology*, 1920, vol. 3, pp. 285-334.
5. Brooks, S., and J. Suchey, Skeletal age determination based on the Os Pubis: A comparison of the Asadi-Nemeskeri and Suchey-Brooks methods, *Human Evolution*, vol. 5, pp. 227-238, 1990.
6. Iscan, M. Yasar, Susan R. Loth, and Ronald K. Wright, Metamorphosis at the sternal rib end: A new method to estimate age at death in white males, *American Journal of Physical Anthropology*, 1984, vol. 65, no. 2, pp. 147-156.
7. Sledzik, Paul, and Nicholas F. Bellantoni, Brief Communications: Bioarchaeological and biocultural evidence of the New England vampire folk belief, *American Journal of Physical Anthropology*, 1994, Vol. 94, no. 2, pp. 269-274.
8. van der Vaart TW, van Thiel PPAM, Juffermans NP, van Vugt M, Geerlings SE, Grobusch MP, et al. Severe murine typhus with pulmonary system involvement. *Emerging Infectious Diseases* [Internet], 2014, August, http://dx.doi.org/10.3201/eid2008.131421

9. Pietrusewsky, Michael, An osteological view of indigenous populations in Oceania, In *Studies In Oceanic Culture History*, Green R.C., and M. Kelly, eds, Pacific Anthropological Records, No. 11 Department of Anthropology, Honolulu: B.P. Bishop Museum, 1979, pp. 1-11.

10. American Board of Commissioners for Foreign Missions, *Instructions from the Prudential Committee of the ABCFM to members of the Mission to the Sandwich Islands*, Boston: Samuel Armstrong, 1819.

11. See Stannard, Davie, *Before the Horror: The Population of Hawai'i on the Eve of Western Contact*, Honolulu: University of Hawai'i Press, 1989, and O.A. Bushnell, *The Gift of Civilization: Germs and Genocide in Hawai'i*, Honolulu: University of Hawai'i Press, 1993.

12. See Diamond, Jared, *Guns, Germs and Steel: The Fates of Human Societies*, New York: W.W. Norton & Co., 1999, p. 214. Kame'eleihiwa, Liliklalā, *Native Lands and Foreign Desires: Ko Hawai'i 'Āina a me, Nā Koi Pu'umake a ka, Po'e Haole*, Honolulu: Bishop Museum Press, 1992 and Silva, Noenoe, *Aloha Betrayed: Native Hawaiian Resistance to American Colonialism*, Durham: Duke University Press, 2004

13. Boshard, Dr. Henry K., *The History of Mokuaikaua: The Oldest and First Founded Christian Church in the State of Hawaii*, Hilo: James Roark Design, 1985, p. 9.

14. Holman, Lucia Ruggles, *Journal of Lucia Ruggles Holman*, Honolulu: Bishop Museum, Special Publication No. 17, 1931, p. 17.

15. John Honoree and George Tamoree were also aboard the *Thaddeus*, but would serve at the Oahu Mission

16. Silva, Noenoe, *Aloha Betrayed: Native Hawaiian Resistance to American Colonialism*, Durham: Duke University Press, 2004, p. 27.

17. Hutchision, William R., *Errand to the World: American Protestant Thought and Foreign Missions*, Chicago: University of Chicago Press, 1987, pp. 69-70.

18. Haley, James L., *Captive Paradise: A History of Hawaii*, New York: St. Martin's Press, 2014, p. 56.

19. American Board of Commissioners for Foreign Missions, *Annual Report*, No. 28, Boston, 1837, p. 96.

20. Ibid., p. 58.

21. Kame'eleihiwa, Liliklalā, *Native Lands and Foreign Desires: Ko Hawai'i 'Āina a me, Nā Koi Pu'umake a ka, Po'e Haole*, Honolulu: Bishop Museum Press, 1992.

22. Boshard, Dr. Henry K., *The History of Mokuaikaua: The Oldest and First Founded Christian Church in the State of Hawaii*, Hilo: James Roark Design, 1985, p. 2.

23. Haley, James L., *Captive Paradise: A History of Hawaii*, New York: St. Martin's Press, 2014, p. 76.

24. Ibid., p. 66.

25. Haley, James L., *Captive Paradise: A History of Hawaii*, New York: St. Martin's Press, 2014, pp. 77-78.

26. Silva, Noenoe, *Aloha Betrayed: Native Hawaiian Resistance to American Colonialism*, Durham: Duke University Press, 2004, p. 32.

27. Ibid.

28. Originally, 'Ōpūkaha'ia's skeleton was to be placed in a small *koa*-wood box, measuring three feet by 16 inches by 20 inches. This container was replaced with a full-sized casket with a *koa* veneer.

29. Krauss, Beatrice H., *Plants in Hawaiian Culture*, Honolulu, University of Hawaii Press, 1993.

30. Haley, James L., *Captive Paradise: A History of Hawaii*, New York: St. Martin's Press, 2014, pp. 108. Also see, Siler, Julia Flynn, *Lost Kingdom: Hawaii's Last Queen, the Sugar Kings, and America's First Imperial Adventure*, New York: Grove Press, 2012, p. 55.

31. Siler, Julia Flynn, *Lost Kingdom: Hawaii's Last Queen, the Sugar Kings, and America's First Imperial Adventure*, New York: Grove Press, 2012, pp. 57-59.

32. Silva, Noenoe, *Aloha Betrayed: Native Hawaiian Resistance to American Colonialism*, Durham: Duke University Press, 2004, p. 36.

33. Humphrey, Heman, "Instructions", Appendix to *The Promised Land*, Boston: Samuel T. Armstrong, 1819, pp. ix, ii.

34. Hutchision, William R., *Errand to the World: American Protestant Thought and Foreign Missions*, Chicago: University of Chicago Press, 1987, p. 71.

35. Ibid., pp. 12-13.

36. Ibid., pp. 77-83.

37. American Board of Commissioners for Foreign Missions, *Annual Report*, No. 7, Boston, 1816, pp. 135-136.

38. See John Demos, *The Heathen School: A Story of Hope and Betrayal in the Age of the Early Republic*, New York: Alfred A. Knopf, 2014, for the most detailed historical review of the Foreign Mission School.

39. Haley, James L., *Captive Paradise: A History of Hawaii*, New York: St. Martin's Press, 2014, pp. 112.

40. Kame'eleihiwa, Lilikalā, *Native Land and Foreign Desires: Ko Hawai'i 'Āiana a me Nā Koi Pu'umake a ka Po' Haole*, Honolulu: Bishop Museum Press, 1992.

41. Levy, N. M., Native Hawaiian Land Rights, *California Law Review*, 1975, vol. 63, p. 853.

42. Ibid., pp. 125-127.

43. Ibid., pp. 128-135.

44. *House Executive Document* 47, 53rd Congress, 2nd Session, 1893.

45. United States-Hawaii Treaty, 1875, 19 *Stat.* 625. Also see, Siler, Julia Flynn, *Lost Kingdom: Hawaii's Last Queen, the Sugar Kings, and America's First Imperial Adventure*, New York: Grove Press, 2012, pp. 150-152.

46. Native Hawaiian Study Commission, *Report on the Culture, Needs and Concerns of Native Hawaiians*, Washington, D. C.: Department of the Interior, 1983, vol. 1, p. 267.

47. Getches, David H., Alternative Approaches to Land Claims: Alaska and Hawaii, In *Irredeemable America: The Indians' Estate and Land Claims*, edited by Imre Sutton, Albuquerque: University of New Mexico Press, 1985, p. 322.

48. Marines put down rebellion with Reciprocity Treaty.

49. Kamakawiwo'ule Osorio, Jonathan K., *Dismembering Lahui: A History of the Hawaiian Nation to 1887*, Honolulu: University of Hawai'i Press, 2002, p. 49.

50. Siler, Julia Flynn, *Lost Kingdom: Hawaii's Last Queen, the Sugar Kings, and America's First Imperial Adventure*, New York: Grove Press, 2012, p. 184.

51. Ibid., p. 146.

52. Silva, Noenoe, *Aloha Betrayed: Native Hawaiian Resistance to American Colonialism*, Durham: Duke University Press, 2004, p. 73.

53. Siler, Julia Flynn, *Lost Kingdom: Hawaii's Last Queen, the Sugar Kings, and America's First Imperial Adventure*, New York: Grove Press, 2012, p. 189.

54. Ibid., pp. 264-265.

55. Ibid., pp. 237-240.

56. Ibid., p. 229.

57. *House Executive Document* 47, 1893, p. XII.

58. Lili'uokalani, *Hawaii's Story by Hawaii's Queen*, Boston: Lee and Shepard, 1898, Also see, Haley, James L., *Captive Paradise: A History of Hawaii*, New York: St. Martin's Press, 2014, pp. 318-320.

59. Quoted in, Getches, David H., Alternative Approaches to Land Claims: Alaska and Hawaii, In *Irredeemable America: The Indians' Estate and Land Claims*, edited by Imre Sutton, Albuquerque: University of New Mexico Press, 1985, p. 324.

60. Lili'uokalani, *Hawaii's Story by Hawaii's Queen*, Boston: Lee and Shepard, 1898, Also see, Haley, James L., *Captive Paradise: A History of Hawaii*, New York: St. Martin's Press, 2014, p. 324 and Noeonoe Silva, *Aloha Betrayed*, Durham: Duke University Press, 2004, p. 146.

61. Silva, Noenoe, Aloha Betrayed, Durham: Duke University Press, 2004.

62. Siler, Julia Flynn, *Lost Kingdom: Hawaii's Last Queen, the Sugar Kings, and America's First Imperial Adventure*, New York: Grove Press, 2012, pp. 284.

63. Getches, David H., Alternative Approaches to Land Claims: Alaska and Hawaii, In *Irredeemable America: The Indians' Estate and Land Claims*, edited by Imre Sutton, Albuquerque: University of New Mexico Press, 1985, p. 319.

64. Ibid., p. 331.

65. Haley, James L., *Captive Paradise: A History of Hawaii*, New York: St. Martin's Press, 2014, pp. 344.

66. Jennings, Peter, and Todd Brewster, *The Century*, New York: Doubleday, 1998, p. 230.

67. Chapman, William, *Hawai'i, the Military, and the National Park: World War II and Its Impacts on Culture and the Environment*, Final Report for the National Park Service, 2014, p. 21.

68. See Public Law 103-150 that details the overthrow of the monarchy and opposition to statehood.

69. Laenui, Pola (Hayden F. Burgess), "Hawaiian Statehood Revisited," IN *Reclaiming Indigenous Voice and Vision*, ed. by Marie Battiste, Vancouver: UBC Press, 2000, pp. 50-56.

70. http://www.marxists.org/history/erol/ncm-1a/hawaii.pdf.

71. http://www.culturalsurvival.org/ourpublications/csq/article/the-struggle-for-hawaiian-sovereignty-introduction

72. Holt, John Dominis, *On Being Hawaiian*, Honolulu: Topgallant Publishing, 1964, p. 7.

73. Haley, James L., *Captive Paradise: A History of Hawaii*, New York: St. Martin's Press, 2014, pp. 349.

74. See, McCollough, Charles, "Why Our Church Apologized to Hawai'i," IN *UCC @ 50-Our History, Our Future*, ed. by J., Martin Bailey, 2006.

75. Renner, Gerald, After 175 Years, a Resting Place in His Hawaiian Homeland, *The Hartford Courant*, Vol. CLV, No. 197, Friday, July 16, 1993, p. A4.

76. Engle, Murry, 'Ōpūkaha'ia is Finally Coming Back Home, *The Honolulu Star Bulletin*, July 28, 1993, p. A-10.

77. Renner, Gerald, After 175 Years, a Resting Place in His Hawaiian Homeland, *The Hartford Courant*, Vol. CLV, No. 197, Friday, July 16, 1993, p. A4.

78. Ibid.

4. "HE WANTS TO COME HOME"

1. Service Program entitled, *The One Hundred and Fiftieth Anniversary of the Death of Henry Opukahaia (Obookiah), Held in Cornwall, Connecticut, Honolulu, Hawaii and Napoopoo, Kealakekua, Sunday, February 1968, A.D.*, published by the First Church of Christ, Cornwall, Connecticut, 1968.

2. Austen, Barbara, "Missionary Legacies: Connecticut to Hawaii," IN *American Ancestors*, Spring 2014, pp. 31-35.

3. Nakashima, Ellen, A Bit of History Returning to Hawaii: Christian Convert Feld in 1808, *The Hartford Courant*, 26 July 1993, pp. C1, C7.

4. Ibid., p. C1.

5. The Cornwall Historical Society had wished to conserve the coffin lid in their collections for public exhibit. However, the Lee family felt that it should be returned to Hawai'i and reburied with 'Ōpūkaha'ia in Kona.

6. Vowell, Sarah, *Unfamiliar Fishes*, New York: Riverhead Books, 2011, pp. 91-92.

7. Boushard, Rev. Henry K., *The History of Mokuaikaua Church: The Oldest and first founded Christian Church in the State of Hawaii*, Hilo: James Roark Design, 1985.

8. Davis' first name has been lost in the written records and family oral traditions.
9. Compiled by Lee, Elizabeth K., *Henry 'Ōpūkaha'ia's Interment Service: Guest Speaker's Messages*, Unpublished manuscript, Office of State Archaeology, University of Connecticut, Storrs, 1993, p.5.
10. Ibid., pp. 6-7.

PART II. THE REPATRIATION OF ALBERT AFRAID OF HAWK

5. THE BUFFALO NATION

1. William Frederick Cody preferred to eliminate the term "Show" and simply call his spectacular, "Buffalo Bill's Wild West" to imply authenticity of the performances.
2. Death of Afraid-of-Hawk: He Fulfilled All he Traditions of His Race by Stoic Demeanor, *New Haven Evening Register*, 2 July 1900, Vol. 57, Issue 153, p. 11.
3. Gooch, George H., *Route-Book buffalo Bill's Wild West 1899*, Buffalo: The Mathews-Northrup Co., 1900, p. 9.
4. Ibid.
5. Soil Nutrient Analysis Laboratory, Department of Plant Sciences, University of Connecticut, on file in the Office of Connecticut State Archaeology, Storrs, CT.
6. Gordon, C.C. and Jane E. Buikstra, Soil, pH, bone preservation, and sampling bias at mortuary sites, *American Antiquity*, vol. 46, pp. 566-571.
7. Brown, Joseph Epes, ed., *The Sacred Pipe: Black Elk's Account of the Seven Rites of the Oglala Sioux*, Norman: University of Oklahoma Press, 1989, pp. 10-30.
8. Swanton, John R., Siouan Tribes and the Ohio Valley, *American Anthropologist*, Vol. 45, No. 1, pp. 49-66.
9. Hyde, George, *Red Cloud's Folk: A History of the Oglala Sioux Indians*, Norman: University of Oklahoma Press, 1937, p. 3.
10. Walker, James R., *Lakota Society*, ed. By Raymond DeMallie, Lincoln: University of Nebraska Press, 1982, p. 14. The term "Sioux" is considered a name given to them by the U.S. government to handle the tribes as a combined group. It does not convene the complexity and diversity among the Seven Council bands and is at times thought of as an insult by the people.
11. Lone Hill, Karen D., "Sioux", In *Encyclopedia of North American Indians*, Frederick E. Hoxie, ed., Boston: Houghton Mifflin Co., 1996, p. 591.
12. Herman, Antonie and James R. Walker, "The Seven Council Fires", In *Lakota Society*, ed. By Raymond J. DeMallie, Lincoln: University of Nebraska Press, 1982, pp. 14-18.
13. Pickering, Katherine, "Articulation of the Lakota Mode of Production and the Euro-American Fur Trade", In *The Fur Trade Revisited, Selected Papers of the Sixth North American Fur Trade Conference*, ed. Brown, Jennifer S. H. Brown,

W. J. Eccles, and Donald P. Heldman, East Lansing: Michigan State University Press, 1994.

14. Interpreting stories from one language to another, and from one culture to another is difficult and loses much of the story's significance. There are many variations in which the White Buffalo Calf Women (or Maiden) story is told though all accounts contain the same basic theme. We have synthesized a number of accounts including those presented by Joseph Marshall and Joseph Chasing Horse.

15. Joseph Chasing Horse says the chief is Standing Hollow Horn of the Itazipcola band.

16. Crow Dog, Leonard and Richard Erdoes, *Crow Dog: Four Generations of Sioux Medicine Men*, New York: Harper Collins, 1995, pp. 4-5, contends this part of the story was invented by Christian Missionaries.

17. Seven rituals included ceremonies associated with the sweat lodge, naming, healing, adoption, marriage, vision quests, and the Sun Dance.

18. Current Keeper of the Sacred Pipe is Arvol Looking Horse, Cheyenne River Sioux Reservation. He represents the nineteenth generation to serve in this sacred capacity.

19. Marshall III, Joseph M., *The Lakota Way: Stories and Lessons for Living*, London: Penguin Compass, 2001, pp. 16-18.

20. Toensing, Gale Courey, White Buffalo Calf named Yellow Medicine Dancing Boy Amid Fire, Water and Thunder, *Indian Country Today Media Network*, 6 August 2015. http://indiancountrytodaymedianetwork.com/2012/08/06/white-buffalo-calf -named-yellow-medicine-dancing-boy-amid-fire-water-and-thunder-127463

21. Wedel, M.M., "Le Sueur and the Dakota Sioux", In *Aspects of Upper Great Lakes Anthropology: Papers in Honor of Lloyd A. Wifford*, ed. By E. Johnson, Minnesota Prehistoric Archaeology Series, 11, St. Paul: Minnesota Historical Society, 1974, pp. 165-166.

22. Hyde, George, *Red Cloud's Folk: A History of the Oglala Sioux Indians*, Norman: University of Oklahoma Press, 1937, p. 21.

23. Ostler, Jeffrey, *The Lakotas and the Black Hills*, New York: Penguin Books, 2010, p. 9.

24. Hoxie, Frederick E., "Travois," In *Encyclopedia of North American Indians*, New York: Houghton Mifflin Co., 1996, p. 643.

25. Cheyenne tradition tells that they had pity on the Sioux and so provided them with horses. Lakota also obtained horses from the Arikaras. See, Grinnell, George Bird, *The Fighting Cheyennes*, Norman: University of Oklahoma Press, 1956 reprint from 1915, p. 37.

26. Erdoes, Richard, *The Sun Dance People: The Plains Indians, Their Past and Present*, New York: Random House, A Vintage Sundial Book, 1972, pp. 18-26.

27. Singer, Ben, A brief history of the horse in America, *Canadian Geographic Magazine*, May 2005.

28. Calloway, Colin G., *One Vast Winter Count: The Native American West Before Lewis and Clark*, History of the American West Series, Lincoln: University of Nebraska Press, 2003, p. 267.

29. Hassrick, Royal B., *The Sioux: Life and Customs of a Warrior Society*, Norman: University of Oklahoma Press, 1964, p. 161.

30. Robes Kipp, Darrell, "Horses and Indians", In *Encyclopedia of North American Indians*, Frederick E. Hoxie, ed., Boston: Houghton Mifflin Co., 1996, p. 257.

31. Erdoes, Richard, *The Sun Dance People: The Plains Indians, Their Past and Present*, New York: Random House, A Vintage Sundial Book, 1972, p. 33.

32. Hassrick, Royal B., *The Sioux: Life and Customs of a Warrior Society*, Norman: University of Oklahoma Press, 1964, p. 30.

33. Ibid., p. 239.

34. DeMallie, Raymond J., ed., *The Sixth Grandfather: Black Elk's Teachings Given to John G. Neihardt*, Lincoln: University of Nebraska Press, 1984, pp. 80-81.

35. Marshall III, Joseph M., *The Day The World Ended at Little Bighorn: A Lakota History*, New York: Viking, 2007, p. 189.

36. Mallery, Garrick, Picture-Writing of the American Indians, *Tenth Annual Report of the Bureau of American Ethnology 1888-89*, Smithsonian Institution, 1893, Washington: Government Printing Office, Section 2, "Winter Counts" pp. 266-273.

37. The term "*wasichus*" is not simply a definition of Euro-Americans, but is also meant to imply someone who is greedy, untrustworthy, lies, and is disrespectful—one "who takes the fat", but never gives back. Use of the term by the Lakota toward the "white man" infers all of these connotations.

38. Mallery, Garrick, and James Gilchrist Swan, Pictographs of North American Indians, *Fourth Annual Report of the Bureau of American Ethnology*, Smithsonian Institution, 1886, p. 134.

39. The doctrine of "Rights of Discovery" was established by monarchies during the so-called "Age of Discovery" and gave them the authority to appropriate newly discovered lands for Christianity. Providing that the lands had not been previously "discovered" by a Christian nation, the Catholic Church authorized European monarchs to colonize the territories of Indigenous Peoples, along with the slavery and servitude of pagans. For a Native perspective see, Robert J. Miller, Esq., *Native America, Discovered and Conquered, Thomas Jefferson, Lewis and Clark and Manifest Destiny*, Westport, CT: Praeger Publishing, 2006.

40. Quoted in Ronda, James P., *Lewis and Clark Among the Indians*, Lincoln: University of Nebraska Press, 1937, p. 30, from the Jefferson Papers in the Library of Congress.

41. Ambrose, Stephen, *Undaunted Courage*, New York: Simon & Schuster, 1997, Chapter 14.

42. Quaife, Milo M., ed., *The Journals of Meriwether Lewis and Sergeant John Ord-way*, Madison: Historical society of Wisconsin, 1916, p. 85, and quoted in Ronda, James P., *Lewis and Clark Among the Indians*, Lincoln: University of Nebraska Press, 1937, p. 30.

43. Mallery, Garrick, and James Gilchrist Swan, Pictographs of North American Indians, *Fourth Annual Report of the Bureau of American Ethnology*, Smithsonian Institution, 1886, p. 142.

44. Dary, David, *Oregon Trail: An American Saga*, New York: Alfred A. Knopf, 2004, p. 227.

45. Ibid., p. 79.

46. Ibid.

47. Stoughton, John A., "Recollections", *Washington Historical Quarterly*, vol. 15, 1924, pp. 208-10.

48. Dary, David, *Oregon Trail: An American Saga*, New York: Alfred A. Knopf, 2004, p. 235.

49. Ibid., p. 227.

50. Ibid., p. 37.

51. Drury, Bob and Tom Clavin, *The Heart of Everything That Is: The Untold Story of Red Cloud, An American Legend*, New York: Simon & Schuster, 2014, p. 32.

52. Andrews, John, The Long Road Home, *South Dakota Magazine*, Vol. 29, No. 2, July/August 2013, p. 58.

53. Miller, Robert, Looking for Historic Bones, *The (Danbury) News-Times*, 14 August 2012, p. A8.

54. Ibid.

55. Miller, Robert, Final Journey for Albert Afraid of Hawk, *The (Danbury) News-Times*, 7 September 2012.

56. Young, Mary-Jo, *The Mosaic That Is Albert Afraid of Hawk's Journey Home*, unpublished manuscript, filed at Office of State Archaeology, University of Connecticut, Storrs.

57. Mallery, Garrick, and James Gilchrist Swan, Pictographs of North American Indians, *Fourth Annual Report of the Bureau of American Ethnology*, Smithsonian Institution, 1886, p. 144.

58. Collins, Charles D., Jr., *Atlas of the Sioux Wars*, 2nd edition, Fort Leavenworth, Kansas: Combat Studies Institute Press, 2006, p. 22.

59. Mallery, Garrick, and James Gilchrist Swan, Pictographs of North American Indians, *Fourth Annual Report of the Bureau of American Ethnology*, Smithsonian Institution, 1886, p. 125.

60. Prucha, Francis, *The Great Father: The United State Government and the American Indian*, Lincoln: University of Nebraska Press, 1986, p. 464.

61. Ibid., p. 562.

62. Drury, Bob and Tom Clavin, *The Heart of Everything That Is: The Untold Story of Red Cloud, An American Legend*, New York: Simon & Schuster, 2014, p. 329-9.

63. Landy, David, "Treaties", In *Encyclopedia of North American Indians*, Frederick E. Hoxie, ed., Boston: Houghton Mifflin Co., 1996, p. 647 and Lee, Patrick A., *Tribal Laws, Treaties and Government: A Lakota Perspective*, iUniverse, 2013, Chapter 4.

64. Kappler, Charles J., ed., Indian Affairs: Laws and Treaties, Washington: Government Printing Office, 1904, p. 1005.

65. Afraid of Hawk's military records show his birth as 13 April 1850, however, U.S. Indian Census data consistently register his birth as September 1848.

66. U.S. Indian Census, Pine Ridge Reservation, Wounded Knee District, 1898, No. 3324, 3325, p. 72 and 1899, No. 3103, 3102, p. 50.

67. Prucha, Francis, *The Great Father: The United State Government and the American Indian*, Lincoln: University of Nebraska Press, 1986, p. 540.

68. Larsen, Robert W., *Red Cloud: Warrior-Statesman of the Lakota Sioux*, Norman: University of Oklahoma Press, 1997, p. 132.

69. Howard, James H., "Dakota Winter Counts As A Source of Plains History", *Bureau of American Ethnology, Smithsonian Institution*, Bulletin 173, 1960, p. 356.

70. Ostler, Jeffery, *The Lakotas and the Black Hills: The Struggle for Sacred Ground*, New York: Penguin Books, 2010, p. 48.

71. Bray, Kingsley, *Crazy Horse: A Lakota Life*, Norman: University of Oklahoma Press, 2006, p. 42-3.

72. See, Cozzens, Peter, Grant's Uncivil War, *Smithsoniam.com*, November 2016

73. See Grua, David W., *Surviving Wounded Knee: The Lakotas and the Politics of Memory*, New York: Oxford University Press, 2015, especially, Chapter 1.

74. Dodge, Richard I., *The Black Hills: A Minute Description of the Routes, Scenery, Soil, Climate, Timber, Gold, Geology, Zoology, Etc....,*, Reprinted Minneapolis: Ross & Haines, 1965, pp. 136-38.

75. Tallent, Annie D., *The Black Hills: Or, the Last Hunting Ground of the Dakotahs*, St. Louis: Nixon-Jones, 1899, p. 111.

76. Lee, Patrick A., *Tribal Laws, Treaties and Government: A Lakota Perspective*, iUniverse, 2013, p. 33

77. Cozzens, Peter, Grant's Uncivil War, *Smithsoniam.com*, November 2016, p. 58.

78. Sheridan always denied that he made this statement, however, his known attitude toward Native Americans and his "scorched earth" policies in pursuing the tribes does not give him the benefit of the doubt.

79. Cozzens, Peter, Grant's Uncivil War, *Smithsonian.com*, November 2016, pp. 48-59.

80. Drury, Bob and Tom Clavin, *The Heart of Everything That Is: The Untold Story of Red Cloud, An American Legend*, New York: Simon & Schuster, 2014, p. 381.

81. In Walker, J.R., *The Sun Dance of the Oglala*, Anthropological Papers of the American Museum of Natural History, Vol. XVI, Part II, 1917, p.p. 152-53, explains that *wakan* means many things, but basically, things that require explanation and are hard to understand. *Wakan Tanka* means all *wakan* things because they are all one. *Wakan Tanka* makes his wishes known through visions or a shaman.

82. Gibbon testimony in letter to General Terry, Fort Shaw, Montana Territory, November 6, 1876.

83. Niehardt, John G., *Black Elk Speaks: Being the Life Story of a Holy Man of the Ogalala Sioux*, The Premier Excelsior Edition, Albany: State University of New York Press, reprinted 2008, p. 85.

84. Michno, Gregory F., *Lakota Noon: The Indian Narrative of Custer's Defeat*, Missoula: Montana Press Publishing Company, 1997, p. 18.

85. Young, Robert, *Afraid of Hawk and Cetan Kokipapi in 19th-century Plains Native American Families*, unpublished manuscript, 2016, p. 13.

86. Michno, Gregory F., *Lakota Noon: The Indian Narrative of Custer's Defeat*, Missoula: Montana Press Publishing Company, 1997, p. 75.

87. Ibid., pp. 251-260.

88. Julia Face quoted in, Ostler, Jeffery, *The Lakotas and the Black Hills: The Struggle for Sacred Ground*, New York: Penguin Books, 2010, p. 98. Also, see Michno, Gregory F., *Lakota Noon: The Indian Narrative of Custer's Defeat*, Missoula: Montana Press Publishing Company, 1997, p. 233.

89. Scott, Douglas D., Richard A. Fox, Jr., Melissa A. Connor, and Dick Harmon, *Archaeological Perspectives on The Battle of Little Bighorn*, Norman: University of Oklahoma Press, 1989, p. 247.

90. Brandon, William, *The American Heritage Book of Indians*, New York: Laurel Edition, 1961, p. 327.

91. Grua, David W., *Surviving Wounded Knee: The Lakotas and the Politics of Memory*, New York: Oxford University Press, 2016, p. 15.

92. Mallery, Garrick, and James Gilchrist Swan, Pictographs of North American Indians, *Fourth Annual Report of the Bureau of American Ethnology*, Smithsonian Institution, 1886, p. 146.

93. *Indian Appropriation Bill* of August 1876, House of Representatives Executive Document 10, pp. 2-3. Also see, Clow, Richard L., "The Sioux Nation and Indian Territory: The Attempted Removal of 1876", *South Dakota History*, 1976, Vol. 6, No. 4, pp. 462-463.

94. Ibid.

95. Michno, Gregory F., *Lakota Noon: The Indian Narrative of Custer's Defeat*, Missoula: Montana Press Publishing Company, 1997, p. 301.

96. Marshall III, Joseph M., *The Day The World Ended at Little Bighorn: A Lakota History*, New York: Viking, 2007, p. 136.

97. Buecker, Thomas R. and R. Eli Paul, *The Crazy Horse Surrender Ledger*, Lincoln: Nebraska State Historical Society, 1994, p. 71.

98. Freedman, Russell, *The Life and Death of Crazy Horse*, New York: Holiday House, 1996, p. 138-139.

99. Register of Enlistments of Soldiers Belonging to the Second Regiment of United States Infantry, Vo. 1874-1877, Indian Scouts,, No. 210, Afraid of a Hawk.

6. "HIS SPIRIT HAS BEEN LIFTED"

1. Pettinelli, Dawn, *Soil pH Results and Recommendations*, University of Connecticut, Department of Plant Science, Soil Nutrient Analysis Laboratory, on file at the Office of State Archaeology, Connecticut Archaeology Center, Storrs.

2. Lund, V. and J. Goksoyr, Effects of water fluctuations on microbial mass and activity in soil, *Microbial Ecology*, 1980, Vol. 6, pp. 115-123.

3. Jenkinson, D.S. and Ladd, J.N., Microbial biomass in soil: Measurements and turnover, edited by E.A. Paul and J.N. Ladd, *Soil Biochemistry*, 1981, Vol. 5, pp. 415-471.

4. Since the casket was rectangular and not hexagonal, we made the assumption that Albert Afraid of Hawk was laid out with his head to the west, facing east, conforming to Christian beliefs at the time. Our assumption proved correct when Albert's cranium appeared.

5. Rose, Christine, The Spirit of Afraid of Hawk Free After 112 Years, *Danbury Patch*, 20 August 2012.

6. The quotes are from, Miller, Robert, Disinterment unearths Afraid of Hawk's skull, *The (Danbury) News-Times*, 16 August 2012, p. A1.

7. Miller, Bonnie M., The Incoherencies of Empire: The "Imperial" Image of the Indian at the Omaha World's Fair of 1898-99, *American Studies*, 2008, 49:3/4, p. 40.

8. *Official Guide Book to the Trans-Mississippi & International Exposition, Omaha, U.S.A., June 1 to November 1, 1898*, Omaha: Megeath Stationary Company, 1898, p. 97.

9. Mooney's Report, In Wakefield, John, A., *A History of the Trans-Mississippi & International Exposition*, Omaha: Omaha Public Library, 1992, p. 634.

10. Ibid., p. 630.

11. Captain Mercer's Report, Submitted to the U.S. Congress, 1898, cited in Wakefield, John, A., *A History of the Trans-Mississippi & International Exposition*, Omaha: Omaha Public Library, 1992, p. 632.

12. Trennert, Robert A., Fairs, Expositions, and the Changing Image of Southwestern Indians, 1876-1904, *New Mexico Historical Review*, No. 62, 1987, p. 143.

13. See Johnson, Michael G., *Tribes of the Sioux Nation*, Kemp House, U.K.: Osprey Publishing, 1012, p. 37.

14. Rydell, Robert W. *All The World's A Fair*, Chicago: University of Chicago Press, 1984, pp. 114-117.

15. Haynes, James B., *History of the Trans-Mississippian & International Exposition of 1898*, Illustrated 1910, published under the direction of the Directors of the Committee on History as authorized by the Board of Directors, June 30, 1902, Omaha: Trans-Mississippi & International Exposition, 1910, p. 230.

16. Clough, Josh, "Vanishing" Indians? Cultural Persistence on Display at the Omaha World's Fair of 1898, *Great Plains Quarterly*, 2005, p. 79.

17. Haynes, James B., *History of the Trans-Mississippian & International Exposition of 1898*, Illustrated 1910, published under the direction of the Directors of the Committee on History as authorized by the Board of Directors, June 30, 1902, Omaha: Trans-Mississippi & International Exposition, 1910, p. 230.

18. Starita, Joe, *The Dull Knives of Pine Ridge: A Lakota Odyssey*, New York: G.P. Putnam's Sons, 1995, p. 39.

19. Ibid., Sherman quote, p. 17.

20. Whipple, Henry B., Bureau of Indian Affairs, *Annual Report*, 1876.

21. Slow Bull would die sometime after 1907 at the age of 87 or older. Enlistment Record.

22. Young, Robert, *Afraid of Hawk and Cetan Kokipapi in 19th-century Plains Native American Families*, unpublished manuscript, 2016, p.23.

23. Ibid. Some United States Indian Census records suggest that Richard was born in Montana or Nebraska, however, Bob Young feels that he was more likely born somewhere in Wyoming.

24. The Pine Ridge Mission Collection at the Center for Western Studies, Augustana College, has only one note referencing the church, "St Mark: First recorded service at Big Turnip's Camp was May 18, 1893."

25. Mallery, Garrick, Picture-Writing of the American Indians, *Tenth Annual Report of the Bureau of Ethnology*, Washington, D.C., Government Printing Office, 1893, p. 3328.

26. The 1892 U.S. Census gives his birth as 1880, while the 1894 Census gives his birthdate in 1881. According to the former Census data, Albert was also called Eagle Weasel.

27. *Letters Sent to the Office of Indian Affairs by the Pine Ridge Agency, 1875-1914*, National Archives and Records Administration, Bureau of Indian Affairs, Record Group 75, 1985, p. 5.

28. Marshall III, Joseph M., *The Day The World Ended at Little Bighorn*, New York: Viking Press, 2007, p. xxii.

29. Coleman, William S.E. *Voices of Wounded Knee*, Lincoln: University of Nebraska Press, 2000, p. 17.

30. See the writings of Joseph M. Marshal III, particularly, *The Lakota Way: Stories and Lessons for Living*, New York: Penguin Press, 2001.

31. Child, Brenda J., Boarding Schools, In *Encyclopedia of North American Indians*, ed. By Frederick E. Hoxie, Boston: Houghton Mifflin Company, 1996, pp. 78-80.

32. Adams, David Wallace, *Education for Extinction: American Indians and the Boarding School Experience, 1875-1928*, Lawrence: University of Kansas Press, 1995, pp. 47-48. Also see Okihiro, Gary Y., *Island World, A History of Hawai'i and the United States*, Berkeley: University of California Press, 2008, pp.125-128.

33. Pratt, Richard H., The Indian Policy, The Advantages of Mingling Indians with Whites, *Official Proceedings of the Nineteenth Annual Conference of Charities and Correction*, 1892, p. 47.

34. Martin, J.W., *The Land Looks After US: A History of Native American Religion*, New York: Oxford University Press, 2001.

35. Neihardt, John G., *Black Elk Speaks*, The Premier Edition, Albany: State University of New York Press, 2008, p. 2.

36. Quoted in Dunbar-Ortiz, Roxanne, *An Indigenous Peoples' History of the United States*, Boston: Beacon Press, 2014, Chapter 10, pp. 158.

37. Banner, Stuart, *How The Indians Lost Their Land: Law and Power on the Frontier*, Cambridge, MA: Harvard University Press, 2005, p. 257-290.

38. Of the five extant photographs of Albert Afraid of Hawk taken by Herman Heyn in Omaha (1898) and housed in the Library of Congress, only two allow examination of the left ear, which show no traces of earrings. In the other two photos, Albert's long hair and an eagle feather headdress cover the ear lobe, but since the portraits can be assumed to have been taken on the same day due to similar clothing, Albert was probably not wearing the earrings at that time.

39. Miller, Robert, Disinterment Unearths Afraid of Hawk Skull, *The (Danbury) News-Times*, 16 August 2012, p. A3.

40. Miller, Robert, His Spirit Has Been Lifted, The *(Danbury) News-Times*, Friday, 17 August 2012, p. A10.

41. Rose, Christine, The Spirit of Afraid of Hawk Free After 112 Years, *Danbury Patch*, 20 August 2012.

42. Marshall III, Joseph M., *The Lakota Way: Stories and Lessons for Living*, New York: Penguin Group Books, 2001, pp. 192-193.

43. DeMallie, Raymond J., ed., *The Sixth Grandfather: Black Elk's Teachings Given to John G. Neihardt*, Lincoln: University of Nebraska Press, 1984, pp. 36-37.

44. Enochs, Ross Alexander, *The Jesuit Mission to the Lakota Sioux: Pastoral theology and Ministry, 1886-1945*, Lanham, Maryland: Rowman and Littlefield, 1996, p. 142.

45. Miller, Robert, His Spirit Has Been Lifted, *Danbury News-Times*, Friday, 17 August 2012, p. A1.

46. Three Stars refers to Major General George Crook whose "treaty" broke up the Great Sioux Reservation. See, Walker, James R., *Lakota Society*, edited by Raymond J. DeMillie, Lincoln: University of Nebraska Press, 1982, p. 151.

47. Deloria, Philip J., *Indians in Unexpected Places*, Lawrence: University of Kansas Press, 2004, p. 43.

48. Robinson, Doane, *History of South Dakota*, Vol. 1, Chicago: Chicago Historical Society, 1930.

49. Green, Jerry, ed., *After Wounded Knee: Correspondences of Major & Surgeon John Vance Lauderdale While Serving With The Army Occupying The Pine Ridge Indian Reservation, 1890-1891*, East Lansing: Michigan State University Press, 1996, p. 21.

50. Neihardt, John G., *Black Elk Speaks*, The Premier Edition, Albany: State University of New York Press, 2008, p. 186.

51. On January 1, 1889, there was a total solar eclipse. See, Walker, James R., *Lakota Society*, edited by Raymond J. DeMillie, Lincoln: University of Nebraska Press, 1982, p. 151.

52. James Mooney lists a number of names associated with Wovoka in his study of the Ghost Dance for the Smithsonian Institution. See, Mooney, James, The Ghost Dance Religion and the Sioux Outbreak, *Fourteenth Annual Report of the Bureau of Ethnology*, Part 2, Washington, D.C.: Government Printing Office, 1896, p. 765.

53. Hittman, Michael, *Wovoka and the Ghost Dance*, Lincoln: University of Nebraska Press, 1990, p. 49.

54. Mooney, James, The Ghost Dance Religion and the Sioux Outbreak, *Fourteenth Annual Report of the Bureau of Ethnology*, Part 2, Washington, D.C.: Government Printing Office, 1896, p. 771-772.

55. The exact date of Wovoka's revelation is unknown, however, a total eclipse of the sun occurred on New Year's Day, January 1, 1889, and has been taken as the start of the Ghost Dance Movement. See Mooney, 1896.

56. Neihardt, John G., *Black Elk Speaks*, The Premier Edition, Albany: State University of New York Press, 2008, p. 189. The story of the hat may have been provided from Neihardt, rather than directly from Black Elk.

57. Coleman, William E., *Voices of Wounded Knee*, Lincoln: University of Nebraska Press, 2000, p. 5.

58. Starita, Joe, *The Dull Knives of Pine Ridge: A Lakota Odyssey*, New York: G.P. Putnam's Sons, 1995, p. 156.

59. Warren, Louis S., *God's Red Son: The Ghost Dance Religion and the Making of Modern America*, New York: Basic Books, 2017.

60. Deloria, Philip J., *Indians in Unexpected Places*, Lawrence: University of Kansas Press, 2004, p. 22.

61. Neihardt, John G., *Black Elk Speaks*, The Premier Edition, Albany: State University of New York Press, 2008, p. 187.

62. Warren, Louis S., *God's Red Son: The Ghost Dance Religion and the Making of Modern America*, New York: Basic Books, 2017, p. 198.

63. Neihardt, John G., *Black Elk Speaks*, The Premier Edition, Albany: State University of New York Press, 2008, p. 190.

64. Warren, Louis S., *God's Red Son: The Ghost Dance Religion and the Making of Modern America*, New York: Basic Books, 2017, p. 213.

65. Neihardt, John G., *Black Elk Speaks*, The Premier Edition, Albany: State University of New York, Press, 2008, p. 193.

66. Ibid., p. 196.

67. Morgan, T.J., *Report of the Commissioner of Indian Affairs for 1891*, vol. 1, pp. 132-135, printed in Mooney, James, The Ghost Dance Religion and the Sioux Outbreak, *Fourteenth Annual Report of the Bureau of Ethnology*, Part 2, Washington, D.C.: Government Printing Office, 1896, p. 829-831.

68. Beasley, Conger, *We Are A People In This World, The Lakota Sioux, Massacre at Wounded Knee*, Little Rock: University of Arkansas Press, 1995, p. 14.

69. Paul, R. Elia, Dakota Resources: The Investigation of Special Agent Cooper and Property Damage Claims in the Winter of 1890-1891, *South Dakota History*, vol. 24, No. 3 and 4, 1994, p. 219. Also see, Grua, David W., *Surviving Wounded Knee: The Lakotas and the Politics of Memory*, New York: Oxford University Press, 2016, p. 108.

70. According to John Loneman's account of the arrest and killing of Sitting Bull, one of the Indians present was Charles Afraid of Hawk, living at the Standing Rock Reservation. See, Vestal, Stanley, *New Sources of Indian History*, Norman: University of Oklahoma Press, 1934, pp. 45-55.

71. Utley, Robert M., *The Lance and The Shield: The Life and Times of Sitting Bull*, New York: Henry Holt and Company, 1993, p.301.

72. *The Chicago Tribune*, vol. 51, No. 5, January 5, 1891, p. 1.

73. Accounts vary as to the actual number of Indian police present that morning and involved in the arrest. McLaughlin's Papers, Letter Box 1881-1890, Roll 20 Frame 957, recommends 39 police officers for recognition. Also cited in Utley, Robert M., *The Lance and The Shield: The Life and Times of Sitting Bull*, New York: Henry Holt and Company, 1993, p.395n23.

74. One of the Standing Rock tribal policemen fighting at Sitting Bull's camp was Charles Afraid of Hawk. However, Bob Young's genealological research shows that he was not related to the Pine Ridge Afraid of Hawk family. See, Young, Robert, *Afraid of Hawk and Cetan Kokipapi in 19ᵗʰ-century Plains Native American Families*, unpublished manuscript, 2016, p.28.

75. Mooney, James, The Ghost Dance Religion and the Sioux Outbreak, *Fourteenth Annual Report of the Bureau of Ethnology*, Part 2, Washington, D.C.: Government Printing Office, 1896, p. 858-859. Also, see, Greene, Jerome A., *American Carnage: Wounded Knee, 1890*, Norman: University of Oklahoma Press, 2014, p.179-183.

76. Walker, James R., *Lakota Society*, edited by Raymond J. DeMillie, Lincoln: University of Nebraska Press, 1982, p. 151.

77. Jensen, Richard E., R. Eli Paul, and John E. Carter, *Eyewitness at Wounded Knee*, Lincoln: University of Nebraska Press, 1991, p. 17.

78. Greene, Jerome A., *American Carnage: Wounded Knee, 1890*, Norman: University of Oklahoma Press, 2014, p.197.

79. *Report to the Secretary of War*, from Sumner to Miles, December 22 and 23, 1890, pp. 235-236.

80. Greene, Jerome A., *American Carnage: Wounded Knee, 1890*, Norman: University of Oklahoma Press, 2014, p. 337.

81. Ostler, Jeffery, *The Plains Sioux and U.S. Colonialism From Lewis and Clark to Wounded Knee*, Cambridge: Cambridge Univeristy Press, 2004, p 333-337. Grua, William W., *Surviving Wounded Knee: The Lakotas and the Politics of Memory*, New York: Oxford University Press, 2016, p. 25.

82. Kelley, William Fitch, *Pine Ridge 1890: An Eye Witness Account of the Events Surrounding the Fighting at Wounded Knee*, San Francisco, Pierre Bovis, 1971, p. 153.

83. Mooney, James, The Ghost Dance Religion and the Sioux Outbreak, *Fourteenth Annual Report of the Bureau of Ethnology*, Part 2, Washington, D.C.: Government Printing Office, 1896, p. 866.

84. Hall, Philip S., *To Have This Land: The Political Road to Wounded Knee, 1888-1891*, Vermillion, SD: University of South Dakota Press, 1991, p.123.

85. McGregor, James H., *The Wounded Knee Massacre From the Viewpoint of the Sioux*, Rapid City: Fenske Media Corporation, 1940, pp. 47.

86. Mooney, James, The Ghost Dance Religion and the Sioux Outbreak, *Fourteenth Annual Report of the Bureau of Ethnology*, Part 2, Washington, D.C.: Government Printing Office, 1896, p. 867.

87. Greene, Jerome A., *American Carnage: Wounded Knee, 1890*, Norman: University of Oklahoma Press, 2014, p.214.

88. It is unknown exactly when and where Richard Afraid of Hawk joined Big Foot's party. Bob Young has found no relatives at Standing Rock he could have been visiting at the time. One theory is that he joined the Miniconjou chief shortly before Wounded Knee, coming from the Stronghold where the Ghost Dance believers were encamped.

89. Taken from Dewey Beard's interview, See Danker, Donald S., The Wounded Knee Interviews of Eli S. Ricker, *Nebraska History*, 1981, vo. 62, p. 190.

90. Richardson, Heather Cox, *Wounded Knee: Party Politics and the Road To An American Massacre*, New York: Perseus Book Group, 2010, 264. Also see, Greene, Jerome A., *American Carnage: Wounded Knee, 1890*, Norman: University of Oklahoma Press, 2014, p.223.

91. Mooney, James, The Ghost Dance Religion and the Sioux Outbreak, *Fourteenth Annual Report of the Bureau of Ethnology*, Part 2, Washington, D.C.: Government Printing Office, 1896, p. 868.

92. Richardson, Heather Cox, *Wounded Knee: Party Politics and the Road To An American Massacre*, New York: Perseus Book Group, 2010, 266.

93. Ibid.

94. Mooney identifies the medicine man as Yellow Bird, See, Mooney, James, The Ghost Dance Religion and the Sioux Outbreak, *Fourteenth Annual Report of the Bureau of Ethnology*, Part 2, Washington, D.C.: Government Printing Office, 1896, p. 868. Other accounts identify the medicine man as being named Good Thunder, Black Fox, Black Coyote, Sits Straight, and Shakes Bird. See, Greene, Jerome A., *American Carnage: Wounded Knee, 1890*, Norman: University of Oklahoma Press, 2014, p.227.

95. Also, identified as Black Fox. See Greene, Jerome A., *American Carnage: Wounded Knee, 1890*, Norman: University of Oklahoma Press, 2014, p.230.

96. Ibid., p. 193.

97. Warren, Louis S., *God's Red Son: The Ghost Dance Religion and the Making of Modern America*, New York: Basic Books, 2017, p. 287.

98. Mooney, James, The Ghost Dance Religion and the Sioux Outbreak, *Fourteenth Annual Report of the Bureau of Ethnology*, Part 2, Washington, D.C.: Government Printing Office, 1896, p. 868.

99. It is uncertain when Richard Afraid of Hawk joined up with Big Foot's group. Bob Young suggests that he may have attached himself to the refuges when they entered the Pine Ridge Reservation, prior to Whitside's encounter (Personal Communication, 2017).

100. Oral family tradition told by Richard's son Daniel Jay Afraid of Hawk.

101. Ruby, Robert H., *The Oglala Sioux: Warriors in Transition*, New York: Vantage Press, 1955, p. 108.

102. Agonito, Joseph, *Lakota Portraits: Live of the Legendary Plains People*, Guildford, CT: TwoDot Press, 2011, p. 172.

103. McGregor, James H., *The Wounded Knee Massacre From the Viewpoint of the Sioux*, Rapid City: Fenske Media Corporation, 1940, contains Richard Afraid of Hawk's account as interpreted by William Bergen, pp. 121-122.

104. Richardson, Heather Cox, *Wounded Knee: Party Politics and the Road To An American Massacre*, New York: Perseus Book Group, 2010, 273.

105. Deloria, Philip J., *Indians in Unexpected Places*, Lawrence: University of Kansas Press, 2004, p. 24.

106. "War With The Savages", *Junction City Republican*, Kansas, 1 January 1891, also quoted in Grua, William W., *Surviving Wounded Knee: The Lakotas and the Politics of Memory*, New York: Oxford University Press, 2016, p. 56.

107. DiSilvestro, Roger, L., *In the Shadow of Wounded Knee: The Untold Story of the Indian Wars*, New York: Walter & Company, 2005, p. 88.

108. Ibid., p. 212.

109. Eastman, Elaine Goodale, *Sister to the Sioux*, Lincoln: University of Nebraska Press, 2nd edition, 1978.

110. Ives, Frank J. *Indians Wounded in Fight at Wounded Knee, South Dakota, December 29, 1890, Treated by Frank J. Ives, Capt. & Asst. Surgeon, USA,*

manuscript (MS H84.38) on file at Fort Robinson Museum, Crawford, NE, and as quoted in Jensen, Richard E., R. Eli Paul, and John E. Carter, *Eyewitness at Wounded Knee*, Lincoln: University of Nebraska Press, 1991, p. 131.

111. Starita, Joe, *The Dull Knives of Pine Ridge: A Lakota Odyssey*, New York: G.P. Putnam's Sons, 1995, p. 128. Also, Dunbar-Ortiz, Roxanne, *An Indigenous Peoples' History of the United States*, Boston: Beacon Press, 2014, p. 155,

112. Jensen, Richard E., R. Eli Paul, and John E. Carter, *Eyewitness at Wounded Knee*, Lincoln: University of Nebraska Press, 1991, p. 106.

113. Ibid., p. 108, provides photographic documentation of a relic hunters among the burial party.

114. Ibid, p. 110.

115. Ibid., p. 113.

116. Mooney, James, The Ghost Dance Religion and the Sioux Outbreak, *Fourteenth Annual Report of the Bureau of Ethnology*, Part 2, Washington, D.C.: Government Printing Office, 1896, p. 876-877.

117. McGregor, James H., *The Wounded Knee Massacre From the Viewpoint of the Sioux*, Rapid City: Fenske Media Corporation, 1940, pp. 73.

118. Ibid., p. 878.

119. Greene, Jerome A., *American Carnage: Wounded Knee, 1890*, Norman: University of Oklahoma Press, 2014, p.302.

120. McGregor, James H., *The Wounded Knee Massacre From the Viewpoint of the Sioux*, Rapid City: Fenske Media Corporation, 1940, pp. 74-75.

121. DiSilvestro, Roger, L., *In the Shadow of Wounded Knee: The Untold Story of the Indian Wars*, New York: Walter & Company, 2005, p. 90.

122. Mooney, James, The Ghost Dance Religion and the Sioux Outbreak, *Fourteenth Annual Report of the Bureau of Ethnology*, Part 2, Washington, D.C.: Government Printing Office, 1896, p. 870-71; Jensen, Richard E., R. Eli Paul, and John E. Carter, *Eyewitness at Wounded Knee*, Lincoln: University of Nebraska Press, 1991, p. 20; Ostler, Jeffrey, *The Lakotas and the Black Hills*, New York: Penguin Books, 2010, p. 123; Greene, Jerome A., *American Carnage: Wounded Knee, 1890*, Norman: University of Oklahoma Press, 2014, p.288.

123. See Warren, Louis S., *God's Red Son: The Ghost Dance Religion and The Making of Modern America*, New York: Basic Books, 2017.

124. Eastman, Charles, *From the Deep Woods to Civilization: Chapters in the Autobiography of an Indian*, Lincoln: University of Nebraska Press, 1977.

125. Fishkin, Shelley Fisher, *Writing America: Literary Landmarks From Waldon Pond to Wounded Knee, A Reader's Companion*, New Brunswick, N.J.: Rutgers University Press, 2015, p. 154.

126. Boyd, James P., *Recent Indian Wars Under the Lead of Sitting Bull and Other Chiefs*, Publisher's Union, 1891, pp. 180-181, reprinted, Digital Scanning Inc., 2000, and quoted in Ronald J. Papandrea, *They Never Surrendered: The Lakota*

Sioux Band That Stayed in Canada, 4ᵗʰ edition revised, La Vergne, TN: Lighting Source, an IGRAM Co., 2012, p. 25.

127. Green, Jerry, The Medals of Wounded Knee, *Nebraska History*, 1994, vol. 75, p. 203. Also, see Green, Jerry, ed., *After Wounded Knee: Correspondences of Major & Surgeon John Vance Lauderdale While Serving With The Army Occupying The Pine Ridge Indian Reservation, 1890-1891*, East Lansing: Michigan State University Press, 1996, p. 39.

128. Deloria, Philip J., *Indians in Unexpected Places*, Lawrence: University of Kansas Press, 2004, p. 34.

129. Green, Jerry, ed., *After Wounded Knee: Correspondences of Major & Surgeon John Vance Lauderdale While Serving With The Army Occupying The Pine Ridge Indian Reservation, 1890-1891*, East Lansing: Michigan State University Press, 1996, p. 38.

130. DeMontravel, Peter A., *A Hero to His Fighting Men: Nelson A. Miles, 1839-1925*, Kent, OH: Kent State University Press, 1998, p. 206.

131. Maddra, Sam, *Hostiles? The Lakota Ghost Dance and Buffalo Bill's Wild West*, Norman: Oklahoma University Press, 2006, p.4.

132. Ibid., p. 25.

133. Deloria, Philip J., *Indians in Unexpected Places*, Lawrence: University of Kansas Press, 2004, p. 67.

134. Maddra, Sam, *Hostiles? The Lakota Ghost Dane and Buffalo Bill's Wild West*, Norman: Oklahoma University Press, 2006, p.25.

135. Ibid., p. 82.

136. Ibid., p. 96.

137. Ibid., p. 101.

138. Delaney, Michele, *Buffalo Bill's Wild West Warriors: A Photographic History by Gertrude Kasebier*, New York: HarperCollins Publishers and the Smithsonian National Museum of American History, 2007, p. 21.

139. Deloria, Philip J., *Indians in Unexpected Places*, Lawrence: University of Kansas Press, 2004, p. 69.

140. Maddra, Sam, Hostiles? *The Lakota Ghost Dane and Buffalo Bill's Wild West*, Norman: Oklahoma University Press, 2006, p.96.

141. Kesson, Joy S., *Buffalo Bill's Wild West: Celebrity, Memory and Popular History*, New York: Hill and Wang, 2000, p. 211.

142. Ibid., 193.

143. Deloria, Philip J., *Indians in Unexpected Places*, Lawrence: University of Kansas Press, 2004, p. 70.

144. Carter, Robert A., *Buffalo Bill Cody: The Man Behind the Legend*, New York: John Wiley & Sons, 2000, p. 196.

145. Kesson, Joy S., *Buffalo Bill's Wild West: Celebrity, Memory and Popular History*, 2000, New York: Hill and Wang, p. 161.

146. Quoted in Carter, Robert A., *Buffalo Bill Cody: The Man Behind the Legend*, New York: John Wiley & Sons, 2000, p. 448.

147. Deloria, Philip J., *Indians in Unexpected Places*, Lawrence: University of Kansas Press, 2004, pp. 67.

148. Starita, Joe, *The Dull Knives of Pine Ridge: A Lakota Odyssey*, New York: G.P. Putnam's Sons, 1995, p. 151.

149. See Deloria, Philip J., *Indians in Unexpected Places*, Lawrence: University of Kansas Press, 2004, pp. 62-65.

150. Delaney, Michele, *Buffalo Bill's Wild West Warriors: A Photographic History by Gertrude Kasebier*, New York: HarperCollins Publishers and the Smithsonian National Museum of American History, 2007, p. 31. Also, see Moses, L. G., *Wild West Shows and the Images of American Indians, 1883-1933*, Albuquerque: University of New Mexico Press, 1996, p. 4.

151. Grua, William W., *Surviving Wounded Knee: The Lakotas and the Politics of Memory*, New York: Oxford University Press, 2016, pp. 117-119.

152. Dunbar-Ortix, Roxanne and Dina Gilio-Whitaker, *"All The Real Indians Died Off" And 20 Other Myths About Native Americans*, Boston: Beacon Press, 2016.

153. Carter, Robert A., *Buffalo Bill Cody: The Man Behind the Legend*, New York: John Wiley & Sons, 2000, pp. 238-341.

154. Delaney, Michele, *Buffalo Bill's Wild West Warriors: A Photographic History by Gertrude Kasebier*, New York: HarperCollins Publishers and the Smithsonian National Museum of American History, 2007, p. 23.

155. Ibid., p. 247.

156. Carter, Robert A., *Buffalo Bill Cody: The Man Behind the Legend*, New York: John Wiley & Sons, 2000, p. 450.

157. Gooch, George H., *Buffalo Bill's Wild West and Congress of Rough Riders of the World, Official Programme*, 1899, Archives, National Museum of American History, Smithsonian Institution, and as reprinted in Delaney, Michele, *Buffalo Bill's Wild West Warriors: A Photographic History by Gertrude Kasebier*, New York: HarperCollins Publishers and the Smithsonian National Museum of American History, 2007, p. 140-141.

158. Carter, Robert A., *Buffalo Bill Cody: The Man Behind the Legend*, New York: John Wiley & Sons, 2000, p. 381.

159. "Wild West In The Arena", *New York Times*, 24 April 1900, p. 2.

160. Gooch, George H., *Route Book: Buffalo Bill's Wild West, Season 1900*, Kansas City: Kimberly Publishing Co., 1901.

161. "Buffalo Bill's Show: Crowds Saw the Street Parade and Scenes Within the Tent", *The Hartford Daily Courant*, 26 January 1900, p. 7.

162. Goochl, George H., *Buffalo Bill's Wild West and Congress of Rough Riders of the World, Official Programme*, 1899, Archives, National Museum of American History, Smithsonian Institution, p. 9, and as reprinted in Delaney, Michele,

Buffalo Bill's Wild West Warriors: A Photographic History by Gertrude Kasebier, New York: HarperCollins Publishers and the Smithsonian National Museum of American History, 2007, p. 140-141.

163. Kesson, Joy S., *Buffalo Bill's Wild West: Celebrity, Memory and Popular History*, New York: Hill and Wang, 2000, p. 211.

164. http://centerofthewest.org/learn/western-essays/wild-west-shows/, Buffalo Bill Center of the West website.

165. Delaney, Michele, *Buffalo Bill's Wild West Warriors: A Photographic History by Gertrude Kasebier*, New York: HarperCollins Publishers and the Smithsonian National Museum of American History, 2007, p. 35.

166. Kesson, Joy S., *Buffalo Bill's Wild West: Celebrity, Memory and Popular History*, New York: Hill and Wang, 2000.

167. "Death of Afraid-of-Hawk: He Fulfilled All he Traditions of His Race by Stoic Demeanor," *New Haven Evening Register*, 2 July 1900, Vol. 57, Issue 153, p. 11. Many other newspapers picked up the by-line on Albert's death including, "Canned Corn Did It", *The Daily Herald* (Delphos, Ohio), 29 June 1900, Friday, p. 1; "Canned Corn Kills an Indian", *The Sterling Standard* (Sterling, Illinois), 29 June 1900, Friday, p. 2; "Sioux Indian's Death: He Succumbed to Canned Corn—Member of Cody's Show", *The Fort Wayne News* (Fort Wayne, Indiana), 29 June 1900, Friday, p. 5.

168. Gooch, George H., *Route Book: Buffalo Bill's Wild West 1900*, Kansas City: Kimberly Publishing Co., 1901.

169. Death of Afraid-of-Hawk: He Fulfilled All he Traditions of His Race by Stoic Demeanor, *New Haven Evening Register*, 2 July 1900, Vol. 57, Issue 153, p. 11.

170. Ibid.

171. Ibid.

172. Gooch, George H., *Route-Book, Buffalo Bill's Wild West, Season 1900*, Kansas City: Kimberly Publishing Co., 1901. Although the Route Book lists Albert's death as June 28th, his death certificate registered in the Danbury Town Clerk's Office cites June 29, 1900.

173. Burying an Indian: Funeral of Man-Afraid-of-Hawk of Col. Cody's Troupe, *Naugatuck Daily News*, 30 June 1900, Friday, p. 5.

174. "Death of Afraid-of-Hawk: He Fulfilled All he Traditions of His Race by Stoic Demeanor," *New Haven Evening Register*, 2 July 1900, Vol. 57, Issue 153, p. 11.

7. AFTER AFRAID OF HAWK

1. Wooster Cemetery Association, Danbury, archival burial card.

2. City of Danbury, Town Clerk's Office, Death Certificate, June 29, 1900.

3. "Death of Afraid-of-Hawk: He Fulfilled All he Traditions of His Race by Stoic Demeanor," *New Haven Evening Register*, 2 July 1900, Vol. 57, Issue 153, p. 11.

4. *United States Indian Census*, Pine Ridge Reservation, Wounded Knee District, 1904, p.64.

5. *United States Indian Census*, Pine Ridge Reservation, Wounded Knee District, 1913, p. 44.

6. *United States Federal Population Census*, Pine Ridge Reservation, Wounded Knee District, 1930, pp. 3-4.

7. Application For Headstone, *War Department, O.Q.M.G. Form No. 623.* Approved, 31 March 1933.

8. Agonito, Joseph, *Lakota Portraits: Lives of the Legendary Plains People*, Guilford, Connecticut: Twodot, Globe Pequot Press, 2011. P. 285.

9. *Land Allotment*, Patent No. 332208, Described as Section 11 in township 40 north of Range 46 west of the 6th Principal Meriden, South Dakota, signed by President William Howard Taft, 17 January 1910

10. Mails, Thomas E., *Fools Crow*, Lincoln: University of Nebraska Press, Bison Books, 1990.

11. Robertson, Paul, *The Power of the Land: Identity, Ethnicity, and Class Among the Oglala Lakota*, New York: Routledge, 2002.

12. Biolsi, Thomas, *Organizing the Lakota: The Political Economy of the New Deal on the Pine Ridge and Rosebud Reservations*, Tucson: University of Arizona Press, 2nd printing, 1998.

13. Robertson, Paul, *The Power of the Land: Identity, Ethnicity, and Class Among the Oglala Lakota*, New York: Routledge, 2002, pp. 123-164.

14. Ibid., p. A10.

15. Miller, Robert, Albert Emerges to Thanks, *The (Danbury) News-Times*, 17 August 2012.

16. DeMallie, Raymond, J. The Teton, *Handbook of North American Indians, Plains*, Vol. 13, Part 2 of 2, ed. By Raymond J. DeMillie, General editor, William, C. Sturtevant, Washington, D.C.: Smithsonian Institution, 2001, p. 816.

17. Ostler, Jeffery, *The Lakotas and the Black Hills: The Struggle for Sacred Ground*, New York: Penguin Books, 2010, p. 143.

18. DeMillie, Raymond, J. The Teton, *Handbook of North American Indians, Plains*, Vol. 13, Part 2 of 2, ed. By Raymond J. DeMillie, General editor, William, C. Sturtevant, Washington, D.C.: Smithsonian Institution, 2001, p. 816.

19. Mails, Thomas E., *Fools Crow*, Lincoln: University of Nebraska Press, Bison Books, 1990, p.

20. *Indian Reorganization Act of 1934*, Wheeler-Howard Act, 73rd Congress, Public Law 73-383.

21. Agonito, Joseph, *Lakota Portraits: Lives of the Legendary Plains People*, Guilford, Connecticut: Twodot, Globe Pequot Press, 2011, p. 293-294.

22. Reinhardt, Akim D., *Ruling Pine Ridge: Oglala Lakota Politics from the IRA to Wounded Knee*, Lubbock: Texas Tech University Press, 2007, p. 210.

23. Kehoe, Alice Beck, *The Ghost Dance: Ethnohistory and Revitalization*, Chicago: Holt, Rinehart and Winston, Inc., 1989, p. 73.

24. http://freepages.genealogy.rootsweb.ancestry.com/~mikestevens/ira_councils .htm

25. Daniel Jay Afraid of Hawk, Richard's son, would turn out to be one of the lead riders in the Annual Chief Big Foot Memorial Ride, covering the 191-mile distance from the Standing Rock Reservation to Wounded Knee to honor the memory of the victims of the massacre.

26. See Pipe on Head and Dewey Beard's testimony on 7 March 1938, House Resolution 2535, *Hearings*, pp. 21-22. Also, Vine Deloria Jr., and Clifford M Lytle, American Indians, American Justice, Austin: University of Texas Press, 1983, p. 162, and Grua, David W., *Surviving Wounded Knee: The Lakotas and the Politics of Memory*, New York: Oxford University Press, 2016, p. 168.

27. National Archives, Record Group 75, *Records of the Bureau of Indian Affairs*, Central Classified Files, 1907-1939, Pine Ridge 15190-1933-Pine Ridge-260. Also, noted by Greene, Jerome A., *American Carnage: Wounded Knee, 1890*, Norman: University of Oklahoma Press, 2014, p. 531n18.

28. National Archives, Record Group 75, *Records of the Bureau of Indian Affairs*, Central Classified Files, 1907-1939, Kansas City, Hi Hawk, James, Philip Blackmoon and Richard Afraid of Hawk, Justification for a Relief Bill, draft, 20 June 1935. Also cited in Grua, David, W., *Surviving Wounded Knee: The Lakotas and the Politics of Memory*, New York: Oxford University Press, 2016, pp. 159-160.

29. McGregor, James H., *The Wounded Knee Massacre From the Viewpoint of the Sioux*, Rapid City: Fenske Media Corporation, 1940, pp. 121-122.

30. Robert Young's genealogical research into the Afraid of Hawk family lists November 1874 for Richard's birth. (See, Young, Robert, *Afraid of Hawk and Cetan Kokipapi in 19th-century Plains Native American families*, unpublished manuscript, 2016, p. 23)

31. The exact genealogical relationship between Emil Afraid of Hawk to Albert's family remains unclear. Some sources suggests that Emil, Richard and Albert were brothers (www.ancestry.com/tree/103172081/person/430025141035/facts) and an interview with Richard's son, Daniel Jay Afraid of Hawk, refers to Emil as his father's brother (Wiping Away the Tears of Seven Generations, part 1, Kifaru Productions, 1992). Bob Young's exhaustive family genealogy suggests that Emil was Albert's half brother, sharing the same father (Emil, Sr.) but having different mothers. Emil, Jr.'s mother appears to be Her Yellow Blanket. (See Young, Robert, *Afraid of Hawk and Cetan Kokipapi in 19th-century Plains Native American families*, unpublished manuscript, 2016, pp. 30-31.)

32. Solon, Sister Eleanor, *We Walk in Faith: The Growth of the Catholic Faith in Western South Dakota*, Eckbolsheim, France: Editions du Signe, 2002, data from the Stipend Lists for the Lumen Christi Award Application of the Diocese of Rapid City. Also, see DeMallie, Raymond J., *The Sixth Grandfather: Black Elk's Teachings Given to John G. Neihardt*, Lincoln: University of Nebraska Press, 1984, p. 26.

33. Peterson, Bruce A., *The Two Masks of Nicholas Black Elk*, Masters Thesis, Department of History, University of Texas–Pan American, 1996. Also see, Baym, Nina, gen. ed., *The Norton Anthology of American Literature 1914-1945*, Vol. D, Seventh Edition, New York: W.W. Norton & Company, 2007, p. 1193.

34. Hinman, Eleanor H., *Oglala Sources on the Life of Crazy Horse*, Nebraska History, 2010, p. 6.

35. Peterson, Bruce A., *The Two Masks of Nicholas Black Elk*, Masters Thesis, Department of History, University of Texas–Pan American, 1996.

36. Neihardt, John G., *Black Elk Speaks*, The Premier Edition, Albany: State University of New York Press, 2008.

37. The Catholic Jesuits and many others were critical of *Black Elk Speaks* because it ended at Wounded Knee and did not relate the conversion of Black Elk to Roman Catholicism. Though Black Elk's declaration of faith to the Catholic Church soothed over many hard feelings, Emil Afraid of Hawk served to get the message of the priest's dissatisfaction across to Black Elk. See, DeMallie, Raymond J., *The Sixth Grandfather: Black Elk's Teachings Given to John G. Neihardt*, Lincoln: University of Nebraska Press, 1984, p. 62.

38. Ostler, Jeffery, *The Lakotas and the Black Hills: The Struggle for Sacred Ground*, New York: Penguin Books, 2010, p. 132.

39. Ibid., p. 134.

40. Ibid., p. 141.

41. Ibid., p. 142.; Also see R. Eli Paul, ed., *The Nebraska Indian Wars Reader 1865-1877*, Lincoln: University of Nebraska Press, 1998, p. 184.

42. For a similar argument, See, *Hearings Before The Committee on Indian Affairs, House of Representatives, 74th Congress, 1st Session*, on Indian Claims Commission Bill H.R. 7837, Statement by Hon. John Collier, Commissioner of the Bureau of Indian Affairs, Department of the Interior, Washington: Government Printing Office, 1935, p. 6.

43. *Sioux Tribe of Indians v. The United States*, 97 Ct. Cl. 613, 1942, as cited in Ostler, Jeffery, *The Lakotas and the Black Hills: The Struggle for Sacred Ground*, New York: Penguin Books, 2010, p. 145, 214n9.

44. Larner, Jesse, *Mount Rushmore: An Icon Reconsidered*, New York: Thunder's Mouth Press, National Books, 2002.

45. Roosevelt, Theodore, *The Winning of the West*, Book IV, New York: G.P. Putnam's Sons, 1896.

46. Delaney, Michelle, *Buffalo Bill's Wild West Warriors: A Photographic History by Gertrude Kasebier*, New York: HarperCollins for the Smithsonian Institution, 2007. See portrait of White Wolf, p. 105.

47. Goldfrank, Esther S., Change and Social Character: A Study of Teton Dakota, *American Anthropologist*, 1943, Vol. 45, No. 1, pp. 67-83.

48. Delaney, Michelle, *Buffalo Bill's Wild West Warriors: A Photographic History by Gertrude Kasebier*, New York: HarperCollins Publishers for the Smithsonian Institution, 2007, p. 4.

49. Fuss, Alison, Cowboys on the Reservation: The Growth of Rodeo as a Lakota National Pastime, *South Dakota History*, Vol. 29, No. 3, 1999, p. 212.

50. *Shannon County News*, August 2, 1929, as quoted in Fuss, Alison, Cowboys on the Reservation: The Growth of Rodeo as a Lakota National Pastime, *South Dakota History*, Vol. 29, No. 3, 1999, p. 227.

51. Fuss, Alison, Cowboys on the Reservation: The Growth of Rodeo as a Lakota National Pastime, *South Dakota History*, Vol. 29, No. 3, 1999, p. 212.

52. Clark, Ann, *Singing Sioux Cowboy Reader*, Washington, D. C.: Department of the Interior Publication of the United States Indian Service, 1954.

53. As recounted in the Executive Proclamation of the Cheyenne River Sioux Tribe of South Dakota, designating 15 February 2014 as "Daniel 'Danny' Afraid of Hawk Day".

54. Mathiessen, Peter, *In The Spirit Of Crazy Horse*, New York: Viking Penguin, 1991, pp. 59-60. Also, see Larner, Jesse, *Mount Rushmore: An Icon Reconsidered*, New York: Thunder's Mouth Press, National Books, 2002, pp. 133-135.

55. Mathiessen, Peter, *In The Spirit Of Crazy Horse*, New York: Viking Penguin, 1991, p. 62.

56. Hertzberg, Hazel W., Indian Rights Movement, 1887-1973, In *Handbook of North American Indians*, ed. By William C. Sturtevant, vol. ed., Wilcomb E. Washburn, History of Indian-White Relations, Vol. 4, Washington: Smithsonian Institution, 1988, p. 318.

57. Marshall III, Joseph M., Wounded Knee Takeover, 1973, In *Encyclopedia of North American Indians: Native American History, Culture, and Life From Paleo-Indians to the Present*, ed. By Frederick E. Hoxie, Boston: Houghton Mifflin Company, 1996, pp. 697-699.

58. Mathiessen, Peter, *In The Spirit Of Crazy Horse*, New York: Viking Penguin, 1991, p. 63.

59. Zimmerman, Bill, *Airlift to Wounded Knee*, Chicago: Swallow Press, 1976, pp. 125-126.

60. Quoted in Kehoe, Alice Beck, *The Ghost Dance: Ethnohistory and Revitalization*, Chicago: Holt, Rinehart and Winston, Inc., 1989, p. 80.

61. Brown, Dee, *Bury My Heart at Wounded Knee*, New York: Holt, Rinehart & Winston, 1970.

62. Kehoe, Alice Beck, *The Ghost Dance: Ethnohistory and Revitalization*, Chicago: Holt, Rinehart and Winston, Inc., 1989, p. 80.

63. Chertoff, Emily, Occupy Wounded Knee: A 71-Day Siege and a Forgotten Civil Rights Movement, *The Atlantic*, October 2012. Also see Mathiessen, Peter, *In*

The Spirit Of Crazy Horse, New York: Viking Penguin, 1991, for detailed account of the siege at Wounded Knee in 1973.

64. Marshall III, Joseph M., Wounded Knee Takeover, 1973, In *Encyclopedia of North American Indians: Native American History, Culture, and Life From Paleo-Indians to the Present*, ed. By Frederick E. Hoxie, Boston: Houghton Mifflin Company, 1996, p. 699.

65. As quoted in Kehoe, Alice Beck, *The Ghost Dance: Ethnohistory and Revitalization*, Chicago: Holt, Rinehart and Winston, Inc., 1989, p. 83.

66. Buddy LaMonte was buried in the Wounded Knee Cemetery. His tombstone resides next to the mass burial trench and Monument.

67. Lyman, Stanley D., *Wounded Knee 1973: A Personal Account*, Lincoln: University of Nebraska Press, 1990, p. 21.

68. Discussion of the skeletal analysis of Albert Afraid of Hawk is as reported in Aronsen, Gary P., *Evaluation of human skeletal remains identified as Albert Afraid of Hawk*, 2012, unpublished Yale University manuscript on file at the Office of State Archaeology, Connecticut Archaeology Center, University of Connecticut, Storrs.

69. Brooks, S., and J. Suchey, Skeletal age determination based on the Os Pubis: A comparison of the Asadi-Nemeskeri and Suchey-Brooks methods, *Human Evolution*, vol. 5, 1990, pp. 227-238.

70. Scott, G., and Christy Turner, III, *The Anthropology of Modern Human Teeth*, Cambridge: Cambridge University Press, 1997.

71. Auerbach, B. M., and C.B. Ruff, Stature estimation formulae for indigenous North American populations, *American Journal of Physical Anthropology*, vol. 141, 2010, pp. 190-207.

72. Molleson, T., and J. Blondiaux, Rider's bones from Kish, Iraq, *Cambridge Archaeological Journal*, vol. 4, 1994, pp. 312-316.

73. Kehoe, Alice Beck, *The Ghost Dance: Ethnohistory and Revitalization*, Chicago: Holt, Rinehart and Winston, Inc., 1989, p. 90.

74. Ostler, Jeffery, *The Lakotas and the Black Hills: The Struggle for Sacred Ground*, New York: Penguin Books, 2010, pp. 176-187.

75. Frank Fools Crow testimony, 42 Indians Claims Commission, 1978, on the Black Hills Claim, Docket 74-B).

76. Kehoe, Alice Beck, *The Ghost Dance: Ethnohistory and Revitalization*, Chicago: Holt, Rinehart and Winston, Inc., 1989, p. 90.

8. "HOME IS WHERE HE BELONGS"

1. Rose, Christine, Buffalo Bill Rough Rider Albert Afraid of Hawk, At Rest, At Last, *Indian Country Today*, September 13, 2012.

2. Lengerich, Ryan, Lakota Performer Comes Home, *Rapid City Journal*, 9 September 2012, p. A1, A6.

3. Young, Mary-Jo, *Reflections on the Repatriation of Albert Afraid of Hawk*, unpublished manuscript on file at the Office of State Archaeology, University of Connecticut, Storrs, 2012, p. 1.

4. *Tunkasila* is the Lakota term for "grandfather" and is used as a sign of respect and honor and demonstrates social kinship relations between individuals. See, Ostler, Jeffrey, *The Lakotas and the Black Hills: The Struggle for Sacred Ground*, New York: Penguin Group, 2010, p. 72.

5. A Lakota Prayer, *In Loving Memory of Albert Afraid of Hawk*, pamphlet for the wake and funeral in Manderson, South Dakota, 8 September 2012.

6. Kent, Jim, Lakota Wild West Rider Returns Home, *Lakota Country Times*, 12 September 2012, vol. 8, issue 51, p. A2.

7. Young, Mary-Jo, *Reflections on the Repatriation of Albert Afraid of Hawk*, unpublished manuscript on file at the Office of State Archaeology, University of Connecticut, Storrs, 2012, p. 1.

8. Lengerich, Ryan, Lakota Performer Comes Home, *Rapid City Journal*, 9 September 2012, p. A6.

9. Young, Mary-Jo, *Reflections on the Repatriation of Albert Afraid of Hawk*, unpublished manuscript on file at the Office of State Archaeology, University of Connecticut, Storrs, 2012, p. 1.

10. Ibid.

11. Ibid., p. 2.

12. Ibid.

13. Associated Press, Ceremony Remembers Buffalo Bill Performer, *Rapid City Journal*, 10 September 2012, p. A4.

References Cited

Adams, David Wallace, *Education for Extinction: American Indians and the Boarding School Experience, 1875-1928*, Lawrence: University of Kansas Press, 1995.

Agonito, Joseph, *Lakota Portraits: Live of the Legendary Plains People*, Guildford, CT: TwoDot Press, 2011.

Alexander, William, D., *A Brief History of the Hawaiian People*, New York: American Book Company, 1891.

Ambrose, Stephen, *Undaunted Courage*, New York: Simon & Schuster, 1997

American Board of Commissioners for Foreign Missions, *Narrative of Five Youths From The Sandwich Islands, Now Receiving An Education In This Country*. New York: J. Seymour, 1816.

_____, *Annual Report*, No. 7, Boston, 1816.

_____, *Instructions from the Prudential Committee of the ABCFM to members of the Mission to the Sandwich Islands*, Boston: Samuel Armstrong, 1819.

_____, *Annual Report*, No. 28, Boston, 1837.

Andrews, John A., "Educating the Heathen: The Foreign Mission School, Controversy and American Ideals", *Journal of American Studies*, Vo. 12, No. 3, 1978, p. 332-333.

Andrews, John, The Long Road Home, *South Dakota Magazine*, Vol. 29, No. 2, July/August 2013, p. 58.

Aronsen, Gary P., *Evaluation of human skeletal remains identified as Albert Afraid of Hawk*, 2012, unpublished Yale University manuscript on file at the Office of State Archaeology, Connecticut Archaeology Center, University of Connecticut, Storrs.

Atalay, Sonya, *Community-based Archaeology*, Berkeley: University of California Press, 2012.

Auerbach, B. M., and C. B. Ruff, Stature estimation formulae for indigenous North American populations, *American Journal of Physical Anthropology*, vol. 141, 2010, pp. 190-207.

Austen, Barbara, "Missionary Legacies: Connecticut to Hawaii," IN *American Ancestors*, Spring 2014, pp. 31-35.

Banner, Stuart, *How The Indians Lost Their Land: Law and Power on the Frontier*, Cambridge, MA: Harvard University Press, 2005.

Barber, John Warner, *Connecticut's Historical Collections, Containing a General Collection of Interesting Facts, Traditions, Biographical Sketches, Anecdotes, etc., Relating to the History and Antiquities of Every Town in Connecticut with Geographical Descriptions*, New Haven: B. L. Hamlen, 1836.

Barrere, Dorothy B., ed., Mary Kawena Pukui, translator, Fragments of Hawaiian History as Recorded by John Papaʻi, *Bernice P. Bishop Museum Special Publication* 70, Honolulu: Bishop Museum Press, 1983.

Baym, Nina, gen. ed., *The Norton Anthology of American Literature 1914-1945*, Vol. D, Seventh Edition, New York: W.W. Norton & Company, 2007.

Beasley, Conger, *We Are A People In This World, The Lakota Sioux, Massacre at Wounded Knee*, Little Rock: University of Arkansas Press, 1995.

Beckwith, Martha, *Hawaiian Mythology*, Honolulu: University of Hawaii Press, 1970.

Beecher, Lyman, *A Sermon Delivered at the Funeral of Henry Obookiah, A Native of OWHYHEE, and A Member of the Foreign Mission School in Cornwall, Connecticut*, Elizabethtown, NJ: Edison Hart, 1819.

Bellantoni, Nicholas, Roger Thompson, David Cooke, Michael Park and Cynthia Trayling, The Life, Death, Archaeological Exhumation and Re-interment of ʻŌpūkahaʻia (Henry Obookiah), 1792-1818, *Connecticut History*, 2007, Vol. 46, No. 2.

Benson, John L., *History of New York City: Embracing an Outline Sketching of Events from 1609 to 1830, and a Full Account of its Development from 1830 to 1884*, Vol. I, New York: Perine Engraving & Publishing Company, 1884.

Biolsi, Thomas, *Organizing the Lakota: The Political Economy of the New Deal on the Pine Ridge and Rosebud Reservations*, Tucson: University of Arizona Press, 2nd printing, 1998.

Boushard, Rev. Henry K., *The History of Mokuaikaua: The Oldest and First Founded Christian Church in the State of Hawaii*, Hilo: James Roark Design, 1985.

Boyd, James P., *Recent Indian Wars Under the Lead of Sitting Bull and Other Chiefs*, Publisher's Union, 1891, pp. 180-181, reprinted, Digital Scanning Inc., 2000.

Brandon, William, *The American Heritage Book of Indians*, New York: Laurel Edition, 1961.

Brooks, S., and J. Suchey, Skeletal age determination based on the Os Pubis: A comparison of the Asadi-Nemeskeri and Suchey-Brooks methods, *Human Evolution*, vol. 5, pp. 227-238, 1990.

Brown, Dee, *Bury My Heart at Wounded Knee*, New York: Holt, Rinehart & Winston, 1970.

Brown, Joseph Epes, ed., *The Sacred Pipe: Black Elk's Account of the Seven Rites of the Oglala Sioux*, Norman: University of Oklahoma Press, 1989.

Brown, Michael F., *Who Owns Native Culture*, Boston: Harvard University Press, 2004.

Brumaghim, Wayne H., *The Life and Legacy of Heneri ʻŌpūkahaʻia: Hawaiʻi's Prodigal Son*, MA Thesis, University of Hawaiʻi, 2011.

Buck, Sir Peter H. (Te Rangi Hiroa), *Vikings of the Sunrise*, Wellington, New Zealand: Whitcombe and Tombs Limited, 1964.

Buecker, Thomas R. and R. Eli Paul, *The Crazy Horse Surrender Ledger*, Lincoln: Nebraska State Historical Society, 1994.

Bushnell, O. A., *The Gift of Civilization: Germs and Genocide in Hawai'i*, Honolulu: University of Hawai'i Press, 1993.

Calloway, Colin G., *One Vast Winter Count: The Native American West Before Lewis and Clark*, History of the American West Series, Lincoln: University of Nebraska Press, 2003.

Carter, Robert A., *Buffalo Bill Cody: The Man Behind the Legend*, New York: John Wiley & Sons, 2000.

Chapman, William, *Hawai'i, the Military, and the National Park: World War II and Its Impacts on Culture and the Environment*, Final Report for the National Park Service, 2014.

Chertoff, Emily, Occupy Wounded Knee: A 71-Day Siege and a Forgotten Civil Rights Movement, *The Atlantic*, October 2012.

Child, Brenda J., Boarding Schools, In *Encyclopedia of North American Indians*, ed. By Frederick E. Hoxie, Boston: Houghton Mifflin Company, 1996, pp. 78-80.

Clark, Ann, *Singing Sioux Cowboy Reader*, Washington, D. C.: Department of the Interior Publication of the United States Indian Service, 1954.

Clough, Josh, "Vanishing" Indians? Cultural Persistence on Display at the Omaha World's Fair of 1898, *Great Plains Quarterly*, 2005, p. 79.

Clow, Richard L., "The Sioux Nation and Indian Territory: The Attempted Removal of 1876", *South Dakota History*, 1976, Vol. 6, No. 4, pp. 462-463.

Coleman, William S. E. *Voices of Wounded Knee*, Lincoln: University of Nebraska Press, 2000.

Collins, Charles D., Jr., *Atlas of the Sioux Wars*, 2nd edition, Fort Leavenworth, Kansas: Combat Studies Institute Press, 2006.

Colwell, Chip, *Plundered Skulls and Stolen Spirits: Inside the Fight to Reclaim Native America's Culture*, Chicago: University of Chicago Press, 2017.

Conlon, Joseph, *The Historical Impact of Epidemic Typhus*, entomology.montana. edu/historybug/Typhus.

Cook, Christopher, *The Providential Life & Heritage of Henry Obookiah*, Waimea, HI: Pa'a Studios, 2015.

Crow Dog, Leonard and Richard Erdoes, *Crow Dog: Four Generations of Sioux Medicine Men*, New York: Harper Collins, 1995.

Danker, Donald S., The Wounded Knee Interviews of Eli S. Ricker, *Nebraska History*, 1981, vo. 62, p. 190.

Dary, David, *Oregon Trail: An American Saga*, New York: Alfred A. Knopf, 2004.

Delaney, Michele, *Buffalo Bill's Wild West Warriors: A Photographic History by Gertrude Kasebier*, New York: HarperCollins Publishers and the Smithsonian National Museum of American History, 2007.

Deloria, Philip J., *Indians in Unexpected Places*, Lawrence: University of Kansas Press, 2004.

Deloria, Vine, Jr., *Custer Died For Your Sins*, London: MacMillan Company, 1969.

_____, *Red Earth, White Lies: Native Americans and the Myth of Scientific Fact*, Golden, Colorado: Fulcrum Publishing, 1997.

DeMallie, Raymond J., ed., *The Sixth Grandfather: Black Elk's Teachings Given to John G. Neihardt*, Lincoln: University of Nebraska Press, 1984.

_____, The Teton, *Handbook of North American Indians, Plains*, Vol. 13, Part 2 of 2, ed. By Raymond J. DeMillie, General editor, William, C. Sturtevant, Washington, D.C.: Smithsonian Institution, 2001.

DeMontravel, Peter A., *A Hero to His Fighting Men: Nelson A. Miles, 1839-1925*, Kent, OH: Kent State University Press, 1998.

Demos, John, *The Heathen School: A Story of Hope and Betrayal in the Age of the Early Republic*, New York: Alfred A. Knoff, 2014.

Dunbar-Ortiz, Roxanna, and Dina Gilio-Whitaker, *"All The Real Indians Died Off" And 20 Other Myths About Native Americans*, Boston: Beacon Press, 2016.

Diamond, Jared, *Guns, Germs and Steel: The Fates of Human Societies*, New York: W.W. Norton & Co., 1999.

DiSilvestro, Roger, L., *In the Shadow of Wounded Knee: The Untold Story of the Indian Wars*, New York: Walter & Company, 2005.

Dodge, Richard I., *The Black Hills: A Minute Description of the Routes, Scenery, Soil, Climate, Timber, Gold, Geology, Zoology, Etc. . .*, Reprinted Minneapolis: Ross & Haines, 1965.

Dongoske, Kurt E., Mark Aldenderfer, and Karen Doebner, *Working Together: Native Americans & Archaeologists*, Washington, D.C.: Society for American Archaeology, 2000.

Drury, Bob and Tom Clavin, *The Heart of Everything That Is: The Untold Story of Red Cloud, An American Legend*, New York: Simon & Schuster, 2014.

Dunbar-Ortiz, Roxanne, *An Indigenous Peoples' History of the United States*, Boston: Beacon Press, 2014.

Dwight, Edwin W., *The Memoirs of Henry Obookiah, A Native of Owhyhee, And A Member of the Foreign Mission School; Who died At Cornwall, Connecticut February 17, 1818, Aged 26 Years*, Honolulu: Woman's Board of Missions For the Pacific Islands, reprint, 2012.

Eastman, Charles, *From the Deep Woods to Civilization: Chapters in the Autobiography of an Indian*, Lincoln: University of Nebraska Press, 1977.

Eastman, Elaine Goodale, *Sister to the Sioux*, Lincoln: University of Nebraska Press, 2nd edition, 1978.

Engle, Murry, ʻŌpūkahaʻia is Finally Coming Back Home, *The Honolulu Star Bulletin*, July 28, 1993, p. A-10.

Enochs, Ross Alexander, *The Jesuit Mission to the Lakota Sioux: Pastoral theology and Ministry, 1886-1945*, Lanham, Maryland: Rowman and Littlefield, 1996.

Erdoes, Richard, *The Sun Dance People: The Plains Indians, Their Past and Present*, New York: Random House, A Vintage Sundial Book, 1972.

Fishkin, Shelley Fisher, *Writing America: Literary Landmarks From Walden Pond to Wounded Knee, A Reader's Companion*, New Brunswick, N.J.: Rutgers University Press, 2015.

Freedman, Russell, *The Life and Death of Crazy Horse*, New York: Holiday House, 1996.

Fuss, Allison, Cowboys on the Reservation: The Growth of Rodeo as a Lakota National Pastime, *South Dakota History*, Vol. 29, No. 3, 1999, p. 212.

Getches, David H., Alternative Approaches to Land Claims: Alaska and Hawaii, In *Irredeemable America: The Indians' Estate and Land Claims*, edited by Imre Sutton, Albuquerque: University of New Mexico Press, 1985, p. 322.

Gold, Theodore, *Historical Records of the town of Cornwall, Litchfield County, Connecticut*, Cornwall, CT: Case, Lockwood & Brainard Company, 2nd edition, 1904.

Goldfrank, Esther S., Change and Social Character: A Study of Teton Dakota, *American Anthropologist*, 1943, Vol. 45, No. 1, pp. 67-83.

Gooch, George H., *Buffalo Bill's Wild West and Congress of Rough Riders of the World, Official Programme*, 1899, Archives, National Museum of American History, Smithsonian Institution.

_____, *Route-Book Buffalo Bill's Wild West 1899*, Buffalo: The Mathews-Northrup Co., 1900.

_____, *Route Book: Buffalo Bill's Wild West, Season 1900*, Kansas City: Kimberly Publishing Co., 1901.

Gordon, C. C. and Jane E. Buikstra, Soil, pH, bone preservation, and sampling bias at mortuary sites, *American Antiquity*, vol. 46, pp. 566-571.

Graves, Michael W. and David J. Addison, The Polynesian Settlement of the Hawaiian Archipelago: Integrating Models and Methods in Archaeological Interpretation, *World Archaeology*, Vol. 26, No. 3, Colonization of Islands, pp. 380-399 (Feb., 1995).

Green, Jerry, The Medals of Wounded Knee, *Nebraska History*, 1994, vol. 75, p. 203.

_____, ed., *After Wounded Knee: Correspondences of Major & Surgeon John Vance Lauderdale While Serving With The Army Occupying The Pine Ridge Indian Reservation, 1890-1891*, East Lansing: Michigan State University Press, 1996.

Greene, Jerome A., *American Carnage: Wounded Knee, 1890*, Norman: University of Oklahoma Press, 2014.

Grinnell, George Bird, *The Fighting Cheyennes*, Norman: University of Oklahoma Press, 1956 reprint from 1915.

Grua, David W., *Surviving Wounded Knee: The Lakotas and the Politics of Memory*, New York: Oxford University Press, 2015.

Haley, James L., *Captive Paradise: A History of Hawaii*, New York: St. Martin's Press, 2014.

Hall, Philip S., *To Have This Land: The Political Road to Wounded Knee, 1888-1891*, Vermillion, SD: University of South Dakota Press, 1991.

Hassrick, Royal B., *The Sioux: Life and Customs of a Warrior Society*, Norman: University of Oklahoma Press, 1964.

Haynes, James B., *History of the Trans-Mississippian & International Exposition of 1898*, Illustrated 1910, published under the direction of the Directors of the Committee on History as authorized by the Board of Directors, June 30, 1902, Omaha: Trans-Mississippi & International Exposition, 1910.

Herman, Antonie and James R. Walker, "The Seven Council Fires", In *Lakota Society*, ed. By Raymond J. DeMallie, Lincoln: University of Nebraska Press, 1982, pp. 14-18.

Hinman, Eleanor H., *Oglala Sources on the Life of Crazy Horse*, Nebraska History, 2010.

Hittman, Michael, *Wovoka and the Ghost Dance*, Lincoln: University of Nebraska Press, 1990.

Holman, Lucia Ruggles, *Journal of Lucia Ruggles Holman*, Honolulu: Bishop Museum, Special Publication No. 17, 1931.

Holt, John Dominis, *On Being Hawaiian*, Honolulu: Topgallant Publishing, 1964.

Hopoo, Thomas, *Memoirs of Thomas Hopoo*, Manuscript, Andover Newton Theological School Library, n.d.

Hough, Richard, *Captain James Cook: A Biography*, New York: W.W. Norton, 1994.

Howard, James H., "Dakota Winter Counts As A Source of Plains History", *Bureau of American Ethnology, Smithsonian Institution*, Bulletin 173, 1960.

Hoxie, Frederick E., "Travois," In *Encyclopedia of North American Indians*, New York: Houghton Mifflin Co., 1996, p. 643.

Humphrey, Heman, "Instructions," Appendix to *The Promised Land*, Boston: Samuel T. Armstrong, 1819.

Hutchision, William R., *Errand to the World: American Protestant Thought and Foreign Missions*, Chicago: University of Chicago Press, 1987.

Hyde, George, *Red Cloud's Folk: A History of the Oglala Sioux Indians*, Norman: University of Oklahoma Press, 1937.

Iscan, M. Yasar, Susan R. Loth, and Ronald K. Wright, Metamorphosis at the sternal rib end: A new method to estimate age in death of white males, *American Journal of Physical Anthropology*, 1984, vol. 65, no. 2, pp. 147-156.

James, Van, *Ancient Sites of Hawai'i: Archaeological Places of Interest on the Big Island*, Honolulu: Mutual Publishing, 1995.

Ives, Frank J. *Indians Wounded in Fight at Wounded Knee, South Dakota, December 29, 1890, Treated by Frank J. Ives, Capt. & Asst. Surgeon, USA*, manuscript (MS H84.38) on file at Fort Robinson Museum, Crawford, NE.

Jenkinson, D. S. and Ladd, J. N., Microbial biomass in soil: Measurements and turnover, edited by E. A. Paul and J. N. Ladd, *Soil Biochemistry*, 1981, Vol. 5, pp. 415-471.

Jennings, Peter, and Todd Brewster, *The Century*, New York: Doubleday, 1998.

Jensen, Richard E., R. Eli Paul, and John E. Carter, *Eyewitness at Wounded Knee*, Lincoln: University of Nebraska Press, 1991.

Johnson, Michael G., *Tribes of the Sioux Nation*, Kemp House, U. K.: Osprey Publishing, 1012.

Kamakawiwo'ule Osorio, Jonathan K., *Dismembering Lahui: A History of the Hawaiian Nation to 1887*, Honolulu: University of Hawai'i Press, 2002.

Kame'eleihiwa, Liliklalā, *Native Lands and Foreign Desires: Ko Hawai'i 'Āina a me, Nā Koi Pu'umake a ka, Po'e Haole*, Honolulu: Bishop Museum Press, 1992.

Kappler, Charles J., ed., Indian Affairs: Laws and Treaties, Washington: Government Printing Office, 1904.

Kehoe, Alice Beck, *The Ghost Dance: Ethnohistory and Revitalization*, Chicago: Holt, Rinehart and Winston, Inc., 1989.

Kelley, William Fitch, *Pine Ridge 1890: An Eye Witness Account of the Events Surrounding the Fighting at Wounded Knee*, San Francisco, Pierre Bovis, 1971.

Kent, Jim, Lakota Wild West Rider Returns Home, *Lakota Country Times*, 12 September 2012, vol. 8, issue 51, p. A2.

Kesson, Joy S., *Buffalo Bill's Wild West: Celebrity, Memory and Popular History*, New York: Hill and Wang, 2000.

Krauss, Beatrice H., *Plants in Hawaiian Culture*, Honolulu, University of Hawaii Press, 1993.

Laenui, Pola (Hayden F. Burgess), "Hawaiian Statehood Revisited," IN *Reclaiming Indigenous Voice and Vision*, ed. by Marie Battiste, Vancouver: UBC Press, 2000, pp. 50-56.

Landy, David, "Treaties", In *Encyclopedia of North American Indians*, Frederick E. Hoxie, ed., Boston: Houghton Mifflin Co., 1996, p. 647.

Larner, Jesse, *Mount Rushmore: An Icon Reconsidered*, New York: Thunder's Mouth Press, National Books, 2002.

Larsen, Robert W., *Red Cloud: Warrior-Statesman of the Lakota Sioux*, Norman: University of Oklahoma Press, 1997.

Lee, Elizabeth K., *Henry 'Ōpūkaha'ia's Interment Service: Guest Speaker's Messages*, Unpublished manuscript, Office of State Archaeology, University of Connecticut, Storrs, 1993.

Lee, Patrick A., *Tribal Laws, Treaties and Government: A Lakota Perspective*, iUniverse, 2013.

Lengerich, Ryan, Lakota Performer Comes Home, *Rapid City Journal*, 9 September 2012, p. A1, A6.

Letters Sent to the Office of Indian Affairs by the Pine Ridge Agency, 1875-1914, National Archives and Records Administration, Bureau of Indian Affairs, Record Group 75.

Levy, N. M., Native Hawaiian Land Rights, *California Law Review*, 1975, vol. 63, p. 853.

Lili'uokalani, *Hawaii's Story by Hawaii's Queen*, Boston: Lee and Shepard, 1898, Also see, Haley, James L., *Captive Paradise: A History of Hawaii*, New York: St. Martin's Press, 2014.

Lone Hill, Karen D., "Sioux", In *Encyclopedia of North American Indians*, Frederick E. Hoxie, ed., Boston: Houghton Mifflin Co., 1996, p. 591.

Lund, V. and J. Goksoyr, Effects of water fluctuations on microbial mass and activity in soil, *Microbial Ecology*, 1980, Vol. 6, pp. 115-123.

Lyman, Stanley D., *Wounded Knee 1973: A Personal Account*, Lincoln: University of Nebraska Press, 1990.

Maddra, Sam, *Hostiles? The Lakota Ghost Dane and Buffalo Bill's Wild West*, Norman: Oklahoma University Press, 2006.

Mails, Thomas E., *Fools Crow*, Lincoln: University of Nebraska Press, Bison Books, 1990.

Mallery, Garrick, and James Gilchrist Swan, Pictographs of North American Indians, *Fourth Annual Report of the Bureau of American Ethnology*, Smithsonian Institution, 1886.

Mallery, Garrick, Picture-Writing of the American Indians, *Tenth Annual Report of the Bureau of American Ethnology 1888-89*, Smithsonian Institution, 1893, Washington: Government Printing Office, Section 2, "Winter Counts" pp. 266-273.

Malo, David, *Hawaiian Antiquities*, Honolulu: Hawaiian Gazette, 1898.

Native Hawaiian Study Commission, *Report on the Culture, Needs and Concerns of Native Hawaiians*, Washington, D. C.: Department of the Interior, 1983, vol. 1.

Marshall III, Joseph M., *The Lakota Way: Stories and Lessons for Living*, London: Penguin Compass, 2001.

_____, *The Day The World Ended at Little Bighorn: A Lakota History*, New York: Viking, 2007.

Martin, J. W., *The Land Looks After US: A History of Native American Religion*, New York: Oxford University Press, 2001.

Mathiessen, Peter, *In The Spirit Of Crazy Horse*, New York: Viking Penguin, 1991.

McCollough, Charles, "Why Our Church Apologized to Hawai'i," IN *UCC@50—Our History, Our Future*, ed. by J. Martin Bailey, 2006.

Michno, Gregory F., *Lakota Noon: The Indian Narrative of Custer's Defeat*, Missoula: Montana Press Publishing Company, 1997.

Miller, Bonnie M., The Incoherencies of Empire: The "Imperial" Image of the Indian at the Omaha World's Fair of 1898-99, *American Studies*, 2008, 49:3/4, p. 40.

McGregor, James H., *The Wounded Knee Massacre From the Viewpoint of the Sioux*, Rapid City: Fenske Media Corporation, 1940,

Miller, Robert J. Esq., *Native America, Discovered and Conquered, Thomas Jefferson, Lewis and Clark and Manifest Destiny*, Westport, CT: Praeger Publishing, 2006.

Miller, Robert, Looking for Historic Bones, The *(Danbury) News-Times*, 14 August 2012, p. A8.

_____, Disinterment Unearths Afraid of Hawk Skull, *The (Danbury) News-Times*, 16 August 2012, p. A3.

_____, His Spirit Has Been Lifted, The *(Danbury) News-Times*, Friday, 17 August 2012, p. A10.

_____, Albert Emerges to Thanks, *The (Danbury) News-Times*, 17 August 2012.

_____, Final Journey for Albert Afraid of Hawk, The *(Danbury) News-Times*, 7 September 2012.

Molleson, T., and J. Blondiaux, Rider's bones from Kish, Iraq, *Cambridge Archaeological Journal*, vol. 4, 1994, pp. 312-316.

Mooney, James, The Ghost Dance Religion and the Sioux Outbreak, *Fourteenth Annual Report of the Bureau of Ethnology*, Part 2, Washington, D.C.: Government Printing Office, 1896.

Nakashima, Ellen, A Bit of History Returning to Hawaii: Christian Convert Feld in 1808, *The Hartford Courant*, 26 July 1993, pp. C1, C7.

New Haven Evening Register, "Death of Afraid-of-Hawk: He Fulfilled All The Traditions of His Race by Stoic Demeanor," 2 July 1900, Vol. 57, Issue 153, p. 11.

Niehardt, John G., *Black Elk Speaks: Being the Life Story of a Holy Man of the Ogalala Sioux*, The Premier Excelsior Edition, Albany: State University of New York Press, reprinted 2008.

Official Guide Book to the Trans-Mississippi & International Exposition, Omaha, U.S.A., June 1 to November 1, 1898, Omaha: Megeath Stationary Company, 1898.

Okihiro, Gary Y., *Island World: A History of Hawai'i and the United States*, Berkeley: University of California Press, 2008.

Orcutt, Samuel, *The History of Torrington, Connecticut from Its First Settlement in 1737, with Biographies and Genealogies*. Albany: J Munsell, Printer, 1878, reprint 1990 edition.

Ostler, Jeffrey, *The Lakotas and the Black Hills*, New York: Penguin Books, 2010.

Papandrea, Ronald J., *They Never Surrendered: The Lakota Sioux Band That Stayed in Canada*, 4th edition revised, La Vergne, TN: Lighting Source, an IGRAM Co., 2012

Park, Michael Alan, *Biological Anthropology*, New York: McGraw-Hill, fifth edition, 2008.

Paul, R. Elia, Dakota Resources: The Investigation of Special Agent Cooper and Property Damage Claims in the Winter of 1890-1891, *South Dakota History*, vol. 24, No. 3 and 4, 1994, p. 219.

_____, ed., *The Nebraska Indian Wars Reader 1865-1877*, Lincoln: University of Nebraska Press, 1998.

Peterson, Bruce A., *The Two Masks of Nicholas Black Elk*, Masters Thesis, Department of History, University of Texas–Pan American, 1996.

Pickering, Katherine, "Articulation of the Lakota Mode of Production and the Euro-American Fur Trade", In *The Fur Trade Revisited, Selected Papers of the Sixth North American Fur Trade Conference*, ed. Brown, Jennifer S. H. Brown, W. J. Eccles, and Donald P. Heldman, East Lansing: Michigan State University Press, 1994.

Pietrusewsky, Michael, An osteological view of indigenous populations in Oceania, In *Studies In Oceanic Culture History*, Green R.C., and M. Kelly, eds, Pacific Anthropological Records, No. 11 Department of Anthropology, Honolulu: B.P. Bishop Museum, 1979.

Bergin & Garvey, *In Remembrance: Archaeology and Death*, Westport: Garvin, 1996.

Pratt, Richard H., The Indian Policy, The Advantages of Mingling Indians with Whites, *Official Proceedings of the Nineteenth Annual Conference of Charities and Correction*, 1892.

Prucha, Francis, *The Great Father: The United State Government and the American Indian*, Lincoln: University of Nebraska Press, 1986.

Pryor, Alton, *Little Known Tales in Hawaiian History*, Roseville, CA: Stagecoach Publishing, 2004.

Quaife, Milo M., ed., *The Journals of Meriwether Lewis and Sergeant John Ordway*, Madison: Historical Society of Wisconsin, 1916.

Reinhardt, Akim D., *Ruling Pine Ridge: Oglala Lakota Politics from the IRA to Wounded Knee*, Lubbock: Texas Tech University Press, 2007.

Renner, Gerald, After 175 Years, a Resting Place in His Hawaiian Homeland, *The Hartford Courant*, Vol. CLV, No. 197, Friday, July 16, 1993, p. A4.

Reuman, Otto G., *The Influence of One Man–Henry Obookiah*, published by the First Church of Christ in Cornwall, CT, 1968.

Richards, Thomas C., *Samuel J. Mills, Missionary, Pathfinder, Pioneer and Promoter*, Boston: The Pilgrim Press, 1906.

Richardson, Heather Cox, *Wounded Knee: Party Politics and the Road To An American Massacre*, New York: Perseus Book Group, 2010, 266.

Riegert, Ray, *Hidden Hawaii The Adventurer's Guide*, Berkeley: Ulysses Press, (6th edition), 1979, p. 1.

Riney, Scott, *The Rapid City Indian School 1898-1933*, Norman: University of Oklahoma Press, 1999.

Robes Kipp, Darrell, "Horses and Indians", In *Encyclopedia of North American Indians*, Frederick E. Hoxie, ed., Boston: Houghton Mifflin Co., 1996, p. 257.

Robinson, Doane, *History of South Dakota*, Vol. 1, Chicago: Chicago Historical Society, 1930.

Robertson, Paul, *The Power of the Land: Identity, Ethnicity, and Class Among the Oglala Lakota*, New York: Routledge, 2002.

Ronda, James P., *Lewis and Clark Among the Indians*, Lincoln: University of Nebraska Press, 1937.

Roosevelt, Theodore, *The Winning of the West*, Book IV, New York: G. P. Putnam's Sons, 1896.

Rose, Christine, The Spirit of Afraid of Hawk Free After 112 Years, *Danbury Patch*, 20 August 2012.

_____, Buffalo Bill Rough Rider Albert Afraid of Hawk, At Rest, At Last, *Indian Country Today*, September 13, 2012

Ruby, Robert H., *The Oglala Sioux: Warriors in Transition*, New York: Vantage Press, 1955.

Rydell, Robert W. *All The World's A Fair*, Chicago: University of Chicago Press, 1984.

Scott, Douglas D., Richard A. Fox, Jr., Melissa A. Connor, and Dick Harmon, *Archaeological Perspectives on The Battle of Little Bighorn*, Norman: University of Oklahoma Press, 1989.

Scott, G., and Christy Turner, III, *The Anthropology of Modern Human Teeth*, Cambridge: Cambridge University Press, 1997.

Service, Elman, *Origins of the State and Civilization: The Process of Cultural Evolution*, New York: W. W. Norton & Company, 1975.

Shelton, Elizabeth W., *Faith, Freedom, and Flag: The Influence of American Missionaries in Turkey on Foreign Affairs, 1830-1880*, Dissertation, Georgetown University, Washington, D.C., 2011.

Siler, Julia Flynn, *Lost Kingdom: Hawaii's Last Queen, the Sugar Kings, and America's First Imperial Adventure*, New York: Grove Press, 2012.

Silva, Noenoe, *Aloha Betrayed: Native Hawaiian Resistance to American Colonialism*, Durham: Duke University Press, 2004.

Silverman, Kenneth, *Timothy Dwight*, New York: Twayne Publishers, 1969.

Singer, Ben, A brief history of the horse in America, *Canadian Geographic Magazine*, May 2005.

Sledzik, Paul, and Nicholas F. Bellantoni, Brief Communications: Bioarchaeological and biocultural evidence of the New England vampire folk belief, *American Journal of Physical Anthropology*, 1994, Vol. 94, no. 2, pp. 269-274.

Solon, Sister Eleanor, *We Walk in Faith: The Growth of the Catholic Faith in Western South Dakota*, Eckbolsheim, France: Editions du Signe, 2002.

Spoeher, Anne Harding, "George Prince Tamoree: Heir Apparent of Kaua'i and Niihau", *Hawaiian Journal of History*, Vol. 15, 1981, p. 38.

Stannard, Davie, *Before the Horror: The Population of Hawai'i on the Eve of Western Contact*, Honolulu: University of Hawai'i Press, 1989.

Starita, Joe, *The Dull Knives of Pine Ridge: A Lakota Odyssey*, New York: G. P. Putnam's Sons, 1995.

Stoughton, John A., "Recollections", *Washington Historical Quarterly*, vol. 15, 1924, pp. 208-10.

Swanton, John R., Siouan Tribes and the Ohio Valley, *American Anthropologist*, Vol. 45, No. 1, pp. 49-66.

Swidler, Nina, Kurt E. Dongoske, Roger Anyon and Alan S. Downer, eds., *Native Americans and Archaeologists: Stepping Stones to Common Ground*, Walnut Creek, CA: Altamira Press, 1997.

Tallent, Annie D., *The Black Hills: Or, the Last Hunting Ground of the Dakotahs*, St. Louis: Nixon-Jones, 1899.

Thomas, David Hurst, *Skull Wars: Kennewick Man, Archaeology and the Battle for Native American Identity*, New York: Basic Books, 2001.

Todd, T. W., Changes in the pubic bone: The male white pubic, *American Journal of Physical Anthropology*, 1920, vol. 3, pp. 285-334.

Toensing, Gale Courey, White Buffalo Calf named Yellow Medicine Dancing Boy Amid Fire, Water and Thunder, *Indian Country Today Media Network*, 6 August 2015. http://indiancountrytodaymedianetwork.com/2012/08/06/white-buffalo-calf-named-yellow-medicine-dancing-boy-amid-fire-water-and-thunder-127463.

Trennert, Robert A., Fairs, Expositions, and the Changing Image of Southwestern Indians, 1876-1904, *New Mexico Historical Review*, No. 62, 1987, p. 143.

Utley, Robert M., *The Lance and The Shield: The Life and Times of Sitting Bull*, New York: Henry Holt and Company, 1993.

van der Vaart TW, van Thiel PPAM, Juffermans NP, van Vugt M, Geerlings SE, Grobusch MP, et al. Severe murine typhus with pulmonary system involvement. *Emerging Infectious Diseases* [Internet], 2014, August, http://dx.doi.org/10.3201/eid2008.131421

Van James, *Ancient Sites of Hawai'i: Archaeological Places of Interest on the Big Island*, Honolulu: Mutual Publishing, 2008.

Vestal, Stanley, *New Sources of Indian History*, Norman: University of Oklahoma Press, 1934.

Vowell, Sarah, *Unfamiliar Fishes*, New York: Riverhead Books, 2011.

Wakefield, John, A., *A History of the Trans-Mississippi & International Exposition*, Omaha: Omaha Public Library, 1992.

Walker, James R., *Lakota Society*, ed. By Raymond DeMallie, Lincoln: University of Nebraska Press, 1982.

Warren, Louis S., *God's Red Son: The Ghost Dance Religion and the Making of Modern America*, New York: Basic Books, 2017.

Wedel, M. M., "Le Sueur and the Dakota Sioux", In *Aspects of Upper Great Lakes Anthropology: Papers in Honor of Lloyd A. Wifford*, ed. By E. Johnson, Minnesota Prehistoric Archaeology Series, no. 11, St. Paul: Minnesota Historical Society, 1974, pp. 165-166.

West, Richard W., Repatriation, IN *Encyclopedia of North American Indians: Native American History, Culture, and Life From the Paleo-Indians to the Present*, ed. By Frederick E. Hoxie, Boston: Houghton Mifflin Company, 1996.

Young, Mary-Jo, *The Mosaic That Is Albert Afraid of Hawk's Journey Home*, unpublished manuscript, filed at Office of State Archaeology, University of Connecticut, Storrs.

_____, *Reflections on the Repatriation of Albert Afraid of Hawk*, unpublished manuscript on file at the Office of State Archaeology, University of Connecticut, Storrs, 2012.

Young, Robert, *Afraid of Hawk and Cetan Kokipapi in 19th century Plains Native American Families*, unpublished manuscript, 2016.

Zimmerman, Bill, *Airlift to Wounded Knee*, Chicago: Swallow Press, 1976.

Index

Garnet Books

Titles with asterisks (*) are also in the Driftless Connecticut Series

*Garnet Poems: An Anthology of
Connecticut Poetry Since 1776**
Dennis Barone, editor

*The Connecticut Prison Association
and the Search for Reformative
Justice**
Gordon Bates

*Food for the Dead: On the Trail of
New England's Vampires*
Michael E. Bell

*The Long Journeys Home: The
Repatriations of Henry 'Ōpūkaha'ia
and Albert Afraid of Hawk**
Nick Bellantoni

*The Case of the Piglet's Paternity:
Trials from the New Haven
Colony, 1639–1663**
Jon C. Blue

Early Connecticut Silver, 1700–1840
Peter Bohan and Philip
Hammerslough

*The Connecticut River:
A Photographic Journey
through the Heart of New England*
Al Braden

*Tempest-Tossed: The Spirit of Isabella
Beecher Hooker*
Susan Campbell

*Connecticut's Fife &
Drum Tradition**
James Clark

Sunken Garden Poetry, 1992–2011
Brad Davis, editor

*Rare Light: J. Alden Weir in
Windham, Connecticut, 1882–1919**
Anne E. Dawson, editor

*The Old Leather Man: Historical
Accounts of a Connecticut
and New York Legend*
Dan W. DeLuca, editor

*Post Roads & Iron Horses:
Transportation in
Connecticut from Colonial
Times to the Age of Steam**
Richard DeLuca

*The Log Books: Connecticut's Slave
Trade and Human Memory**
Anne Farrow

*Birding in Connecticut**
Frank Gallo

Dr. Mel's Connecticut Climate Book
Dr. Mel Goldstein

*Hidden in Plain Sight: A Deep
Traveler Explores Connecticut*
David K. Leff

Renée Tribert and James
F. O'Gorman

*Connecticut in the American Civil
War: Slavery, Sacrifice,
and Survival**
Matthew Warshauer

*Inside Connecticut and the Civil War:
One State's Struggles*
Matthew Warshauer, editor

*Prudence Crandall's Legacy:
The Fight for Equality in the 1830s,
Dred Scott, and Brown v. Board of
Education**
Donald E. Williams Jr.

*Riverview Hospital for Children and
Youth: A Culture of Promise**
Richard Wiseman

*Stories in Stone: How Geology
Influenced Connecticut
History and Culture*
Jelle Zeilinga de Boer

*New Haven's Sentinels: The Art and
Science of East Rock and West Rock**
Jelle Zeilinga de Boer and John
Wareham

About the Author

Nicholas F. ("Nick") Bellantoni is an Associate Adjunct Professor in the Anthropology Department at the University of Connecticut. Bellantoni is also *Emeritus* Connecticut State Archaeologist at the Connecticut State Museum of Natural History. He has published numerous articles in journals and newsletters including, "The Life, Death, Archaeological Exhumation and Re-internment of ʻŌpūka-haʻia (Henry Obookiah)" (*Connecticut History*, 2007), "The Search for Graves with Ground-penetrating Radar in Connecticut" (*Journal of Archaeological Sciences*, 2010), and "Critical Issues in Connecticut Archaeological Preservation" (*Bulletin of the Archaeological Society of Connecticut*, 2005). He lives in Newington, Connecticut.

About the Driftless Connecticut Series

The Driftless Connecticut Series is a publication award program established in 2010 to recognize excellent books with a Connecticut focus or written by a Connecticut author. To be eligible, the book must have a Connecticut topic or setting or an author must have been born in Connecticut or have been a legal resident of Connecticut for at least three years.

The Driftless Connecticut Series is funded by the Beatrice Fox Auerbach Foundation Fund at the Hartford Foundation for Public Giving.

For more information and a complete list of books in the Driftless Connecticut Series, please visit us online at http://www.wesleyan.edu/wespress/driftless.